University of Chicago
Studies in Library Science

Patterns
in the use of books
in large research
libraries

Patterns
in the use of books
in large research
libraries

Herman H. Fussler
and Julian L. Simon

The University of Chicago Press
Chicago & London

Z
711
.3
.F88
1969

The University of Chicago Studies in Library Science
This is a reedited version under the same title as that of a report originally published in a very small preliminary edition by the University of Chicago Library
in 1961.

Standard Book Number: 226–27556–6
Library of Congress Catalog Card Number 72-79916

THE UNIVERSITY OF CHICAGO PRESS, CHICAGO 60637
The University of Chicago Press, Ltd., London W.C. 1
© 1961, 1969 by The University of Chicago
All rights reserved. Published 1969
Printed in the United States of America

Library
UNIVERSITY OF MIAMI

Contents

List of tables

List of Figures

List of appendices

Introduction

The seemingly limitless growth of general research libraries has produced stresses and strains difficult for many institutions to resolve. Resulting problems include the rising costs of space for library buildings and bookstacks, the scarcity of land convenient to the campus, aesthetic and functional limitations on the height and bulk of library buildings, and the increasing complexity of organizing materials and services for efficient use.

Library growth reflects, of course, both the growth of recorded knowledge and major expansion in the scope of university teaching and research interests. Efficient access to this growing body of knowledge is essential to sound scholarship. In turn, such access may require a steady growth in the size of individual libraries. It seems desirable therefore to examine alternate methods that might be more efficient or economical than conventional ones for coping with library growth.

A common response to some aspects of the problem of growth has been to subdivide libraries into smaller units; most university libraries have already done so. But subdivision has its limits, and while facilitating access for some users, it makes it more difficult for others. It certainly does not reduce costs. Another possible answer would be radical technological change. Microfacsimile and other methods of optical or electronic information storage have long been considered possibilities. These or similar techniques may in time relieve the problems of growth, but up to now the cost of these steps has made them an unattractive alternative to acquiring and retaining books, except in special circumstances or as a supplement to conventional collections. Some relief may also be provided for the development of stronger regional or national supporting collections to which universities may turn with formal assurance of availability of certain categories of infrequently used materials.

A fourth possibility is to differentiate in the way books are stored and made available. It has long been assumed in American university libraries that all books not actually in use should be immediately available and shelved with all other books on the same subject. The presumed necessity for the immediate availability of books may deserve closer

1

examination when the cost of providing it is compared with possible alternatives, particularly when the number of books is extremely large. As for subject relationships, they have already become much too complex for large research collections to allow more than broad relationships in complex subjects.

Book storage programs are already in operation at Michigan, Harvard, Yale, and Iowa State Universities, and at the libraries of many of the institutions belonging to the Center for Research Libraries and the New England Deposit Library. Neither a local nor a cooperative storage program eliminates growth, but properly handled such programs can mitigate some of the more serious stresses resulting from growth.

The more compact housing of books is worth investigating for three reasons: (a) book housing in large research libraries requires a very substantial proportion of the available space, (b) library space is expensive, (c) the efficiency in the use of conventional book stack space is very poor (it has been estimated that only 10 percent of the cubic space in a conventional book stack is occupied by books[1]). The number of books that can be shelved within a given space may be doubled, or more, by arranging them by size rather than by subject, shelving some or all on edge, reducing aisle space, making the shelving a bit higher, and possibly using different types of shelving equipment (see chapter 10). Furthermore, if storage space need not be at the center of campus, cheaper land can often be used for this purpose. In this case storage facilities can be constructed, equipped, and operated at a cost substantially less per book

than conventional book stack space. If regional or national cooperative access programs are successful, even greater economies would result, in part through the reduction in the total number of copies of a single title that need be retained.

But the limits and efficacy both of storage and of other major programs such as microfacsimile depend at least in part on the ways in which research materials are normally used. Obviously, a procedure that destroys effective scholarly access to needed materials is a false economy. The study that follows explores this fundamental question: *Will any kind of statistical procedure predict with reasonable accuracy the frequencies with which groups of books with defined characteristics are likely to be used in a research library?*

To answer this and related questions raises the need to define what a research library is and how scholars use print. The main problem of definition has to do with *use* as a relevant criterion. A good general research library could never result from a census of heavily used books. Many infrequently used books are absolutely essential to good research, and reasonably quick access to them is essential if research is not to be impaired. In short, the relevance, importance, or value of a single book or a class of books is not established primarily by the frequency of its use.[2] On the other hand, it is safe to generalize that frequently used books should be housed as accessibly as possible. The question of use as a criterion, then, falls primarily on those books that are used either not at all or very infre-

---

[1] Fremont Rider, *Compact Book Storage* (New York: Hadham Press, 1949), p. 8.

[2] For a theoretical discussion of the valuation of books and book use, see chapters 5 and 6 of Julian Simon, "Economics of Book Storage Plans for a Large University Library" (Ph.D. diss., University of Chicago, 1961).

quently. Among very infrequently used books there are some that are important and others that are inferior, marginal, or substantively, although not necessarily historically, obsolete. Only skilled judgment can distinguish the one from the other, and such judgment should be brought to bear on the question. We believe that measures of use, together with screening by skilled judges, are relevant to our fundamental question. A careful analysis of use should (a) indicate whether any discrimination in access is at all likely to be feasible; (b) if it is, indicate the probable character and extent of such discrimination; and (c) reduce the mass of material to which skilled judgment might otherwise have to be applied.

The objective of the study then is to obtain the information required to create a library that would provide immediate access to three categories of books: (a) those that are "used," with a very liberal definition of use; (b) those that by statistical or related analytical techniques fall into *groups* of books likely to be used, even though the individual books may have had little or no use; and (c) those that fall outside groups (a) and (b) but which are judged by experts to be relevant and important in a *general* research context. Books that fall outside these three groups might be stored where they would still be accessible, but not as immediately.

It is extremely important to recognize that the primary objective of this differential treatment of books is *not* necessarily to reduce library expenditures. Instead it might be designed to increase the amount of research material that could be made accessible for a fixed sum for physical plant and operating expense. This point deserves close attention because the cost of a library's physical plant is usually ignored in computing the costs of library operations.

In this study we have assumed, for the sake of simplicity, a "working library" housing the bulk of a research collection, and a local, expansible storage facility absorbing much of the least-used material. The findings, we believe, are of equal relevance to cooperative storage and acquisition programs and to cooperative or individual programs for large-scale microfacsimile operations.

The study has been based primarily upon an analysis of use of groups of books at the University of Chicago. But an analysis of use at several other institutions has been incorporated in an effort to explore the general applicability of the data. Various subordinate questions on the effects of a storage operation are explored in a preliminary way, and data have been collected on some of these issues. Insofar as possible, the approach has been practical; it is a study of some aspects of the *use of libraries* and does not pretend to ascertain what scholars "should" read or what they actually do read. No attempt is made to ascertain differences in use of books among individual scholars or groups of scholars, nor to weight the use by the level of the reader or any similar criterion.

The study was based on certain assumptions that can be briefly stated as follows:

1. The recorded circulation use of books is a reasonably reliable index of *all* use, including the unrecorded, consultative, or browsing use within the library;

2. There are certain patterns in the use of books that are common to major research libraries;

3. Within homogeneous subject areas and types of books (that is, monographs

and serials), *use* is a suitable *initial* criterion for segregating materials into different levels of accessibility;

4. Economic factors may make it highly desirable to segregate books, on the basis of their value and use, into two or more levels of accessibility.

Julian L. Simon, associate director of the project, was responsible for working out most of the procedures, devising several lines of investigation, supervising the staff, and developing the initial interpretation of the data. He prepared most of the first draft on which the preliminary edition of 1961 was based. Herman H. Fussler was responsible for the specification of the general problem, the general administration of the project, the setting of the general scope of the study, and indicating the general lines of investigation.

David Kleinman, the project statistician, prepared the first draft of chapter 6 and carried out much of the data analysis for it. With the aid of empirical cost studies by John Baroco, Kenneth W. Soderland worked out the transfer procedures and prepared the first draft of chapter 9 and a substantial revision of that chapter for the current edition, based upon experience at the University of Chicago library in the actual transfers

of materials to storage. Mrs. Hope Hodgess Rodger drafted most of the technical appendices, edited an earlier draft of the manuscript, and directed the data collection. Professors Robert L. Graves, Paul Meier, and Howard L. Jones, all of the University of Chicago faculty, served as consultants in statistics. Professor William E. Kruskal was unfailingly generous with his time and advice on problems relating to the design of the study and a variety of statistical questions.

The present text is a revision, prepared primarily by Raymond L. Glasscote of Washington, D.C., of the 1961 text. Julian Simon did not participate in this revision. The intent of the revision was to retain a detailed description of the methodology and findings while simplifying some of the language of the 1961 report. It was deemed inadvisable to revise the report of this study to include references to other studies of book and literature use published since 1961.

The study was made possible by a grant to the University of Chicago from the Council on Library Resources, and we are indebted to Verner W. Clapp, president of the Council, for his unfailingly sympathetic interest and advice.

1

Methodological and sampling techniques in the study

A. Major purpose of the study

The major purpose of the study was to answer this question: *Will any kind of statistical procedure predict with reasonable accuracy the frequencies with which groups of books with defined characteristics are likely to be used in a research library?*

Subordinate but closely related questions were:

1. What kinds of statistical procedures, convertible into practical working rules, are most effective for predicting use among the little-used books in a research library? Procedures differ for different kinds of library situations (e.g., storing monographs versus serials) and so a full answer to the question should indicate which kinds of procedures are appropriate for particular situations.

2. In terms of specific library policy decisions, how may we best compare

Since the methods of developing information in this study may be relevant to future studies, an unusually detailed account of the techniques chosen will be given. A full statement of the working details is included in the appendix. The comments in the first part of this chapter will apply to the investigations of monographs and serials alike. The latter part of the chapter refers to the study of monograph use only.

various procedures as to the expected relationships between the number of books moved to storage and the number of books that will be recalled from storage in any future period of any specified length in a specified subject field? More specifically, what accuracy can be anticipated for statements about (a) the number of books that will be taken to storage with a specified procedure generated from a specified size of sample and (b) the number of books that will be withdrawn from storage for use in future periods.

B. Random model of book use

Throughout the study, it is assumed that at *any given moment* each book in a library has a random probability of being used within some specific period of time. Thus, whether or not a book will be used in any single period of time depends only upon its underlying probability of use and not upon whether it was used in some given previous period (although previous use may be used to estimate the probability of future use). The probabilities may change from year to year, of course, and this complicates our task.

TABLE 1

Use history of groups of titles used once or more in 1951, 1952, or 1953

Year	Number of titles used once or more[a]	1952	1953	1954	1955	1956	1957	1958
				Also used in				
1951	214	55	51	53	44	40	51	43
1952	204		66	64	40	47	52	45
1953	205			52	52	55	56	52

[a] A single title is entered in the tabulation for each year in which it was used.

It is almost impossible to estimate the probability of use of many single books in a given period of time because of the short period during which one may observe use and the small probability that any single book will be used at all. Therefore it is necessary to group books together on the basis of common characteristics in order to estimate the probability of use. This probability may then be applied both to the group and to single books from the group. Two considerations encourage the use of relatively short observation periods in estimating the probability: (a) the probability is likely to change with time, and (b) records of use are generally available only for the relatively recent past.

In short,[1] we assume that whether a particular book will be used within a specified period of time is an entirely random process, depending only upon the underlying probability which we estimate by observing the use of a group of books with common characteristics.

We know of no way to test our assumption that, over short periods of time, the amount of use that a book generates in one time period is independent of the use that it gen-

[1] Some of the more technical aspects of the study and its procedures are given throughout the text in smaller type so that the reader who is not especially concerned with methodology can more easily identify and skip over these sections if he wishes to do so.

erated in a previous time period. (See latter part of this chapter for the definition of "use.") But we may test whether there are specific relationships between time periods that would need to be taken into account in estimating the probability of use.

If instead of having its uses randomly distributed in time, each book was actually used at some regular interval, the results of this study might not be applicable. This effect was tested by examining from several subject areas a group of titles which were used one or more times in 1951, 1952, or 1953 (table 1). If there had been a pattern of use at regular intervals and the pattern were much the same for many books, the use in subsequent years would rise and fall in some regular fashion. We found no evidence of such an effect.

Table 1 may be read as follows: "Of the 214 titles used once or more in 1951, 55 were used again in 1952, 51 in 1953," and so on.

We also tested to see if the use of books is contagious—that is, whether the use of a book in one year substantially raises the probability that it will be used in the next year. If that were the case, a group of books that was used in a given year would show progressively greater uses in following years. Our test was made less than perfect by the overall decrease in the use of books over time, and by changes in university population and book use. Nevertheless, our assumption of independence of use from one time period to another seemed to be supported by the data.

We also assumed that the use pattern of one book is independent of the patterns of use of other books. This assumption will not always hold, of course, since some books refer the reader to others; this particular relationship would be difficult to evaluate, and in any case we do not think it would affect our results greatly.

C. Development of a measure of the "value" or "usefulness" of books

Recognizing that it is only one of many factors determining "value," *frequency of use* was chosen as an index of the "value" or "usefulness" of a book.

1. Historical vs. cross-sectional
   approaches to determining
   the past use of individual
   books

There are two ways to trace the use of books—historical and cross-sectional. Both involve using information from the circulation book cards showing withdrawals. The historical approach requires studying the use of each book in a sample for the whole period in which it has been in the library. The cross-sectional approach requires information for a restricted time period.

The cross-sectional approach was chosen for two reasons:

1. Data are more consistently available. The further back one goes, the fewer records are found because book cards are replaced when they are filled. Furthermore, there have probably been changes both in circulation rules and in procedures for recording circulation.

2. Changes in university population and in teaching and research interest and methods probably have altered patterns of use over the past 60 years.

The years 1949–53 and 1954–58 were chosen as base periods.

2. Definitions of the unit of use

a. Renewals. Librarians who contemplate separating books into first and second levels of accessibility are interested in retaining the highest possible proportion at the first level, partly because it may cost more to obtain a book from a second level of accessibility, and partly because readers may not use certain categories of books unless they are immediately accessible. Consequently, in a study focusing on the physical location of books, it is appropriate to count only original borrowing charges and not renewals.

Only one withdrawal was recorded for a book withdrawn twice or more in succession by the same person, unless twelve months had elapsed between the date on which he returned the book and the date on which he next withdrew it, or unless another reader withdrew the book in between.[2] The theory was the same as that for not counting renewals.

b. Reserve charges. Multiple reserve charges were not counted, because they would not constitute an access problem in a storage operation. Placement on reserve was counted as a single use. We will indicate later how we evaluated the use during the time a book was on reserve. Our underlying criterion of accessibility led us to count an interlibrary loan as a use, but charges to the bindery were excluded.

c. Estimation of missing data. Some books did not have complete use records for the two five-year sampling periods chosen. Instead of excluding them, we estimated their use as accurately as possible. They are probably among the highest-use books, and to remove them from the sample would have given a biased

---

[2] Unfortunately, an absolutely uniform procedure was not evolved until some of the data had been collected. For details see appendix A.

picture both of the library's circulation and of the average use of groups of similar books.

The principal methods of estimation were as follows:

Books without charge cards. The most likely reason for the absence of a charge card was that the book had been acquired when cards were not created until a book was initially withdrawn. All books without cards were old and appeared to have been used little or not at all. In such cases no use was attributed to the book for the base periods.

Books with replacement charge cards. If a book had replacement charge cards that covered use for only part of the base periods, use was estimated for the total time on the assumption that the rate of the earlier, unrecorded use was at least as great as that during the known period. This method of estimation was used because at the time of data collection no data on obsolescence trends were available. Subsequent information about obsolescence trends did not offer a firm basis for establishing rates of obsolescence for books that had had their cards replaced. The obsolescence pattern for one group of books differed from that of other groups. Furthermore, since the period of estimation was always less than ten years, it is unlikely that the obsolescence trend is great enough to invalidate a simple average of uses.

If other copies of the same book in the same location had cards covering a longer period, a combined estimate of use for the unknown period was made from the copy's circulation and the known circulation in the period covered. We doubt that many errors were made in confusing new cards with replacements.

Restricted-use books. It was necessary to take account of variation in circulation rules. For example, in the University of Chicago social science reading room and in the reference room books circulate only overnight. When there were copies elsewhere in the library, those copies were used in making estimates. When there were no regularly circulating copies, we arbitrarily attributed a high amount of use to the restricted-circulation volumes. Although there seemed to be no other choice, it was not a happy one because the location of some books in these and other restricted categories may reflect the judgment of a single person about the value of the book, and that judgment may be highly subjective.

Reserve books. For books that were on reserve less than the ten years of the combined base periods, the circulation during the nonreserve period was extrapolated for the reserve period, and one use was arbitrarily added to the extrapolated total for each year on reserve in order to reflect the handling necessary to bring the book to reserve. Only a very few were on reserve for the entire combined base periods, and those books were arbitrarily assigned a high amount of use.

For many parts of the study, error in measuring the *amount* of use is not important, since in most of the analysis the books were divided into only two classes —those that had some use during the base periods, and those that had none. This distinction was relatively easy to make with great accuracy.

Because of differences in circulation rules from one departmental library to another and from one university library to another, intercomparisons of subject areas could not be made.

The procedure for estimating use data is covered more fully in appendix A.

D. Definition of sampling units

1. Excluded materials

We excluded the following: maps, unbound periodicals, newspapers, microtexts, and unbound books, all mainly because they do not have charge cards; the rare book collection and other special collections, because books from them are not considered for storage and are usually used *in situ;* materials at libraries away from the main campus; and books acquired after 1953, because they would have had only a limited period in which to accumulate use.

It was assumed that books acquired since 1953 would show much the same patterns of use as those acquired in the period 1949–53. However, the highest-use books exhaust their charge cards most quickly, and examining books when they are at least five years old precludes an inspection of the highest-use books in their initial circulation period. But books used so much as to exhaust their bookcards within five years are probably no more than a minute portion of the population.[3]

2. Separation into "serials" and "monographs"

All materials not excluded were classified as *monographs* or *serials*. A serial was defined as "any publication issued at regular or irregular intervals with some scheme for consecutive numbering and intended to be continued indefinitely, containing work by several writers." We excluded any serial that had fewer than five volumes in the library (details

given in serial section). As a rule, any material for which the shelf list card indicated "See Serial Record," past or present, was included in the serial group. This was a sufficient but not a necessary condition for definition as a serial.

If a book was not classified as a serial, by process of elimination it was a monograph.

3. The monograph sampling unit

The basic unit for monograph sampling was the *title,* which included all copies of all volumes of all editions of the book that were in *the same language,* housed anywhere in the library system. There were many ambiguous cases. For example, are two collections of articles the same title if one is a collection containing all that are in the second, but the second contains fewer than the first?

The title was chosen as the unit for sampling because it was easier to define than was a *copy,* a *volume,* or an *edition* and because it would have been extremely difficult to sample the other units with equal probability. The sum of the recorded use shown in all copies, volumes, and editions for a title was the controlling measurement.

There were other reasons why the title was also the basic unit of analysis. Despite the fact that we sampled titles, we could have estimated use from age, employing copies or editions as the observation unit. Indeed, for some purposes units other than the title were employed for analysis.

Also, it is not important to a reader whether he uses one *copy* of a book or another if they are identical. Two copies may increase the probability that a reader will chance upon or be able to find a book; but more important, two copies will probably split the use that would have occurred if there were only one

[3] An inspecton of more than one hundred recently *exhausted* charge cards revealed that the highest-use book took two-and-one-half years to accumulate the 25 uses provided on one card. (Individual reserve use is not entered on the book cards.)

copy. This is the rationale behind adding the use of copies.

If two *editions* are similar, there are occasions when either might be equally acceptable to a reader; and such editions could be combined as if they were mere copies of each other. But if a later edition brings an earlier edition up to date or substantively amends it, we would expect all but the historically minded to use the later edition. In other cases, for example an edited text with annotations, the editions are essentially different works and the later edition is not necessarily preferred or more accurate. Despite such variations, editions were arbitrarily treated as part of the same title.

The problem of different *volumes* within a title also presented difficulties. Presumably most libraries would avoid breaking up monographs by placing some volumes in storage while keeping other volumes in conventional stacks. Thus, since we wanted to predict title use, if use were predicted for any volume in the title all of the volumes were kept.

4. The serial sampling unit

The basic unit for serial sampling was the *volume,* including all copies of a single volume of the serial. Again there were ambiguities. In one departmental library two bibliographical volumes might be bound together, while in another library they might be bound separately. Our rule was that the binding arrangement in the departmental library that we first worked in defined the volume, and we either split or added use for the other binding arrangements accordingly.

E. Determination of subject area size

A sample of the books used in a library could be based upon the entire collec-

tion. But there are reasons to expect that the use of various parts of the collection would differ, and any general sample of use would disguise these differences. Furthermore large libraries are likely to vary in composition. If two libraries were to analyze their use patterns by broad samples, it would be impossible to determine whether the differences resulted from the composition of the collections, the behavior of the users, a combination of the two, or still other factors. We concluded that analysis by broad subject fields would probably be a more useful approach, using the previously indicated distinction between serials and monographs. The definition of subject was set for practical reasons by conventional library systems of subject classification.

The minimum number of titles or volumes to be sampled was determined by the size of a subject that could be defined more or less comparably in more than one classification system (for example, Library of Congress and Dewey). For subjects such as economics or chemistry, there is probably a great overlap among the books that would be included under various classification systems. If there is such overlap, and all else is equal, a procedure for predicting future use that would work for one system would work for another within the same subject.

The maximum number of titles or volumes to be sampled was determined by grouping subject areas together when experience suggested that most of the users of the area collections were likely to be from the same department.

Most of the subject areas were of the same scope as traditional academic departments, except for a few cases where we combined two areas—for example, sociology and anthropology.

F. Choice of subject areas to study

Within the University of Chicago library, subject areas were chosen on the basis of (a) the kinds of historical records available in the main and departmental libraries, (b) the type of regulations governing entry into the stacks, (c) the frequency with which the subject area was held by research libraries (many universities do not have a school of social work, for example), and (d) the assumed strength or evenness of the Chicago collection. The primary objective was to choose the areas of concentrated study from the humanities and the physical, biological, and social sciences so as to ascertain the probable *ranges* in the patterns of use of different disciplines. The applied sciences and disciplines such as medicine, law, and engineering were omitted.

G. Requirements of monograph sampling plan

The basic approach to investigating monograph use was to select a sample from among all of the titles in the shelf list in two widely disparate subject areas —Teutonic literatures and languages (PD, PF, PT in the Library of Congress classification system) and economics (HB–HJ in the Library of Congress classification system)—as well as smaller samples in other subject areas. Since entries in a shelf list represent all the library's holdings arranged by classification number, selecting the sample from the shelf list is equivalent to selecting it from the shelves when none of the books are out.

The object of choosing the sample from among all the titles was to allow each *title* in the chosen subject areas the same probability of entering into the sample. Giving each *card* in the catalog the same probability will not satisfy this requirement, because some titles are entered in the shelf list with more than one card.

H. Description of monograph sampling technique

In each subject area in which a sample was taken, the cards were compressed in the shelf list tray with a bench clamp. A series of 600 equal intervals were measured through the shelf list cards and the intervals marked with a pen. The third card following the interval boundary was chosen. We expected about 200 of the cards chosen to be excluded for one reason or another, and if a card was excluded, the entire interval was excluded (except in physics, when the card following the excluded card was chosen). The purpose of not taking the interval boundary card was to insure that the height or thickness of the top edge of a card would not affect its probability of being chosen, even if the height of a card did influence where the pen mark fell. It was assumed that there is no cyclical relationship between high and low cards, and therefore, taking the third card following the interval boundary would not bias the sample by including an undue proportion of either high or low cards.

To insure that each *title* had the same probability of entering into the sample, even though some titles had more than one catalog card in the shelf list, a title was included only if the *first* card for the title was chosen.

Data were recorded for the title in its entirety, including data on any cards subsequent to the first card.[4]

We wanted to compose our final samples of subject areas so that each decade prior to 1940 would be represented by about the same number of titles. Consequently, the distributions of books by publication date were determined from each of the initial systematic samples. In most cases, the number of titles

4 Variations in procedure from subject area to subject area are discussed in appendix C. We found that the bias of this sampling method would not alter the results appreciably. A full discussion of bias in sampling may be found in appendix J.

was larger for the periods after 1940 and before 1870, so no further samples were needed for these periods. For the remaining decades, the five cards following each initially chosen card were resampled to equalize the number of titles in each decade according to the kinds of rules shown below:

We arbitrarily set the rule that in summarizing, the latest accession date and the earliest publication date among the units being summarized would be the dates taken, on the grounds that if an old book was worth acquiring at some later date, it probably represented a continuing need.

Publication date	Economics	Teutonic languages and literatures
1870–89	Take all titles	Take 1 of every 2 titles
1890–94	Take all titles	Take 1 of every 3 titles
1895–99	Take 2 of every 5 titles	Take 1 of every 3 titles
1900–1904	Take 2 of every 5 titles	Take 1 of every 5 titles
1905–14	Take 1 of every 5 titles	Take none
1915–24	Take 1 of every 10 titles	Take none

To illustrate how this worked: in economics, one of every five titles with a publication date of 1905–14 was selected. The instructions to the data collectors specified which of the five was to be taken—for example, "1905–14, take 1 in 5—the 2nd." Note that each five-card set formed only part of one large sample, within which the "one out of five," etc., was chosen.

I. Data collection procedure

After the data were collected for each book, the use of all its copies was summarized. The total was recorded on a single sheet as part of the *volume* deck, along with the titles which had only one edition, volume, copy, etc. The volumes were then summarized into editions and a new deck was created. The final deck, used for most analyses, was created when the editions were summarized into titles.

The process of summary created some difficulties. Units to be summarized were different on some qualitative, nonsummarizable dimensions. Some of these we could disregard because they would not enter into the analysis—for example, *library location*. By definition, *language* was the same for all units within the title. But the accession date could differ within a title, as could the publication date.

Because in cases of titles with a large number of copies, volumes, or editions, collecting data would have cost a disproportionate amount of time, we followed a subsampling procedure when there were more than five units at any one level within a single title. (See appendix A.)

Publication date was almost always given. When it was not we searched the text for hints as to when the book was published.

Accession date was particularly troublesome. There were two sources of information on the shelf list card, the cataloging date and the accession number. If the book had not been recataloged, the cataloging date was a good indicator and served as the basic source unless the date suggested by the accession number was more than five years earlier than the cataloging date.

Accession numbers were fairly accurate until 1928, when a block system of distributing numbers was inaugurated. We adjusted the accession numbers on the assumption that the quantity of accessions was regular from year to year.

J. Sample size determination

The correct statistical approach to fixing the sample size for this study was to minimize the cost of sampling plus the cost of errors in practice which result from the use of the predictive procedures derived from sampling information. It was difficult to obtain a satisfactory cost estimate as a guide to establishing sample size, because it requires information on how a procedure derived from the sample will be used operationally. For example, a procedure used in one small segment of one small library with an error of 10 percent may cost only a few dollars, no matter how the costs are computed. But when the same procedure is applied to huge portions of many libraries, the same error may cost many thousands of dollars. So it would be necessary, in order to get a cost estimate, to assume that some arbitrary number of libraries would apply the procedures. Also, it was difficult to estimate the cost of the loss in browsing that would result from storing books on the basis of procedures derived from the study.

It was considerably easier to develop a notion of the sample size necessary to reduce variability to an acceptable point with reference to the number of books that would actually be moved to storage under a stated rule, for a stated proportion that a library might want to move. Assuming that enough books would be moved at one time so that variability due to sampling error from that source would be low, we would only have to consider variability in the mean of the population estimated from our sample information. For example, if we wished to remove 25 percent of a given collection to storage using a given rule, and if we estimated the composition of the population (into those that would fall above and below a given cutting point) on the basis of a sample of 400, then we could be 95 percent confident (in the statistical sense) that we would take out between 21 percent and 29 percent of the collection.[5] Confidence limits that assume the variance to be no greater than that of a simple random sample seem to be satisfactory.

The increase in the sample size to 600 (our original sample plus the stratified resamples) will reduce these limits, but the major reason for increasing the simple size with the stratified samples was to reduce the variability of our estimates of use and to test our assumption of use as a simple function of book age.

$$^5 \text{S.D.} = \sqrt{\frac{pq}{n}} = \sqrt{\frac{.25 \times .75}{400}} \approx .02 \text{ or } 2\%$$

Then 2 S.D. $\approx 4\%$, and $25\% \pm 4\% = 21\%$ to 29%

where p = the sample proportion sent to storage with given cutting point and a given rule.

q = the sample proportion not sent to storage.

n = the sample size.

S.D. = one standard deviation.

$\approx$ = approximately equal.

2

Developing and applying procedures to identify monograph titles for storage

A. Purpose of the chapter

The purpose of this chapter is to examine procedures of predicting the future use of monograph titles in the collections of a major research library. We wish to determine which procedures will, under operating conditions, best succeed in making these predictions, on the basis of data about the prior use of individual titles.

When we use the word *function* we refer to a procedure or formula that, when entered with particular values of book age, language, amount of prior use, or other variables, yields a numerical value or prediction of the future use of the title. When combined with policy decisions and used to identify books to be stored on the basis of relative future use, a function may be thought of as an operating *rule*. To give an example, a group of titles may be ranked on the basis of their future use as predicted by a function based on the dates of publication. If the policy decision is to store 25 percent of the group with the lowest prospect of future use, the function becomes a rule indicating which of the titles should be placed in storage under that policy decision.

We sought to determine such things as the efficacy of including *language* in a function, or including both *language* and *country of publication*. In this chapter we do not attempt to determine the relative importance of the various predictor variables in a manner that would hold for all subject areas, since the relative importance of such variables differs from one subject to another and must be separately established. (This is discussed in chapter 3.)

Economics and Teutonic languages and literatures were chosen for the basic analysis of different *forms* of functions because these two subjects probably are as unlike one another as major sections of literature are likely to be. The collections at Chicago in both are believed to be strong, and the two subject departments have been active and relatively strong over a long period of time.

Two kinds of functions for predicting book use were investigated. The first kind involved one or two predictor variables whose distributions we had inspected to select appropriate cutoff points for storage.

The second kind of function was based on statistical regression equations solved with the aid of a Univac computer. Here the effects of *more* than two predictor variables, free of all qualitative judgments, could be tested. The regression equations produced results little if any better than the simple inspectional functions.

For both of these approaches, the techniques and results for unsatisfactory functions as well as for the best function will be described for two reasons: (a) we believe further investigation in this field is desirable, and reports of negative results and the methodologies used may aid subsequent investigators; (b) any given function that is suggested as *most satisfactory* attains that status only in comparison with other known alternative functions.

We experimented with two classes of predictor variables: (a) variables such as the *age* of the book and the *language* in which it was written; and (b) various measures of the *past use* of individual books. *Past use, where sufficient data are available, was found to be the best single predictor of the future use of a book.*

Because research libraries vary in the adequacy of use records, functions were considered for three different situations: (a) where no record of past use is available, (b) where a record of use for the past five years is available, and (c) where the record of past use for 20 years is available. Some of the by-products of the data for this part of the investigation are themselves of interest, and we shall include them as appropriate.

The analysis is entirely in terms of *titles,* which we have previously defined as including all copies, volumes, and editions, in the same language, of a single monograph. In a small pilot study, crude functions at the volume and edition levels appeared to justify this definition.

B. Functions for libraries with no records of prior use

1. Use as a function of publication date (function 1)

This function is the simplest that we shall examine. It is based on the assumption that as books grow older they are progressively less used by readers. Therefore the single predictor variable is *publication date.* In the case of titles having editions or volumes printed in different years, the earliest publication date for any book within the title was used.

If we employ different measures, we arrive at different relationships of publication date to use, as examined initially in a library *with* past use records in order to ascertain whether a predictable relationship exists. One such measure is "average use," whose value is the ratio of the sum of the recorded uses in 1954–58 for all the titles in the sample that were printed within a given time period, to the number of such titles. A second measure is a measure of average use based on the assignment of the values 1–5, only, for the number of uses during the five-year period 1954–58 (instances of more than five uses are counted as five in order to reduce the effect on the ratio of the possible heavy use of a few titles). A third measure considers whether a title was "used or not used," assigning the value "0" if not used and "1" if used one or more times. The results of the investigation of these three measures are shown in figure 1 for Teutonic languages and literatures and in figure 2 for economics.

The functions of "average use," "average use 0–5," and "proportion used" *all* lead to the same rule. They merely predict in different terms the use that would have occured *if the titles had remained in conventional housing.* (If readers are not inhibited by the difficulties of storage access, recorded

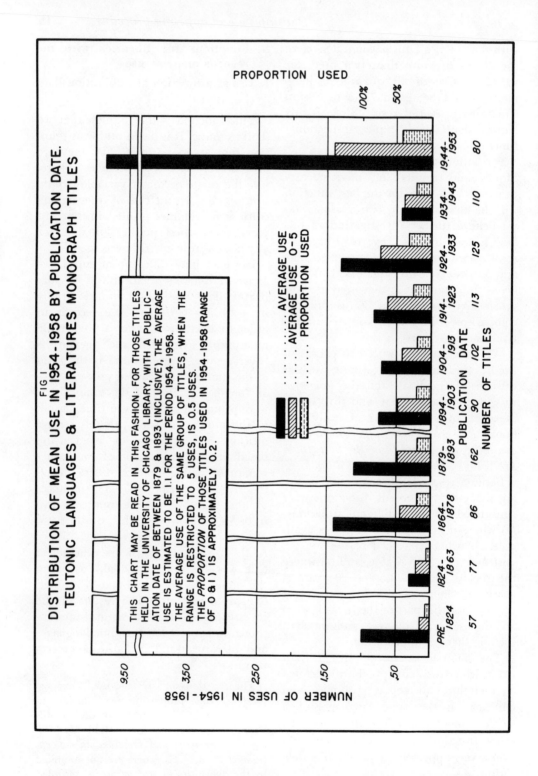

FIG I
DISTRIBUTION OF MEAN USE IN 1954-1958 BY PUBLICATION DATE.
TEUTONIC LANGUAGES & LITERATURES MONOGRAPH TITLES

PROPORTION USED

THIS CHART MAY BE READ IN THIS FASHION: FOR THOSE TITLES
HELD IN THE UNIVERSITY OF CHICAGO LIBRARY, WITH A PUBLIC-
ATION DATE OF BETWEEN 1879 & 1893 (INCLUSIVE), THE AVERAGE
USE IS ESTIMATED TO BE 1.1 FOR THE PERIOD 1954 - 1958.
THE AVERAGE USE OF THE SAME GROUP OF TITLES, WHEN THE
RANGE IS RESTRICTED TO 5 USES, IS 0.5 USES.
THE *PROPORTION* OF THOSE TITLES USED IN 1954-1958 (RANGE
OF 0 & 1) IS APPROXIMATELY 0.2.

.... AVERAGE USE
.... AVERAGE USE 0-5
.... PROPORTION USED

NUMBER OF USES IN 1954-1958

PUBLICATION DATE

NUMBER OF TITLES

16

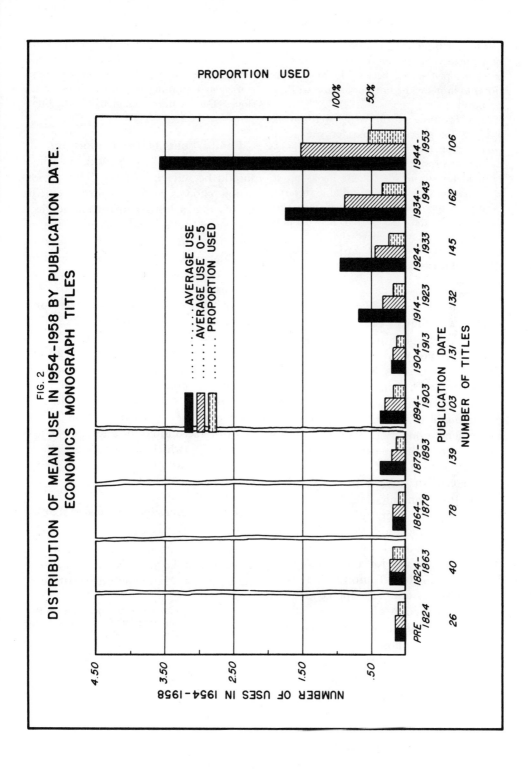

FIG. 2
DISTRIBUTION OF MEAN USE IN 1954-1958 BY PUBLICATION DATE.
ECONOMICS MONOGRAPH TITLES

PROPORTION USED

.... AVERAGE USE
------ AVERAGE USE 0-5
·-·-·- PROPORTION USED

NUMBER OF USES IN 1954-1958

PUBLICATION DATE
NUMBER OF TITLES

17

use for all titles within storage libaries will undoubtedly be greater than for the same titles in open stacks, because in the storage libraries browsing or unrecorded use will not be possible.)

If a function of this type were to be adopted for selecting books for storage, it would probably be assumed that average use decreases with age. The functions would be used for storing the oldest books up to whatever point was deemed suitable in terms of use or space needs. Although there are variations in the results that may dispute this assumption, we believe that it is satisfactory for most practical purposes. Appendix K discusses an investigation of this phenomenon.

We see in figures 1 and 2 that the ratio of the number of titles used to the total number of titles in a given age group does not vary widely among publication date periods. Thus it is not subject to huge irregularities caused by a single very highly used title or to the *contagion* effect in which word-of-mouth recommendations raise the probability that a title will be used two or more times after a period of no use.

It may be of interest to compare the samples for economics and for Teutonic languages and literatures, since they come from widely different substantive areas. From figures 1 and 2 it is evident that the mean use for the samples (in 1954–58, 0.95 for Teutonic languages and literatures and 1.15 for economics) and the proportion of titles used (0.240 in Teutonic languages and literatures and 0.259 in economics) are much the same. But there is little significance in these similarities, since these quantities depend heavily upon the number of faculty and students enrolled in the University who would use those books, and also upon the size of the total collection in those areas.[1]

We also note that for all three measures the slopes of the functions for the economics samples are considerably steeper and more consistent beginning with 1913 than are the slopes for Teutonic languages and literatures.

Comparisons between functions are presented in tables 2 and 3, which should be self-explanatory. This presentation chooses a few arbitrary cutting points that a library might employ as a matter of policy and compares the results that the functions would produce at these points. For function 1, titled "Use as a function of publication date," we may read table 3 as follows: The oldest 25 percent of the titles were published prior to approximately 1905. They represent 203 of the 812 titles in the sample. Thirty-three of them, or 16 percent of those that would have been placed in storage under a rule based upon storing the oldest 25 percent, were used once or more in 1954–58. Those 203 titles accounted for a total of 41 uses in 1954–58, which was 4 percent of the total of 937 uses that were shown by the entire sample of 812 titles.

2. Use as a function of accession date (function 2)

Accession date may also be considered a measure of the age of a book. In a study done at the Massachusetts Institute of

---

[1] To some extent titles can be made to substitute for one another; and all other things being equal, we would expect that the larger the collection in a particular area, the less will any particular title be used. In other words, it is assumed that for a population of given size an increase in the size of a library, beyond some point, may not by itself increase the amount of reading. However, it seems reasonable to assume that a collection of larger size will facilitate the matching of a reader's needs with exactly the "right" book, and that it may also result in the use of a larger number of titles, for portions of their content, if not a larger amount of reading.

TABLE 2

Results of functions for Teutonic languages and literatures monograph titles
(830 titles generating 789 uses in 1954–58)

Function number and description	Cumulative % of titles to be stored taken in increasing order of predicted use	For functions of age only, upper cutting point for group in terms of publication or accession date	Number that would be stored	No. of those stored that would be used once or more in 1954–58	% of those stored that would be used once or more in 1954–58	Number of uses generated by this group	Proportion of uses generated by this group to uses generated by entire sample in percent
A. *Functions for libraries with no use records*							
1. Use as a function of publication date	25	1808	208	20	10	197	25
	35	1895	291	38	13	258	33
	50	1912	415	61	15	351	45
	75	1940	623	121	19	558	71
2. Use as a function of accession date	25	1924	208	34	16	96	12
	35	1927	291	47	16	138	18
	50	1932	415	66	16	199	25
	75	1942	623	108	17	347	44
3. Use as a function of publication date, excluding post-1939 accessions	25	1899	208	19	9	76	10
	35	1908	291	36	12	140	18
	50	1917	415	55	13	197	25
4. Use as a function of publication date and language	25		208	18	9	184	23
	35		291	32	11	218	28
	50		415	47	11	262	33
5. Formal multiple linear regression functions of publication date, accession date, and language:							
a. Average use constrained	25		206	22	11	45	6
	35		288	27	9	74	10
	50		411	46	11	116	15
b. Average use unconstrained	25		206	33	16	63	8
	35		288	39	14	76	10
	50		411	57	14	112	15
c. 0–5 use constrained	25		206	21	10	38	5
	35		288	31	11	86	11
	50		411	48	12	115	15
d. 0–5 use unconstrained	25		206	19	9	33	4
	35		288	25	9	66	9
	50		411	53	13	125	16
e. Proportion used constrained	25		205	19	9	43	6
	35		288	25	9	84	11
	50		411	43	10	120	16
f. Proportion used unconstrained	25		206	15	7	24	3
	35		288	25	9	68	9
	50		411	37	9	101	13
B. *Functions for libraries with five-year past use records*							
6. Use as function of publication date and use in last five years	25	1887	208	13	6	42	5
	35	1915	291	20	7	54	7
	50	1921	415	35	8	79	10
	75	1950	623	78	13	128	16

TABLE 2—*Continued*

Function number and description	Cumulative % of titles to be stored taken in increasing order of predicted use	For functions of age only, upper cutting point for group in terms of publication or accession date	Number that would be stored	No. of those stored that would be used once or more in 1954–58	% of those stored that would be used once or more in 1954–58	Number of uses generated by this group	Proportion of uses generated by this group to uses generated by entire sample in percent
7. Use as function of publication date, language, and use in last five years	25		208	12	6	41	5
	35		291	20	7	52	7
8. Formal multiple regression functions of accession date, publication date, language, and use in the last five years:							
a. Average use	25		208	10	5	34	4
	35		292	17	6	43	5
	50		417	25	6	58	7
	75		625	61	10	105	13
b. 0–5 use	25		208	10	5	35	4
	35		292	16	5	43	5
	50		417	26	6	59	7
	75		625	61	10	105	13
c. Proportion used	25						
	35						
	50						
	75						
C. Functions for libraries with long records of past use							
9. Use as a function of years since last use	25		208	7	3	8	1
	35		291	11	4	12	1
	50		415	23	5	23	2
	75		623	66	11	121	13
10. Use as function of years since last use and years since accession	25		208	7	3	9	1
	35		291	10	3	12	2
	50		415	22	5	23	3
11. Formal regression function of years since last use, publication date, and language:							
a. Average use constrained	25		207	9	4	10	1
	35		289	17	4	14	2
	50		413	24	6	31	4
b. Average use unconstrained	25		207	7	3	8	1
	35		289	15	5	44	6
	50		413	28	7	64	8
c. 0–5 use constrained	25		207	6	3	9	1
	35		289	10	3	14	2
	50		413	23	6	51	7
d. 0–5 use unconstrained	25		207	8	4	9	1
	35		289	15	5	45	6
	50		413	28	7	65	9
e. Proportion used constrained	25		207	8	4	9	1
	35		289	12	4	14	2
	50		413	23	6	50	7
f. Proportion used unconstrained	25		207	9	4	32	4
	35		289	24	8	49	6
	50		413	30	7	65	9

The figures have been adjusted to facilitate comparison.

TABLE 3

Results of functions for economics monograph titles
(812 titles generating 937 uses in 1954–58)

Function number and description	Cumulative % of titles to be stored taken in increasing order of predicted use	For functions of age only, upper cutting point for group in terms of publication or accession date	Number that would be stored	No. of those stored that would be used once or more in 1954–58	% of those stored that would be used once or more in 1954–58	Number of uses generated by this group	Proportion of uses generated by this group to uses generated by entire sample in percent
A. Functions for libraries with no records of prior use							
1. Use as a function of publication date	25	1905	203	33	16	41	4
	35	1913	284	42	15	52	6
	50	1925	406	65	16	147	16
	75	1943	609	117	19	349	37
2. Use as a function of accession date	25	1924	203	32	16	43	5
	35	1930	284	47	17	66	7
	50	1939	406	85	21	163	17
	75	1944	609	118	19	260	28
3. Use as a function of publication date, excluding post-1939 accessions	25	1908	203	29	15	36	4
	35	1919	284	42	15	61	7
	50	1939	406	60	15	95	10
4. Use as a function of publication date and language	25		203	25	17	31	3
	35		284	35	12	44	5
	50		406	59	15	71	10
5. Formal multiple linear regression functions of publication date, accession date, and language:							
a. Average use constrained	25		204	18	9	23	2
	35		285	32	11	37	4
	50		408	54	13	84	9
b. Average use unconstrained	25		204	22	11	26	3
	35		285	32	11	55	6
	50		408	55	13	87	9
c. 0–5 use constrained	25		204	18	9	23	2
	35		285	34	12	42	4
	50		408	54	13	86	9
d. 0–5 use unconstrained	25		204	21	10	25	3
	35		285	30	11	49	5
	50		408	56	14	80	9
e. Proportion used constrained	25		204	18	9	24	2
	35		285	33	12	41	4
	50		408	53	13	65	7
f. Proportion used unconstrained	25		204	14	7	15	2
	35		285	33	12	25	3
	50		408	52	13	71	8
B. Functions for libraries with five-year past use records							
6. Use as a function of publication date and use in the past five years	25	1909	203	20	10	22	2
	35	1919	284	28	10	32	3
	50	1934	406	45	11	52	6

TABLE 3—*Continued*

Function number and description	Cumulative % of titles to be stored taken in increasing order of predicted use	For functions of age only, upper cutting point for group in terms of publication or accession date	Number that would be stored	No. of those stored that would be used once or more in 1954–58	% of those stored that would be used once or more in 1954–58	Number of uses generated by this group	Proportion of uses generated by this group to uses generated by entire sample in percent
7. Use as a function of publication date, language, and use in past five years	25		203	12	6	15	2
	35		284	18	6	21	2
8. Formal multiple regression functions of accession date, publication date, language, and use in past five years:							
a. Average use	25		203	13	6	13	1
	35		285	28	10	32	3
	50		407	41	10	47	5
	75						
b. 0–5 use	25		203	13	6	13	1
	35		285	28	10	32	3
	50		407	41	10	47	5
	75						
c. Proportion used	25		203	13	6	14	1
	35		285	22	8	25	3
	50		407	41	10	47	5
	75						
C. Functions for libraries with long records of past use							
9. Use as a function of years since last use	25		203	11	5	13	1
	35		284	18	6	22	2
	50		406	56	14	71	8
	75		609	132	22	445	47
10. Use as a function of years since last use and years since accession	25		203	10	5	12	1
	35		284	20	7	25	3
	50		406	35	9	42	4
11. Formal regression function of years since last use, publication date, and language:							
a. Average use constrained	25		203	19	9	22	2
	35		284	23	8	27	3
	50		406	42	10	48	5
b. Average use unconstrained	25		203	19	9	22	2
	35		284	24	8	28	3
	50		406	41	10	47	5
c. 0–5 use constrained	25		203	20	10	23	2
	35		284	26	9	30	3
	50		406	42	10	48	5
d. 0–5 use unconstrained	25		203	19	9	22	2
	35		284	26	9	30	3
	50		406	42	10	47	5
e. Proportion used constrained	25		203	17	8	20	2
	35		284	21	7	25	3
	50		406	40	10	45	5
f. Proportion used unconstrained	25		203	17	8	20	2
	35		284	24	8	28	3
	50		406	40	10	45	5

The figures have been adjusted to facilitate comparison.

22

TABLE 4

Use of titles published prior to 1914, in various monograph fields,
as a function of accession date

Accession date	Pre-1904	1904–13	1914–23	1924–33	1934–43	1944–53
Total number of titles	305	408	394	430	317	191
Number of titles unused 1954–58	253	320	314	369	239	136
Percentage of titles unused 1954–58	83.0%	78.4%	79.4%	85.8%	75.4%	71.2%

This table may be read as follows: For those titles that were published before 1914 and acquired between 1914 and 1923, 79.7 percent were not used at all in 1954–58.

Technology,[2] accession date was more closely related to the use of a book than was publication date. Therefore, we next looked at the use of books measured by accession date. Again we considered the three different predictor variables: average use in five years, average use excluding uses above five, and books used as a proportion of the total number of books within the age group. See figures 3 and 4, which may be read in the same fashion as figures 1 and 2.

We see in tables 2 and 3 that accession date produces less satisfactory results than does publication date for all categories except the 75 percent storage level Teutonic languages and literatures. This is explained by a single title—*Goethe's Collected Works.*

3. Use as a function of both publication and accession dates (function 3)

The third function in tables 2 and 3 supplements the use-related-to-publication-date function with information from accession dates.

It is unlikely that librarians would store books less than 20 years old, and we know from a large-scale analysis of titles in many fields (see table 4) that all

but the latest accession dates fail to distinguish between high- and low-use books. We therefore subtracted from the sample all titles acquired after 1939 and constructed a use-on-publication-date function in exactly the same manner as we constructed function 1.[3]

Function 3 seems to do little better at any point than functions 1 or 2.

4. Use as a function of publication date plus language (function 4)

When we use two predictor variables in a function, decisions about cutting points for storage must be made by inspection or by the use of a multiple regression equation. In the former case, the operation begins with tables for each of the language groups that give the use values as a function of publication date, as in tables 5 and 6.[4]

[2] Martin L. Ernst and Bertram Shaffer, "A Survey of Circulation Characteristics of Some General Library Books" (unpublished study, Massachusetts Institute of Technology, Cambridge, Mass., 1954).

[3] Note that in tables 2 and 3 the *denominators of the fractions* in the comparison ratios used to compare functions continue to be the same as in the original sample. We remove as many books as would constitute 25 percent of the *entire sample,* and *not* 25 percent of the subsample that has been stripped of post-1939 accessions. Similarly, the use shown by that 25 percent of the books is compared to the use that the original sample generated. Only in this way can we estimate the results that would occur if we used the function as a rule to remove 25 percent of the universe.

[4] We separated *language* into English, French, German, and other. On the data sheets and IBM cards, language is coded into eleven

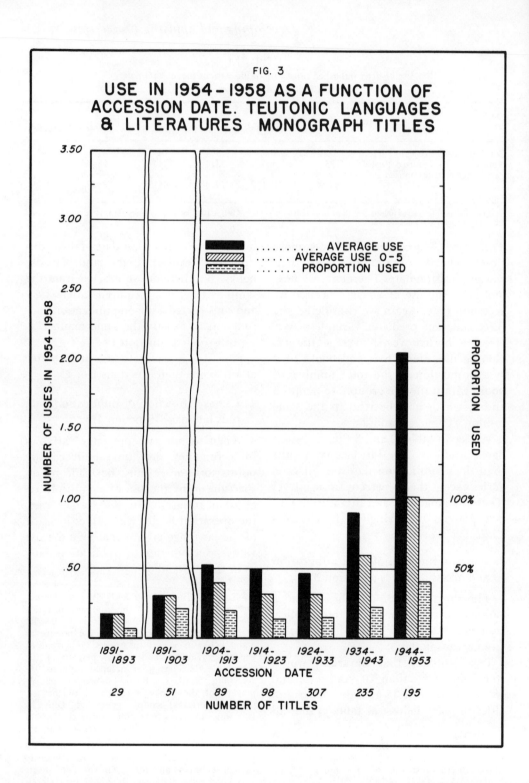

FIG. 3

USE IN 1954-1958 AS A FUNCTION OF
ACCESSION DATE. TEUTONIC LANGUAGES
& LITERATURES MONOGRAPH TITLES

.... AVERAGE USE
...... AVERAGE USE 0-5
.... PROPORTION USED

NUMBER OF USES IN 1954-1958

PROPORTION USED

1891-1893	1891-1903	1904-1913	1914-1923	1924-1933	1934-1943	1944-1953

ACCESSION DATE

| 29 | 51 | 89 | 98 | 307 | 235 | 195 |

NUMBER OF TITLES

24

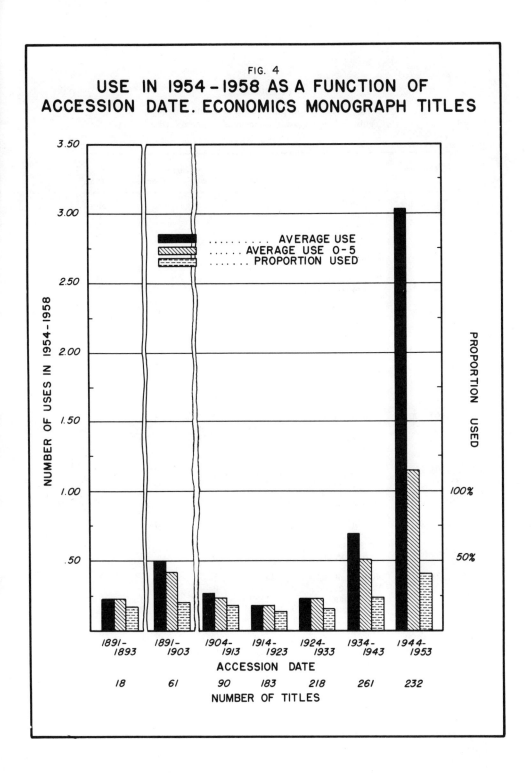

FIG. 4

USE IN 1954 – 1958 AS A FUNCTION OF ACCESSION DATE. ECONOMICS MONOGRAPH TITLES

NUMBER OF USES IN 1954-1958

PROPORTION USED

.... AVERAGE USE
...... AVERAGE USE 0 - 5
.... PROPORTION USED

3.50
3.00
2.50
2.00
1.50
1.00
.50

100%
50%

1891-1893	1891-1903	1904-1913	1914-1923	1924-1933	1934-1943	1944-1953

ACCESSION DATE

| 18 | 61 | 90 | 183 | 218 | 261 | 232 |

NUMBER OF TITLES

TABLE 5

Use as a function of publication date and language,
Teutonic languages and literatures monograph titles
(1954–58)

Publication date		English	French	German	Other
			Language		
Pre-1824	Number of titles	0	0	25	30
	Average use	0	0	2.28	0
	0–5 Average use	0	0	.32	0
	Proportion used	0	0	.12	0
1824–63	Number of titles	3	2	62	10
	Average use	2.33	0	.24	0
	0–5 Average use	1.67	0	.16	0
	Proportion used	0.33	0	.05	0
1864–78	Number of titles	4	2	68	13
	Average use	.50	0	1.68	.23
	0–5 Average use	.50	0	.47	.23
	Proportion used	.50	0	.16	.23
1879–93	Number of titles	6	1	118	32
	Average use	5.33	0	1.15	.22
	0–5 Average use	2.50	0	.47	.22
	Proportion used	.67	0	.20	.13
1894–1903	Number of titles	8	6	65	16
	Average use	5.33	.50	.31	.25
	0–5 Average use	2.50	.50	.30	.25
	Proportion used	.63	.33	.15	.19
1904–13	Number of titles	6	1	79	15
	Average use	1.50	0	.78	0
	0–5 Average use	1.33	0	.44	0
	Proportion used	.50	0	.22	0
1914–23	Number of titles	14	2	80	18
	Average use	1.43	0	.79	.50
	0–5 Average use	.93	0	.63	.44
	Proportion used	.29	0	.29	.22
1924–33	Number of titles	14	1	96	15
	Average use	2.07	0	1.31	.47
	0–5 Average use	1.50	0	.68	.40
	Proportion used	.50	0	.32	.13
1934–43	Number of titles	14	0	78	18
	Average use	1.50	0	.24	.56
	0–5 Average use	1.21	0	.23	.56
	Proportion used	.50	0	.14	.17
1944–53	Number of titles	13	4	39	25
	Average use	6.62	.25	1.28	.40
	0–5 Average use	3.69	.25	1.28	.32
	Proportion used	1.00	.25	.36	.12

TABLE 6

Use as a function of publication date and language,
economics monograph titles

(1954–58)

Publication date		English	Language French	German	Other
Pre-1824	Number of titles	17	6	1	2
	Average use	.24	0	1	0
	0–5 Average use	.24	0	1	0
	Proportion used	.18	0	1	0
1824–63	Number of titles	30	6	2	2
	Average use	.17	.17	0	1.50
	0–5 Average use	.17	.17	0	1.50
	Proportion used	.17	.17	0	.50
1864–78	Number of titles	49	12	12	5
	Average use	.18	.42	0	0
	0–5 Average use	.18	.42	0	0
	Proportion used	.12	.25	0	0
1879–93	Number of titles	95	11	26	7
	Average use	.49	.27	.04	.29
	0–5 Average use	.24	.27	.04	.29
	Proportion used	.17	.18	.04	.29
1894–1903	Number of titles	54	19	25	5
	Average use	.48	.32	.08	.40
	0–5 Average use	.39	.32	.08	.40
	Proportion used	.25	.32	.08	.20
1904–13	Number of titles	76	23	21	11
	Average use	.25	.04	.10	.27
	0–5 Average use	.22	.04	.10	.27
	Proportion used	.14	.04	.10	.27
1914–23	Number of titles	98	10	16	8
	Average use	.91	0	.06	0
	0–5 Average use	.43	0	.06	0
	Proportion used	.22	0	.06	0
1924–33	Number of titles	104	12	26	3
	Average use	1.26	.08	.08	.33
	0–5 Average use	.57	.08	.08	.33
	Proportion used	.30	.08	.04	.33
1934–43	Number of titles	128	3	19	12
	Average use	2.18	0	0	.25
	0–5 Average use	1.09	0	0	.25
	Proportion used	.41	0	0	.25
1944–53	Number of titles	86	5	7	8
	Average use	4.31	.40	.43	.38
	0–5 Average use	1.90	.40	.43	.38
	Proportion used	.59	.40	.29	.13

TABLE 7

Order in which titles were ranked for storage for function 4 derived from table 5, Teutonic languages and literatures monographs

Language	Publication date
Other languages	Pre-1824
French	Pre-1824
Other	1824–63
French	1824–63
French	1864–78
Other	1864–78
German	Pre-1879
French	1879–1940
Other	1879–93
German	1879–93
Other	1894–1923
German	1894–1903
Other	1824–1933
German	1904–13

TABLE 8

Order in which titles were ranked for storage for function 4 derived from table 6, economics monographs

Language	Publication date
German	Pre-1904
French	Pre-1879
Other languages	Pre-1879
French	1879–1903
Other	1879–1903
English	Pre-1879
German	1904–13
French	1904–13
French	1914–23
German	1914–23
Other	1904–23
French	1924–33
German	1924–33
English	1879–1913
French	1934–43
German	1934–43
Other	1924–43
English	1914–23

When a book was printed in two languages but the texts were equivalent—for example, dictionaries and books giving both a text and its translation—a special code was used. This group was pooled with "other" for purposes of analysis. If a book was printed in two languages and the text in one language was not exactly equivalent to that in the other—for example, a collection of essays, some in English and some in French—the title was coded into the more popular language in that subject area. English took preference over all other languages, French and German over all but English, and so on.

The order in which cells were designated for storage in function 4 is shown in tables 7 and 8. It was fixed by inspection of all three predicted variables. The reader may decide whether he agrees with the judgments of the writers.[5]

The effect of function 4 in terms of numbers of titles that would be withdrawn may be seen in tables 2 and 3. There is a substantial improvement over use predictions based on age alone.

5. Formal multiple linear regression equation functions of publication date, accession date, and language (functions 5a–5f)

The purpose of our regression functions is to predict the amount of title use from publication date, accession date, and language of publication (in later functions, by a category of past use, also). The role of any regression function is to extrapolate statistically from one category to another, and in that sense the functions we have discussed in previous pages are regressions. If we had data available for a sufficiently large number of titles in each characteristic's group, we would have no need of the regression technique.

To illustrate, we might have in our sample several titles published in English with given publication dates, accession dates, and category of past use, but our sample may have no titles published in French in that group. Without a regression we have no means of

---

groups, in case finer analysis is required. The particular nature of the separation for analysis should be dictated by the special nature of the subject area under consideration.

[5] A problem in logical inference arises here. The choice of predicted variable will affect the choice of cutting points. And if the predicted variable was chosen *after* inspection of the various sets of data (choosing the most consistent of the data sets, for example), then we might logically not believe that they would be unbiased estimates of future samples. We believe that alerting the reader to the possible difficulties should help prevent misinterpretation.

estimating use for French titles in that group. But the regression technique extends the use relationship from other groups, where we have data on both English and French titles, to the group where we have only English titles. If English titles are used twice as often in the groups where we have data, we assume that in the group for which we have no sample observations, English titles will be used twice as much as French titles.

All six of the regression functions used the same predictor variables. They differ in the variables they predicted and in the method of combining the predictor variables. Functions 5a and 5b employ the *total use* measure, 5c and 5d employ the *0–5 use* measure, and functions 5e and 5f employ the *proportion used* measure. Functions 5a–5f enter the *publication date* and *accession date* variables as well as *language,* as *dummy variables* coded into various time periods. A discussion of our regression techniques, including the use of dummy variables, may be found in appendix L.

Results are presented in tables 2 and 3 above.[6] The procedure that led to these results was as follows: (a) solve the regression equations and obtain *predicted* values for each observation; (b) rank the observations by predicted value from low to high; (c) consider that some arbitrary proportion of the total (say 25 percent) would be stored, and take the lowest 25 percent along the predicted value dimension; (d) examine the use of those books to be stored in the next (five-year) time period.

In the cases of functions that employed age periods coded into dummy variable periods, we inserted another step into the procedure

6 For the following reasons we shall not present either regression coefficients or measures of association among the variables: first, no statistic of correlation has meaning in this situation except insofar as it leads us to expect "good" results as measured by tables 2 and 3; second, because of the results we shall present, we do not expect any library to employ these formal functions.

to estimate the results that the function would produce *when constrained to rank titles for storage consistently by age.* Even if the calculated use value was lower for the period 1904–13 (say) than for 1894–1903, we ranked the titles in the earlier period lower than those in the later period. In this manner we took into account the likely working assumption of decrease in use with age, and reduced the possibility that sampling variation would cause a speciously good fit. For contrast, we show the results of the function both when constrained and when *not* constrained to mark titles consistently by age.

Tables 2 and 3 reveal no clear indication that any one of the formal regression functions will give substantially better results than will the informal functions of language and age—this despite the fact that the formal regression functions employed accession date in addition to publication date and language.

None of the next few functions to be discussed employ accession date as a predictor variable. Accession date is certainly not superior to publication date, and it has the liability of lack of transferability from library to library. Therefore, whenever there is a choice we will employ publication date. Function 3 showed that combining accession date and publication date did not improve on the predictions based on publication date alone.

C. Functions that require five-year past use records

1. Use as a function of publication date and use in the last five years (function 6)

In this function all titles that were used in the period 1949–53 were subtracted from the original sample. This is roughly equivalent to adding a predictor variable: *proportion used in past five years.* The function was applied at the end of 1953 and tested on data from the period 1954–58 to observe its effects.

Denominators for tables 2 and 3 are again those of the original sample, just as they were for function 3.

Function 6 is superior to mere *age* functions. In comparison with functions 1–3, function 6 results in considerably less error for both Teutonic languages and literatures and economics, in the percentage used and in the number of uses generated by the stored titles.

From a statistical standpoint, such a function should be tested on an independently drawn sample, although this was not attempted.

2. Use as a function of publication date plus language plus use in the past five years (function 7)

Function 7 differs from function 6 by adding *language* as a variable. And as we might expect from previous results, this function improves on function 6, as well as on function 3. For libraries that have records of past use for approximately five years, this function seems to work well.

3. Formal multiple regression functions of accession date plus publication date plus language plus use in the last five years (functions 8a–8c)

Use in the past five years was introduced into these functions implicitly by dropping from the sample those titles that were used once or more in 1949–53. Publication and accession dates were entered by means of an arbitrary scaling technique discussed in appendix L. Function 8a employs the *total use* measure; function 8b, the *0–5 use* measure; and function 8c, the *proportion used* measure.

The results are no better than the results of function 7.

D. **Functions employing long records of past use**

For libraries with data over a long period for each book, the independent

variable *years since last use* promises to provide maximum advantage. Definition of this predictor variable is complicated by the fact that some titles are never used at all. As in the case of function 3, we considered the year of accession as the date of the last use for titles that had never been used. However, the efficacy of this variable is limited by changes in size of university population over long periods of time, changes in types of use records maintained, and differences in rates of use decay between books.

1. Use as a function of years since last use (function 9)

Function 9, employing *years since last use* as the only variable, gives strikingly good results. We see in table 2 that this function can identify 25 percent of the collection in Teutonic languages and literatures in such a way that perhaps as little as 3 percent of that group would be used in the subsequent five-year period—a probability of use for each title of approximately one use per hundred per year. For economics (table 3) the results are less striking but still good.

2. Use as a function of years since last use and years since accession (function 10)

Function 10 is similar to function 9 but also takes account of whether a title has ever been used. Because of the manner in which the data cards were punched, it was possible to make this distinction only for titles that had not been used in the years 1935–58. Those titles that had been acquired prior to 1935 and had not been used since then were necessarily grouped together.

Since we generated the function as of the end of 1953 and tested it in the period 1954–58, we speak of a title that has not been used since 1934 as having gone *20* years without use.

Figures 5 and 6 plot the relationship of use in 1954–58 to *years since accession if never used* and *years since last use,* respectively. The very satisfactory results of function 10 may be seen in tables 2 and 3.[7]

3. Formal regression functions of years since last use plus publication date plus language (functions 11a–11f)

Functions 11a–11f are the three predicted-variable functions of *years since last use* (expressed as a coded variable), *publication date,* and *language.* There are again constrained and unconstrained forms. The constrained form demands that for any given *years since last use* value, titles are ranked consecutively by publication date, and for a given publication date, titles are ranked consecutively by *years since last use.* The unconstrained form only demanded consecutive ranking by age with *years since last use* value.

These functions do not show more satisfactory results than function 9.

Several other functions were examined, including a few nonlinear functions of *age* and *years since last use,* but the results were not promising. As a result of this empirical evidence, we concluded that it was unlikely that we would find a function for the variables listed that would perform much better than the simple functions investigated. We were also led to this conclusion because of the high variability of use among books with similar objective characteristics.

E. General conclusions about functions to provide rules for storage

By far the best predictor of the *future* use of a title is its *past* use. Because of

the low probability of use in any one year for titles in the marginal value range in a library the size of that at the University of Chicago, a 15- or 20-year observation period produces considerably better results than an observation period of five years.

Some research libraries have no records of past use. If these libraries wish to begin storage immediately, our results should (a) help them select the best possible functions and (b) suggest the extent of the errors that will arise. Our results also suggest the wisdom of postponing storage for perhaps five years and collecting records of use during that time. If a library initiates a storage plan without waiting to collect such records, it should consider a system whereby high-use books sent to storage could be easily restored to the working collection.

In Teutonic languages and literatures, it is not surprising to find that characteristics such as the age of a book and its language are less satisfactory in predicting future use than is past use. It is doubtful that any other variable will suddenly appear on the research scene and greatly increase predictive accuracy. Some other variables such as *country of publication, number of subject headings on the main entry card,* and *whether the title is or has a translation* were briefly explored. None of them was of much help. Since we do not wish to consider any variable that cannot be coded with ease by a clerk with no knowledge of the subject area or the language in which the book is written, we are doubtful that further investigation will uncover some other simple, objective variable of great predictive value.

When considering the efficacy of an objective selection system, we must take into account the possibility of adding an inspection by the faculty of those titles recommended for storage. Eco-

---

[7] This function was developed in response to a suggestion of a faculty member at the Graduate School of Business of the University of Chicago.

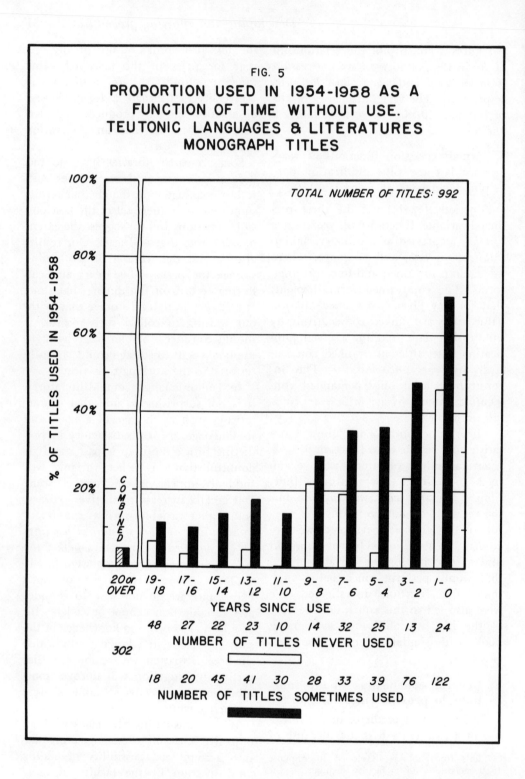

FIG. 5
PROPORTION USED IN 1954-1958 AS A
FUNCTION OF TIME WITHOUT USE.
TEUTONIC LANGUAGES & LITERATURES
MONOGRAPH TITLES

TOTAL NUMBER OF TITLES: 992

% OF TITLES USED IN 1954-1958

COMBINED

| 20 or OVER | 19-18 | 17-16 | 15-14 | 13-12 | 11-10 | 9-8 | 7-6 | 5-4 | 3-2 | 1-0 |

YEARS SINCE USE

NUMBER OF TITLES NEVER USED

| | 48 | 27 | 22 | 23 | 10 | 14 | 32 | 25 | 13 | 24 |

302

NUMBER OF TITLES SOMETIMES USED

| | 18 | 20 | 45 | 41 | 30 | 28 | 33 | 39 | 76 | 122 |

32

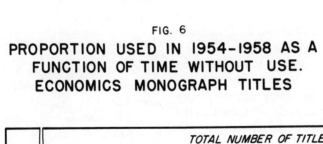

FIG. 6

PROPORTION USED IN 1954-1958 AS A FUNCTION OF TIME WITHOUT USE. ECONOMICS MONOGRAPH TITLES

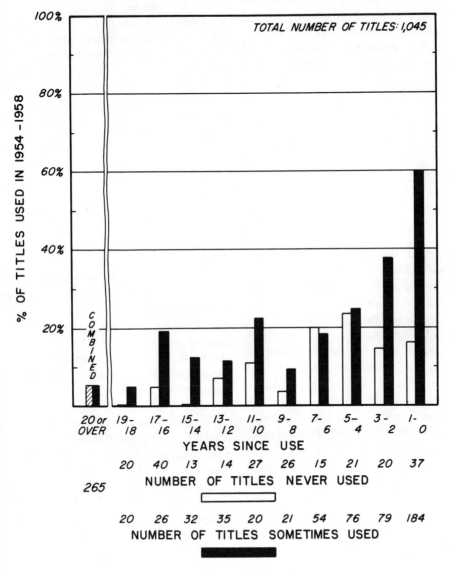

nomically this is far different from asking a scholar to select titles for storage from the entire collection. If a mechanical or objective criteria system can preselect, say, 25 percent of the titles to be considered for storage, the other 75 percent need not be inspected, a saving probably well in excess of three-fourths of the time of an expert selector.

There is little doubt that the accuracy of selection would be improved considerably if one or more scholars reviewed the recommended titles. Necessarily, some important titles would be recommended for storage by a system, even if a considerable record of past use is available, because during any single period some of a group of highly used titles will be used very little.

Chapter 8 discusses an investigation of expert selection in comparison to an objective system of selection.

F. Determining the accuracy of prediction

We must establish the accuracy of prediction of two quantities, listed below.

1. *The proportion of titles that will actually be sent to storage under a rule that attempts to send a given proportion.* This proportion does not depend upon the form of the function employed, but only upon the size of the sample from which the rule was generated. The larger the sample, the closer the actual proportion will come to the expected one. To illustrate: We surveyed the publication dates of 2,874 titles in economics. Thus, for a publication date rule, the 95 percent confidence limits around an expected 25 percent storage would be $2\sqrt{\dfrac{.25\times.75}{2,874}}$, or 1.7 percent. Our selection then would result in from 23.3 to 26.7 percent of economics titles being sent to storage with a confidence of 95 percent. But we did not survey all these

titles as to language, and if we wished to employ function 3, the 95 percent confidence limits would be $2\sqrt{\dfrac{.25\times.75}{812}}$ or 2.8 percent, resulting in from 22.2 to 27.8 percent of economics titles being sent to storage.

2. *The number of titles that will be withdrawn (or number of withdrawals) among a given group sent to storage.* We may look at the accuracy of this prediction in several ways, depending upon the particular interest of the library. Perhaps the most important statistic is the probability that a library patron will have to wait for a book that he wishes to withdraw because the book is in the storage library. The estimate of this quantity is the ratio of the estimated withdrawals from storage divided by the estimated total number of withdrawals. The accuracy of this estimate depends not only upon the accuracy of the predicted number of withdrawals from storage, but also upon the accuracy of prediction of the total number of withdrawals. Our estimates of the variation of the ratio naturally will also depend upon the cutting point chosen. An exact statement of the statistic requires a good many assumptions and a rather complex proof which we shall not attempt here.

Another statistic of interest is the accuracy of prediction of number of withdrawals if a given number of books is sent to storage. This is a simpler problem which may be approached solely in terms of binomial confidence limits. For example, if the function were computed from a sample of 400 and the prediction is that one out of 100 books in the storage group would be used in an average year, we would be 95 percent confident that the real value would not exceed two books used in a hundred. We arrive at this result with the same formula illustrated in the footnote on page 13.

3

Descriptions of monographic use in several subject areas

A. Distribution by age of holdings of titles in the various subject fields

1. Publication date

Chapter 2 stated that in terms of the number of books sent to storage the effect of any rule based on publication date depends heavily upon the distribution of holdings by age. Figures 7a–7c show holdings by publication date for various subject areas, derived from either unstratified systematic samples or stratified samples. In almost every case, the samples contained more than a thousand observations.

Distribution by publication date for the various subject areas is certainly related to the particular nature of the subject area, but also to acquisition policies. To indicate differences between institutions, figure 8 shows similar distributions for the library of the University of California at Berkeley for three subject areas.

2. Accession date

Figures 9a–9c show the distributions of holdings by accession date, similar in all other respects to the distribution of holdings by publication date in figures 7a–7c. The time periods differ from those based on publication dates because the University of Chicago library did not begin its collection until the last decade of the nineteenth century.

B. Some functional relations of use to independent variables

The functional relationships described in this chapter were chosen on the basis of the experience outlined in chapter 2. From the range of functions described there, plus others with which we experimented less successfully, we chose those that seem most likely to be helpful to a storage operation. For a full explanation concerning the derivation and significance of the tabular material that follows in this chapter, see the descriptions of the corresponding functions in chapter 2.

1. Use in relation to publication date

Table 9 shows the relationship of use to publication date. For the predicted variable we arbitrarily chose the mean of use restricted to a 0–5 range, because it seemed to have the most desirable characteristics of the three dependent variables we checked. The time periods were coded into slightly longer intervals than

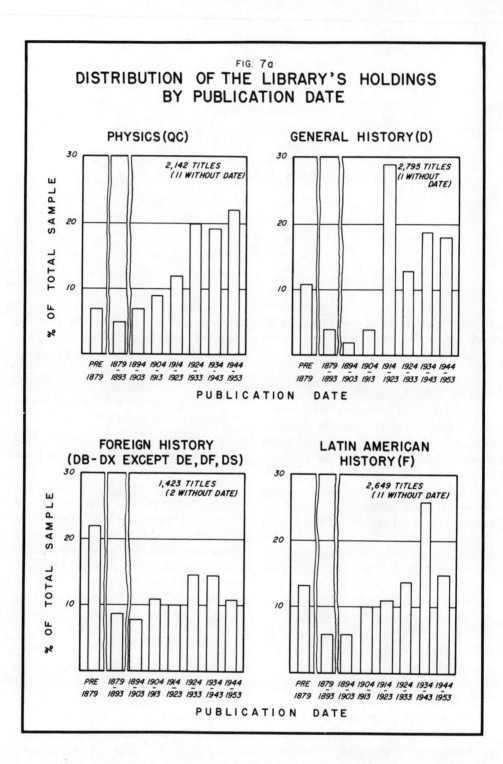

FIG. 7a

DISTRIBUTION OF THE LIBRARY'S HOLDINGS
BY PUBLICATION DATE

PHYSICS(QC)

GENERAL HISTORY(D)

FOREIGN HISTORY
(DB-DX EXCEPT DE,DF,DS)

LATIN AMERICAN
HISTORY(F)

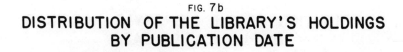

FIG. 7b

DISTRIBUTION OF THE LIBRARY'S HOLDINGS
BY PUBLICATION DATE

ANTHROPOLOGY (GF-GT)

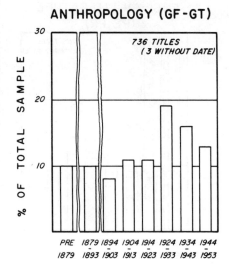

736 TITLES
(3 WITHOUT DATE)

% OF TOTAL SAMPLE

PRE 1879 1894 1904 1914 1924 1934 1944
1879 1893 1903 1913 1923 1933 1943 1953

PUBLICATION DATE

SOCIOLOGY (HM-HT)

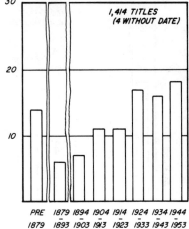

1,414 TITLES
(4 WITHOUT DATE)

PRE 1879 1894 1904 1914 1924 1934 1944
1879 1893 1903 1913 1923 1933 1943 1953

PHILOSOPHY
(B-BJ,EXCEPT BF)

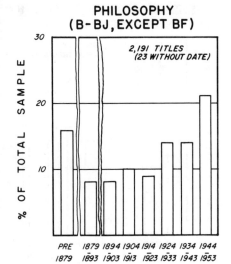

2,191 TITLES
(23 WITHOUT DATE)

% OF TOTAL SAMPLE

PRE 1879 1894 1904 1914 1924 1934 1944
1879 1893 1903 1913 1923 1933 1943 1953

PUBLICATION DATE

ROMANCE LANGUAGES
& LITERATURES (PC,PQ)

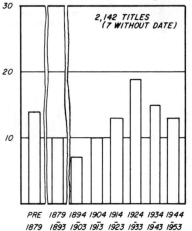

2,142 TITLES
(7 WITHOUT DATE)

PRE 1879 1894 1904 1914 1924 1934 1944
1879 1893 1903 1913 1923 1933 1943 1953

PUBLICATION DATE

37

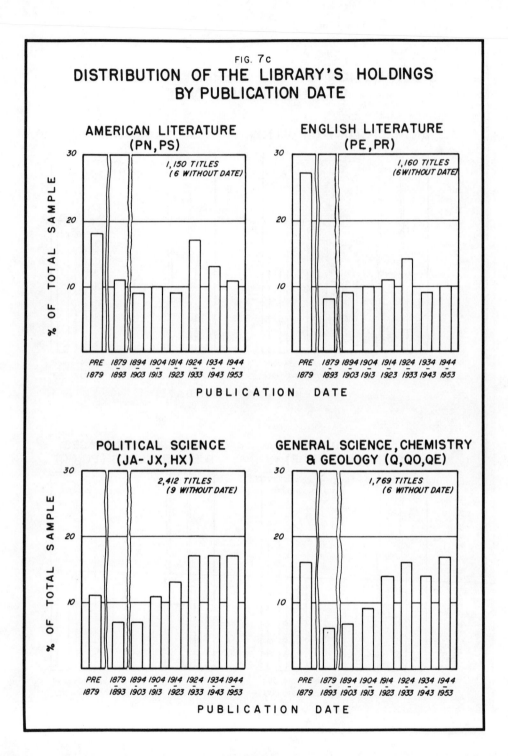

FIG. 7c

DISTRIBUTION OF THE LIBRARY'S HOLDINGS
BY PUBLICATION DATE

AMERICAN LITERATURE
(PN, PS)

1,150 TITLES
(6 WITHOUT DATE)

ENGLISH LITERATURE
(PE, PR)

1,160 TITLES
(6 WITHOUT DATE)

% OF TOTAL SAMPLE

PUBLICATION DATE

POLITICAL SCIENCE
(JA-JX, HX)

2,412 TITLES
(9 WITHOUT DATE)

GENERAL SCIENCE, CHEMISTRY
& GEOLOGY (Q, QO, QE)

1,769 TITLES
(6 WITHOUT DATE)

% OF TOTAL SAMPLE

PUBLICATION DATE

FIG. 8
DISTRIBUTION OF TITLES BY PUBLICATION DATE FOR THE UNIVERSITY OF CHICAGO & THE UNIVERSITY OF CALIFORNIA AT BERKELEY

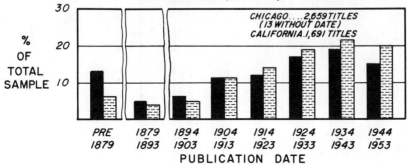

ECONOMICS (HB-HJ)

CHICAGO.....2,659 TITLES
(13 WITHOUT DATE)
CALIFORNIA.1,691 TITLES

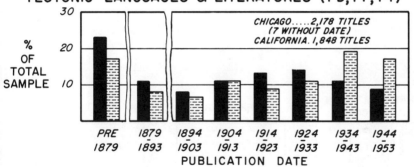

TEUTONIC LANGUAGES & LITERATURES (PD, PF, PT)

CHICAGO......2,178 TITLES
(7 WITHOUT DATE)
CALIFORNIA. 1,848 TITLES

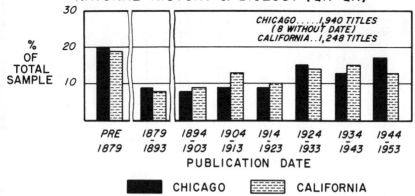

NATURAL HISTORY & BIOLOGY (QH-QR)

CHICAGO.....1,940 TITLES
(8 WITHOUT DATE)
CALIFORNIA..1,248 TITLES

CHICAGO   CALIFORNIA

39

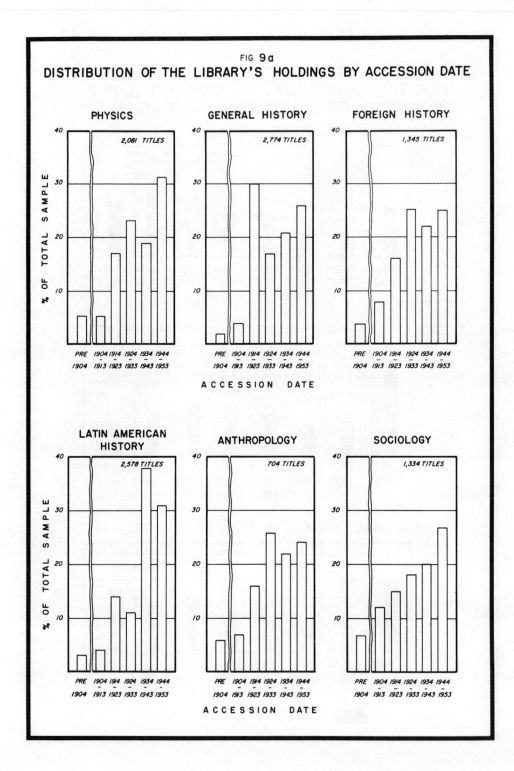

FIG. 9a

DISTRIBUTION OF THE LIBRARY'S HOLDINGS BY ACCESSION DATE

40

FIG. 9b

DISTRIBUTION OF THE LIBRARY'S HOLDINGS BY ACCESSION DATE

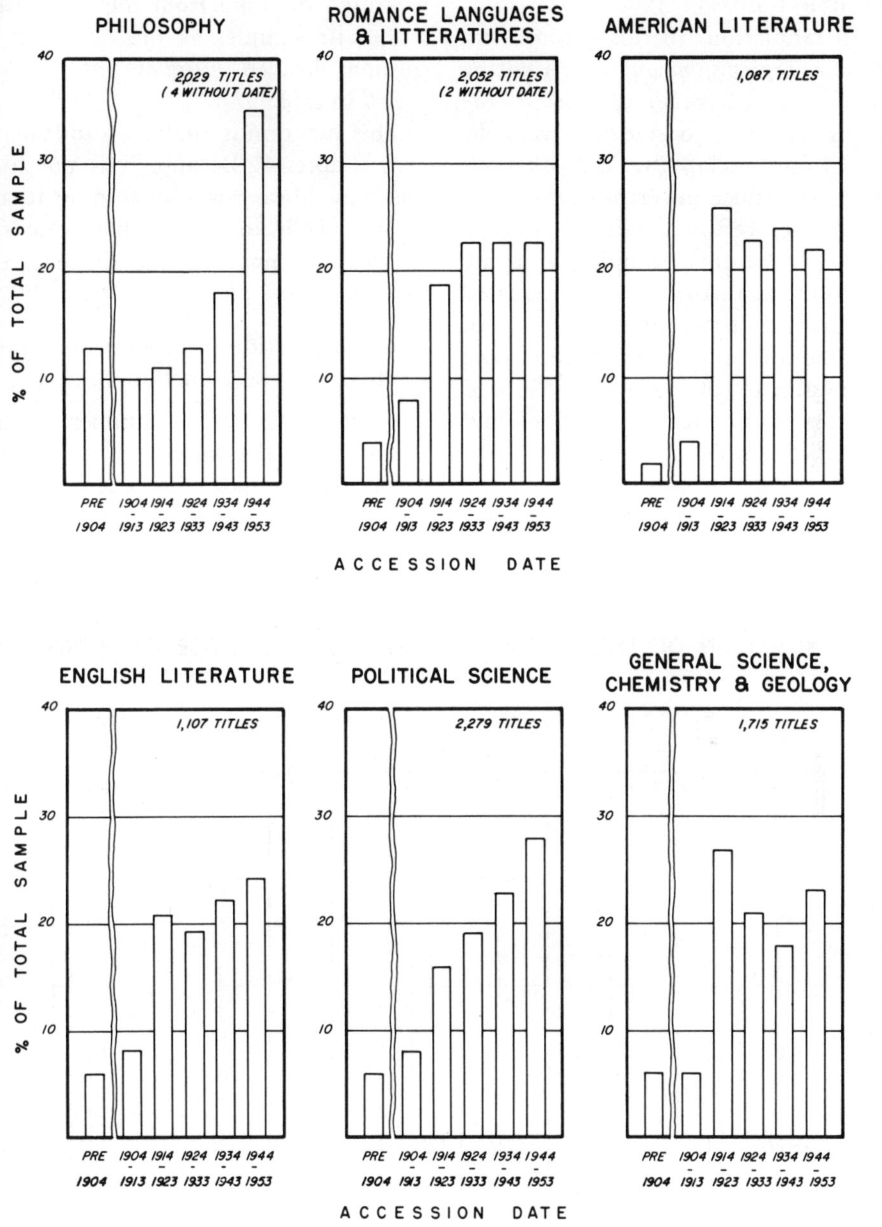

41

in chapter 2 in order to reduce the sampling variations. (The samples taken for economics and for Teutonic languages and literatures were larger than for the other subject areas.)

In all tabulations in this section, two statistics are given, *mean use* (limiting use to 0–5) and *number of titles in the subgroup*. These two statistics were developed from overlapping, but different, samples. To reduce the error of sampling for mean use, we took stratified samples, either as the original samples or as adjuncts to them. In this way we increased the number of observations for books of earlier publication date, producing more reliable estimates of mean use. We used the observations both from stratified and nonstratified samples as the basis for estimates of mean use. Since we fixed the distribution by age that enters a strati-

fied sample, such a sample is not an appropriate basis for estimating the relative numbers of books that would be affected if any rule were used. We therefore used the data from the unstratified systematic samples as the basis for the columns headed *number (of titles) in group* in table 9.

This function is analogous to function 1 in chapter 2. Because it is not likely that any library would employ it as a basis for rules to identify books for storage, we did not tabulate the effects of various cutting points.

2. Use in relation to publication date plus language (function 4)

Table 10 shows the number of titles that fell into the various groups defined by publication date plus language in the different subject areas. It also shows the

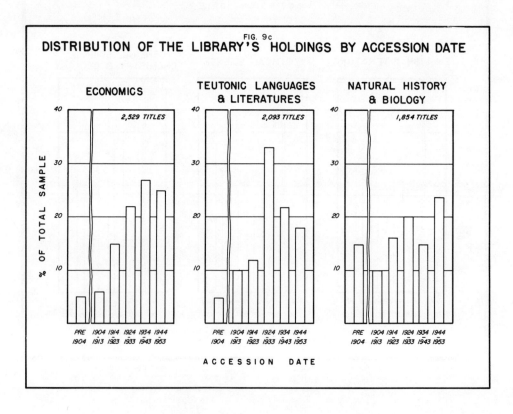

FIG. 9c
DISTRIBUTION OF THE LIBRARY'S HOLDINGS BY ACCESSION DATE

TABLE 9

Relationships of publication date to use in 1954–58 and
distribution of samples by publication date

(Restricted to five uses per title)

	Publication date							
	Pre-1904		1904–33		1934–43		1944–53	
Subject area	No. in group	Mean use	No. in group	Mean use	No. in group	Mean use	No. in group	Mean use
Physics	82	.34	134	.73	69	1.81	75	1.59
History[a]	323	.37	366	.52	216	.74	142	1.65
Anthropology and Sociology	118	.39	156	.89	48	1.31	51	2.57
Philosophy	140	.77	145	.94	55	1.58	84	1.60
Romance Languages and Literatures	57	.63	82	.51	36	.42	34	.98
American and English Literatures	159	.50	169	1.02	51	1.16	38	2.07
Political Science	132	.54	168	.59	71	.87	59	2.07
General Science, Chemistry, and Geology	142	.29	202	.56	48	1.67	60	2.31
Economics	201	.22	342	.32	162	.88	106	1.61
Teutonic Languages and Literatures	345	.39	325	.61	90	.41	71	1.39
Natural History and Biology	144	.27	139	.66	56	1.36	52	2.51

[a] Includes general, foreign, and Latin American History.

mean use (restricted to the range 0–5 uses) for the various groups during 1954–58.

We then employed the data in table 10 as the basis for choosing groups for storage to determine the effects of storing 25 percent, 35 percent, and 50 percent of the subject area subcollections. The results are shown in table 11.

The order in which groups of titles were cut for storage is given in appendix B. For more details of the procedure, see the discussion of function 4 in chapter 2.

We found that when 25 percent were stored in each subject area, the percent that would be used at all in a five-year period ranged from 9 percent (Teutonic languages and literatures) to 26 percent (philosophy), a spread which indicates the need for a storage policy that differs for various subject areas. The *proportion* of total use in each subject area ranged from 1 percent (anthropology and sociology) to 23 percent (Teutonic languages

and literatures). It is doubtful that many research libraries would be satisfied with such results.

3. Use in relation to publication date and to use in the past five years (function 6)

Table 12 shows the relationship of age to use, after subtracting from the sample those titles that had been used in the period 1949–53. As we have said before, this is roughly equivalent to including as a predictor variable *proportion used in 1949–53*.

4. Use in relation to publication date plus language plus use in the past five years

Table 13 shows the effects of storing various proportions of the subject area collections, employing the same ranking of subgroups as in function 4, but also excluding those titles that were used in 1949–53. This function is analogous in

TABLE 10

Relationships of publication date and language to use in 1954–58
and distribution by publication date and language

(Restricted to five uses per title)

Language	Pre-1904 No. in group	Mean use	1904–13 No. in group	Mean use	1914–23 No. in group	Mean use	1924–33 No. in group	Mean use	1934–43 No. in group	Mean use	1944–53 No. in group	Mean use
PHYSICS												
English	35	0.52	15	0.75	24	0.80	49	1.15	49	2.33	50	1.94
French	16	0.18	1	0.50	4	0.20	8	0.44	6	0.83	5	0.40
German	24	0.17	10	0.39	5	0.50	11	0.71	7	0.57	10	0.70
Other	7	0	1	0	2	0.17	4	0.50	7	0.29	10	1.30
HISTORY Excluding American, British, Classical Antiquity, Greek, and Asian												
English	22	0.65	33	0.78	112	0.39	70	1.28	89	1.23	85	2.52
French	80	0.37	24	0.31	27	0.27	22	0.50	17	1.10	19	0.72
German	78	0.14	18	0.68	26	0.21	33	0.24	34	0.47	9	1.15
Other	71	0.30	24	0.20	39	0.52	38	0.15	76	0.27	29	0.37
ANTHROPOLOGY AND SOCIOLOGY												
English	66	0.63	20	1.06	27	1.02	49	1.71	27	2.23	35	3.24
French	13	0.22	7	0	8	0.46	6	0.71	4	0.67	7	0.86
German	33	0.14	13	0.04	7	0.09	9	0.15	13	0.04	6	1.17
Other	6	0.14	2	0.25	4	0.29	4	0.13	4	0	3	0
PHILOSOPHY												
English	59	1.47	14	1.39	25	1.58	27	1.36	28	2.57	25	3.04
French	16	0.33	5	1.17	3	0.33	5	1.20	6	0.50	28	0.93
German	52	0.30	20	0.29	8	1.25	21	0.19	8	0.25	10	1.90
Other	13	0.35	4	0	6	0.33	7	0.43	13	0.77	21	0.62
ROMANCE LANGUAGES AND LITERATURES												
English	7	1.52	1	0.91	2	1.14	5	1.38	7	0.64	2	1.25
French	31	0.66	10	1.03	4	0.39	15	0.64	8	0.13	8	1.93
German	4	0.12	3	0	3	0.11	2	0	4	0	0	0
Other	15	0.39	7	0.37	16	0.32	14	0.10	15	0.58	14	0.48
AMERICAN AND ENGLISH LITERATURE												
English	14	0.53	43	1.16	41	0.93	63	1.29	42	1.38	30	2.22
French	3	0.40	1	0	0	0	3	0	1	0	3	0.23
German	10	0.27	7	0.50	3	0	6	0.67	4	0	0	0
Other	3	0.33	0	0	1	0	1	0	4	0	5	0.80
POLITICAL SCIENCE												
English	80	0.71	28	0.43	37	1.06	33	0.87	44	1.22	42	2.62
French	21	0.46	9	0.31	3	0.60	6	0	7	0.63	6	0.83
German	19	0.28	7	0.27	12	0.50	14	0.47	11	2.27	5	1.00
Other	12	0.07	6	0.22	5	0	8	0	9	0	6	0.33

TABLE 10—*Continued*

| | Publication date | | | | | | | | | | | |
| | Pre-1904 | | 1904–13 | | 1914–23 | | 1924–33 | | 1934–43 | | 1944–53 | |
Language	No. in group	Mean use	No. in group	Mean use	No. in group	Mean use	No. in group	Mean use	No. in group	Mean use	No. in group	Mean use
GENERAL SCIENCE, CHEMISTRY, AND GEOLOGY												
English	75	0.42	33	0.71	57	0.40	54	1.14	42	1.79	44	2.90
French	17	0.14	5	0.25	8	0.55	2	0.50	1	1.00	3	0.33
German	48	0.17	13	0.09	12	0.15	11	0.33	4	1.00	7	0.86
Other	7	0	3	0	2	0.25	2	0	1	0	6	0.57
ECONOMICS												
English	57	0.23	52	0.22	86	0.43	103	0.57	128	1.09	86	1.90
French	29	0.28	16	0.04	7	0	12	0.08	3	0	5	0.40
German	32	0.06	16	0.10	10	0.06	28	0.08	19	0	57	0.43
Other	12	0.33	6	0.28	5	0	3	0.33	12	0.25	8	0.38
TEUTONIC LANGUAGES AND LITERATURES												
English	16	1.52	4	1.33	14	0.93	14	1.50	11	1.21	12	2.89
French	9	0.25	2	0	1	0	0	0	0	0	3	0.25
German	245	0.37	68	0.44	80	0.63	96	0.68	64	0.23	34	1.28
Other	55	0.14	13	0	19	0.44	14	0.40	15	0.56	22	0.32
NATURAL HISTORY AND BIOLOGY												
English	58	0.34	22	0.69	29	0.71	49	1.09	48	1.44	41	2.83
French	17	0.25	2	0.71	3	0.83	2	0	3	0	1	5.00
German	50	0.17	10	1.11	4	0.71	16	1.18	5	1.40	4	1.25
Other	19	0.32	1	0	0	0	1	0	0	0	6	0.67

all respects to function 7 described in chapter 2. As expected, the results are better than those for function 4.

5. Use in relation to years since last use or years since accession if never used

Table 14 shows the data for mean use in relation to years since last use or, if never used, years since accession. From these data we determined that the order of storing groups of books in all the areas would be as follows:

a. Never used since accession 13 years before
b. Not used in past 20 years
c. Not used in past 19 years
d. Never used since accession 12 years before

e. Not used in the past 18 years . . . and so on

Identifying groups for storage in this manner produced the results seen in table 15 which, for almost every subject group, are better than the results of any other function.

C. Conclusion

The results described in this chapter for several different subject areas confirm the conclusions based on the intensive study of economics and of Teutonic languages and literatures regarding the efficacy of various functions investigated and the storage rules derived from them. It becomes evident that books can be separated into groups that will generate significantly different amounts of use. Be-

TABLE 11

Result of basing the rule for storage on use as a function
of publication date and language

Subject area	Cumulative % of titles to be stored taken in increasing order of predicted use	Number that would be stored	Number of those stored that would be used once or more in 1954–58	Percent of those stored that would be used once or more in 1954–58	Number of uses generated by this group	Proportion of uses generated by this group to uses generated by entire sample in percent
Physics	25	90	12	13	40	3
	35	126	26	21	93	8
	50	180	35	19	136	12
History	25	287	48	17	96	9
	35	401	68	17	139	13
	50	574	97	17	190	18
Anthropology and Sociology	25	93	10	11	12	1
	35	131	14	11	17	2
	50	186	31	17	51	5
Philosophy	25	106	28	26	45	4
	35	148	44	30	79	7
	50	212	73	34	125	11
Romance Languages and Literatures	25	49	8	16	21	7
	35	69	13	19	32	11
	50	98	21	21	60	20
American and English Literature	25	104	16	15	40	6
	35	146	28	19	76	11
	50	208	50	24	112	17
Political Science	25	108	14	13	53	7
	35	134	21	16	64	9
	50	215	42	20	187	26
General Science, Chemistry, and Geology	25	113	15	13	20	2
	35	158	24	15	37	5
	50	226	41	18	111	14
Economics	25	203	25	12	31	3
	35	284	35	12	44	5
	50	406	59	15	91	10
Teutonic Languages and Literatures	25	208	18	9	184	23
	35	291	32	11	218	28
	50	415	47	11	262	33
Natural History and Biology	25	98	16	16	15	2
	35	137	25	18	29	3
	50	196	48	24	63	8

TABLE 12

Results of basing the rule for storage on use as a function of
publication date and use in the past five years

Subject area	Cumulative % of titles to be stored taken in increasing order of predicted use	Number that would be stored	Number of those stored that would be used once or more in 1954–58	Percent of those stored that would be used once or more in 1954–58	Number of uses generated by this group	Proportion of uses generated by this group to uses generated by entire sample in percent
Physics	25	90	9	10	12	1
	35	126	15	12	24	2
	50	180	27	15	50	4
History	25	287	42	15	66	6
	35	401	57	14	86	8
	50	574	81	14	119	11
Anthropology and Sociology	25	93	14	15	19	2
	35	131	23	18	23	2
	50	186	31	17	41	4
Philosophy	25	106	19	18	27	2
	35	148	25	17	37	3
	50	212	49	23	91	8
Romance Languages and Literatures	25	49	6	12	18	6
	35	69	8	12	23	8
	50	98	13	13	28	9
American and English Literatures	25	104	15	14	25	4
	35	146	21	14	31	5
	50	208	32	15	46	7
Political Science	25	108	12	11	13	2
	35	134	14	10	17	2
	50	215	31	14	37	5
General Science, Chemistry, and Geology	25	113	14	12	23	3
	35	158	20	13	30	4
	50	226	22	10	33	4
Economics	25	203	20	10	22	2
	35	284	28	10	31	3
	50	406	45	11	52	6
Teutonic Languages and Literatures	25	208	13	6	42	5
	35	291	20	7	54	7
	50	415	35	8	79	10
Natural History and Biology	25	98	7	7	9	1
	35	137	9	7	12	1
	50	196	19	10	24	3

47

TABLE 13

Results of basing the rule for storage on use as a function of
publication date, language, and use in the past five years

Subject area	Cumulative % of titles to be stored taken in increasing order of predicted use	Number that would be stored	Number of those stored that would be used once or more in 1954–58	Percent of those stored that would be used once or more in 1954–58	Number of uses generated by this group	Proportion of uses generated by this group to uses generated by entire sample in percent
Physics	25	90	11	12	19	2
	35	126	16	13	26	2
	50	180				
History	25	287	29	10	47	4
	35	401	44	11	71	7
	50	574	82	14	130	12
Anthropology and Sociology	25	93	6	6	6	1
	35	131	13	10	15	2
	50	186	27	15	32	3
Philosophy	25	106	21	20	23	2
	35	148	31	21	35	3
	50	212	44	21	70	6
Romance Languages and Literatures	25	49	4	8	5	2
	35	69	6	9	7	2
	50	98	11	11	25	8
American and English Literature	25	104	12	12	18	3
	35	146	19	13	31	5
	50	208	30	14	45	7
Political Science	25	108	9	8	12	2
	35	134	13	10	17	2
General Science, Chemistry, and Geology	25	113	10	9	15	2
	35	158	16	10	26	3
	50	226	22	10	32	4
Economics	25	203	12	6	15	2
	35	284	18	6	21	2
Teutonic Languages and Literatures	25	208	12	6	41	5
	35	291	20	7	52	7
Natural History and Biology	25	98	5	5	5	1
	35	137	10	7	13	2
	50	196	18	9	22	3

TABLE 14

Relationship of "years since last use or years since accession
if never used" to mean use in 1954–58

(Restricted to five uses per title)

	Number of years since use or accession									
	0–4		5–9		10–14		15–19		20	
	No. in group	Mean use	No. in group	Mean use	No. in group	Mean use	No. in group	Mean use	No. in group	Mean use
PHYSICS (353 titles)										
Titles used some time since accession	134	1.98	37	0.62	14	0.14	16	0.19	a	
Titles never used since accession	31	1.36	25	0.64	12	0.08	6	0.00	a	
Combined	165	1.86	62	0.63	26	0.12	22	0.14	78	0.12
HISTORY (1,139 titles)										
Titles used some time since accession	350	1.43	149	0.41	76	0.25	29	0.17		
Titles never used since accession	78	0.73	86	0.30	81	0.14	42	0.14		
Combined	428	1.27	235	0.37	157	0.19	71	0.16	248	0.07
ANTHROPOLOGY AND SOCIOLOGY (365 titles)										
Titles used some time since accession	136	2.07	39	0.54	15	0.20	27	0.11		
Titles never used since accession	24	1.25	15	0.20	14	0.07	9	0.11		
Combined	160	1.95	54	0.44	29	0.14	36	0.11	86	0.11
PHILOSOPHY (414 titles)										
Titles used some time since accession	187	1.83	38	0.47	15	0.47	13	0.39		
Titles never used since accession	45	1.13	24	0.21	9	0.11	6	0.00		
Combined	232	1.70	62	0.37	24	0.33	19	0.26	77	0.08
ROMANCE LANGUAGES AND LITERATURES (195 titles)										
Titles used some time since accession	79	1.46	21	0.57	16	0.56	6	0.00		
Titles never used since accession	14	0.64	11	0.09	5	0.00	9	0.11		
Combined	93	1.33	32	0.41	21	0.43	15	0.07	34	0.03

[a] Information not available; see chapter 2.

TABLE 14—*Continued*

	Number of years since use or accession									
	0–4		5–9		10–14		15–19		20	
	No. in group	Mean use	No. in group	Mean use	No. in group	Mean use	No. in group	Mean use	No. in group	Mean use
AMERICAN AND ENGLISH LITERATURE (413 titles)										
Titles used some time since accession	158	1.82	45	0.47	17	0.35	16	0.19		
Titles never used since accession	25	1.56	23	0.04	24	0.08	19	0.21		
Combined	183	1.79	68	0.32	41	0.20	35	0.20	86	0.08
POLITICAL SCIENCE (444 titles)										
Titles used some time since accession	157	1.66	44	0.50	15	0.15	16	0.21		
Titles never used since accession	38	0.52	23	0.14	16	0.00	47	0.08		
Combined	195	1.51	67	0.40	31	0.09	63	0.15	88	0.07
GENERAL SCIENCE, CHEMISTRY, AND GEOLOGY (445 titles)										
Titles used some time since accession	143	1.65	52	0.25	38	0.27	29	0.11		
Titles never used since accession	25	1.38	13	0.13	9	0.40	14	0.06		
Combined	168	1.61	65	0.24	47	0.30	43	0.10	122	0.04
ECONOMICS (1,005 titles)										
Titles used some time since accession	240	0.97	112	0.25	64	0.16	67	0.16		
Titles never used since accession	66	0.21	53	0.15	49	0.42	65	0.03		
Combined	306	0.81	165	0.22	113	0.15	132	0.10	289	0.00
TEUTONIC LANGUAGES AND LITERATURES (992 titles)										
Titles used some time since accession	219	1.92	79	0.49	89	0.21	65	0.15		
Titles never used since accession	45	0.91	63	0.18	46	0.11	84	0.06		
Combined	264	1.75	142	0.35	135	0.18	149	0.10	302	0.05
NATURAL HISTORY AND BIOLOGY (383 titles)										
Titles used some time since accession	139	1.82	29	0.35	28	0.11	17	0.29		
Titles never used since accession	26	1.62	7	0.29	9	0.00	4	0.00		
Combined	165	1.79	36	0.33	37	0.08	21	0.24	124	0.03

TABLE 15

Results of basing the rule for storage on use as a function of "years since last use or years since accession if never used"

Subject area	Cumulative % of titles to be stored taken in increasing order of predicted use	Number that would be stored	Number of those stored that would be used once or more in 1954–58	Percent of those stored that would be used once or more in 1954–58	Number of uses generated by this group	Proportion of uses generated by this group to uses generated by entire sample in percent
Physics	25	90	7	8	13	1
	35	126	12	10	21	2
	50	180	26	14	55	5
History	25	287	20	7	22	2
	35	401	33	8	37	4
	50	574	62	11	92	9
Anthropology and Sociology	25	93	8	9	10	1
	35	131	10	8	12	1
	50	186	26	14	33	3
Philosophy	25	106	9	8	12	1
	35	148	19	13	27	2
	50	212	48	23	126	11
Romance Languages and Literatures	25	49	2	4	2	1
	35	69	4	6	4	1
	50	98	11	11	28	9
American and English Literature	25	104	9	9	9	1
	35	146	11	8	11	2
	50	208	21	10	23	3
Political Science	25	108	6	6	7	1
	35	134	9	7	10	1
	50	215	20	9	24	3
General Science, Chemistry, and Geology	25	113	4	4	8	1
	35	158	6	4	13	2
	50	226	18	8	27	3
Economics	25	203	10	5	12	1
	35	284	20	7	25	3
	50	406	35	9	42	4
Teutonic Languages and Literatures	25	208	7	3	9	1
	35	291	10	3	12	2
	50	415	22	5	23	3
Natural History and Biology	25	98	3	3	3	0.5
	35	137	5	4	5	1
	50	196	13	7	17	2

cause of the differences between the patterns of holdings in various matters and in various libraries, the effects of any given rule cannot be predicted without knowing more about the subject area and the library. But an inexpensive and quick set of surveys should in most cases provide all the information necessary for applying the rules successfully.

Our data also indicate considerable variation from subject to subject in (a) the choice of function that would be most promising under any condition of information about prior use, (b) the effectiveness of the results that would be achieved under any condition of information about prior use, and (c) the aptness of the policy recommendation that seems implicit in the data. On the basis of our data, some fields would be highly suitable for a storage program while others would present very difficult problems in terms of probable impairment of reader access.

4

Comparisons of book use in several institutions

The findings of this study would be primarily of local interest unless the results could be applied to some extent in other research libraries. We must therefore ask:

1. Can other libraries apply the procedures of the University of Chicago library directly to their own collections?

2. If not, can other libraries use the basic findings when they are supplemented with their own data?

A. Factors affecting the validity of the comparison

A major difference in any of several dimensions might make the analysis of use at Chicago inapplicable to another library. Several of these dimensions are discussed below.

1. *Differences in specific subject areas.* If a much higher proportion of another library's collection in history, for example, consists of relatively new works, direct application of the Chicago rules might designate for storage a much smaller proportion of the other library's collection than that designated at Chicago. Or if a different proportion of the other library's collection were in foreign languages, the same result would occur. The same general rule might still be applicable, but adjustments would be necessary.

2. *Substantial differences in size of collections.* The average use of smaller collections is likely to be higher if the number of users is the same, but the use within the collection may be distributed differently. In such a case, application of Chicago rules without further investigation might lead either to a different number of books designated for storage or to a higher number of withdrawals from storage than was expected.

3. *Major differences in the number of users.*

4. *Differences in the nature of the users.* These may involve, for example, the interests and command of foreign languages of faculty and students, and the relative numbers of faculty, graduate, and undergraduate students.

5. The following technical factors could make the use patterns appear different and, therefore, make comparisons difficult between libraries. These factors can make it difficult to adapt the functions derived for one library to another library.

a. *The nature of use records available.*

The most reliable predictor of the use of monographs at Chicago was *number of years since the last use* (or *since accession if never used*). A library having no record of use, or a very recent one, will be unable to use this variable. Some libraries have no clear record of accession dates, which would be a further limitation. Appendix G summarizes some of the information obtained from a study of use records of a number of major research libraries.

b. *Variations in circulation rules.* If it is impossible to determine from the records whether a book was taken out by several different readers or several times in succession by the same reader, the length of the circulation period could make a considerable difference in the patterns of use shown by various classes of books.

c. *Differences in cataloging procedures.* For example, if the *political science* category in the Library of Congress scheme contains many books that would appear under *law* or *sociology* in the classification used by another library, then the description and the rules for storage for the political science category at Chicago would not apply very well to the political science section of the other library. Furthermore, certain cataloging procedures may make it more difficult to perform supplementary investigations in a particular library for the purpose of corroborating the Chicago results. In some cataloging systems (for example, that of Yale), editions of the same title are not next to each other in the shelf list if other works in the same subject area with the same author initial have been purchased in the years between editions. This makes it very difficult to sample from such a shelf list with an equal probability for all titles.

B. Amount of use of the same titles at different institutions

In the first part of this investigation we sought to establish whether differences of scholarly interest would make it possible to generalize from one institution to another. Insofar as possible, we attempted to do so apart from the effects of differences in the collections.

Our procedure was as follows: From lists of titles in the random samples of monographs taken at Chicago, each having approximately 400 titles, we derived lists of items that were also held in certain other libraries. We compared the sample lists in biology, Teutonic languages and literatures, and philosophy against the holdings at Yale; the lists in physics, Teutonic languages and literatures, and economics against the holdings at Northwestern University; and the lists in economics, Teutonic languages and literatures, and biology against the holdings at the University of California at Berkeley. In each comparison, the titles on the original list that were held by both institutions formed the new sample. Any book unit within the title (see definition of "title" in chapter 1) was sufficient to constitute a holding.[1] The mechanics are described in appendix G.

Each comparison sample constituted a group of similar items that were available to different scholars in different institutions. It was, of course, a very biased sample of the holdings of the libraries compared, but at least the use of each title could be compared between institutions. The choice of subject areas was based primarily on certain similarities between institutions; for example, the existence of a school of business in both or in neither. The research libraries used

[1] For other possible analyses we determined whether the holdings in each title were identical as to edition and volume.

TABLE 16

Comparisons of the use of the same titles at Chicago, Yale,
Northwestern, and California at Berkeley

Use at Yale in 1949–53	No. in Group	Use at Chicago 1954–58								Use at Yale 1954–58							
		Number of cases used						Total Use	Total Use (0–5)	Number of cases used						Total Use	Total Use (0–5)
		0	1	2	3	4	5+			0	1	2	3	4	5+		
PHILOSOPHY																	
0	79	58	11	6	0	1	3	57	42	70	7	1	1	0	0	12	12
1	18	13	3	2	0	0	0	7	7	10	4	3	0	1	0	14	14
2	14	7	3	1	1	0	2	18	18	6	4	1	1	2	0	17	17
3	2	1	0	0	1	0	0	3	3	0	1	0	0	0	1	6	6
4+	19	6	4	3	1	3	2	65	35	4	2	2	1	3	7	105	56
Total	132	85	21	12	3	4	7	150	105	90	18	7	3	6	8	154	105
TEUTONIC LANGUAGES AND LITERATURES																	
0	109	93	9	3	1	1	2	43	32	102	7	0	0	0	0	7	7
1	15	7	4	1	1	0	2	25	19	6	7	1	1	0	0	12	12
2	6	4	1	1	0	0	0	3	3	2	3	0	1	0	0	6	6
3	7	3	1	2	1	0	0	8	8	2	2	2	0	0	1	18	11
4+	12	2	4	0	2	1	3	73	29	0	3	3	1	1	4	69	36
Total	149	109	19	7	5	2	7	152	91	112	22	6	3	1	5	112	72
BIOLOGY																	
0	84	70	8	1	2	1	2	61	30	77	3	2	1	1	0	14	14
1	7	4	1	0	1	0	1	10	9	5	1	0	1	0	0	4	4
2	6	3	0	0	2	0	1	11	11	3	2	0	1	0	0	5	5
3	1	1	0	0	0	0	0	0	0	1	0	0	0	0	0	0	0
4+	17	3	1	3	2	1	7	147	52	3	1	1	0	1	11	188	62
Total	115	81	10	4	7	2	11	229	102	89	7	3	3	2	11	211	85

for comparison were chosen to include one library larger than that of Chicago, one about the same size, and one somewhat smaller. We sought libraries that had satisfactory records of past use and that employed classification schemes that could be made to correspond roughly to the Library of Congress classification.

We then asked whether titles that are used *little* or *much* in one institution are also used little or much in other institutions. We identified titles as *high-use* or *low-use* by their use in the period 1949–53 at the other libraries. In table 16 the titles in each joint-holdings sample are separated into groups in this manner. We excluded from our samples all titles that did not have at least one book unit

present in both libraries in the comparison pairs during the two five-year periods, 1949–53 and 1953–1958. We also excluded those titles for which it would have been necessary to estimate some part of the recorded use (to avoid intercorrelation between periods).

We examined each use group of titles (identified by use in 1949–53) in each comparison sample to see how the groups behaved in 1954–58 in the two institutions in each pair. See, for example, table 16 for philosophy at Chicago and Yale.[2]

[2] Because of the manner in which we constructed these charts, it is definitely not possible to make any comparison between the amount of use in the period 1949–53 versus the period 1954–58. Contrary to obsolescence effects, the latter period will show some increase

TABLE 16—*Continued*

Use at NW. in 1949–53	No. in Group	Use at Chicago 1954–58								Use at Northwestern 1954–58							
		Number of cases used						Total Use	Total Use (0–5)	Number of cases used						Total Use	Total Use (0–5)
		0	1	2	3	4	5+			0	1	2	3	4	5+		
ECONOMICS																	
0	40	25	10	3	0	0	2	34	26	33	6	0	0	0	1	13	11
1	21	15	3	2	0	0	1	36	12	14	5	1	0	0	1	17	12
2	14	10	2	2	0	0	0	6	6	6	7	0	0	1	0	11	11
3	6	1	0	0	1	0	4	62	23	1	1	3	1	0	0	10	10
4+	8	4	1	0	0	0	3	58	16	1	1	2	1	1	2	28	22
Total	89	55	16	7	1	0	10	196	83	55	20	6	2	2	4	79	66
TEUTONIC LANGUAGES AND LITERATURES																	
0	34	26	2	0	0	2	4	32	30	29	3	0	2	0	0	9	9
1	15	10	1	1	0	1	2	31	17	11	2	2	0	0	0	6	6
2	4	0	2	1	0	0	1	12	9	4	0	0	0	0	0	0	0
3	2	1	0	1	0	0	0	2	2	1	1	0	0	0	0	1	1
4+	6	2	0	0	1	1	2	45	17	1	1	0	1	1	2	31	18
Total	61	39	5	3	1	4	9	122	75	46	7	2	3	1	2	47	34
PHYSICS																	
0	34	20	5	3	3	0	3	72	35	29	3	0	0	0	2	22	13
1	11	3	3	0	0	2	3	47	26	4	4	0	0	0	3	22	19
2	10	3	2	2	1	1	1	18	18	6	2	1	0	0	1	9	9
3	6	1	2	2	0	1	0	10	10	4	1	1	0	0	0	3	3
4+	20	1	2	2	0	2	13	248	79	1	3	2	3	3	8	91	68
Total	81	28	14	9	4	6	20	395	168	44	13	4	3	3	14	147	112

Of the 79 philosophy titles that had no use at Yale in 1949–53, 58 were not used at Chicago and 70 were not used at Yale during the next five years.[3] In the areas of Teutonic languages and literatures and of biology, the similarities are greater. Certainly for the libraries and

in use *in these charts* because the charts included titles that were not present in the Chicago library for a full five-year period, 1949–53. This means that they had a period somewhat shorter than five years in which to accumulate the original use on which they were grouped, and therefore are likely to show more use in the later period. This effect is present for *both* Yale and Chicago and therefore does not introduce a distortion. These books contribute to creating a satisfactory sample size.

[3] Part of the differences in these samples could, of course, be caused by differences in the availability of possible substitutes for the titles in the sample by other titles *not* in the sample.

subjects under examination, use at one library predicts use at another library with results far better than chance.

But this is not to suggest that there are no noticeable differences between libraries. For all three scholarly areas, those titles not used at Yale in 1949–53 contained more cases of high use (five or more uses) at Chicago than at Yale in 1954–58, while fewer were not used at all at Chicago. Because of the greater disparity in total use between Chicago and Northwestern and Chicago and California than between Chicago and Yale, it is difficult to make similar comparisons; but the data would still not contradict the statements made about the Yale-Chicago data.

As a crude method of summarizing one

TABLE 16—*Continued*

Use at Calif. in 1949-53	No. in Group	Use at Chicago 1954-58								Use at California 1954-58							
		Number of cases used						Total Use	Total Use (0-5)	Number of cases used						Total Use	Total Use (0-5)
		0	1	2	3	4	5+			0	1	2	3	4	5+		
ECONOMICS																	
0	45	40	4	1	0	0	0	6	6	39	3	3	0	0	0	9	9
1	24	17	6	1	0	0	0	8	8	12	8	0	1	2	1	24	24
2	7	4	1	1	0	0	1	8	8	1	1	4	0	0	1	15	14
3	4	2	1	1	0	0	0	3	3	2	1	0	1	0	0	4	4
4+	14	6	4	1	2	0	1	24	17	3	4	1	1	1	4	45	33
Total	94	69	16	5	2	0	2	49	42	57	17	8	3	3	6	97	84
TEUTONIC LANGUAGES AND LITERATURES																	
0	123	102	13	1	4	0	3	44	42	112	7	3	1	0	0	16	16
1	26	18	6	0	1	0	1	14	14	11	9	1	3	0	2	37	30
2	7	2	2	0	1	1	1	19	14	2	1	2	1	0	1	16	13
3	6	1	2	0	2	0	1	15	13	0	4	0	1	0	1	14	12
4+	7	2	0	1	0	0	4	78	22	0	0	1	1	3	2	48	27
Total	169	125	23	2	8	1	10	170	105	125	21	7	7	3	6	131	98
BIOLOGY																	
0	53	42	6	3	0	0	2	26	22	38	10	2	1	1	1	30	26
1	14	11	2	1	0	0	0	4	4	8	5	1	0	0	0	7	7
2	14	7	4	0	3	0	0	13	13	5	2	3	2	1	1	26	23
3	12	7	3	0	1	0	1	12	11	4	0	3	1	2	2	45	27
4+	13	5	2	3	1	0	2	49	21	4	1	1	1	2	4	59	34
Total	106	72	17	7	5	0	5	104	71	59	18	10	5	6	8	167	117

aspect of common book use between institutions, we may look at the ratio of the number of titles *correctly* predicted as having no use in 1954–58 at Yale on the basis of Yale past-use data divided by the number of titles correctly predicted at Chicago on the basis of *Yale* data. Because of differences in the overall proportions of titles used in the various libraries, we must normalize the results so that the two figures are comparable. This was done on the basis of the ratio of total titles used in the pairs of samples. For example, of the 132 titles held commonly by Yale and Chicago in philosophy, 85 were not used at all in 1954–58 at Chicago, while 90 were not used at all at Yale. We therefore multiplied by 90/85 the 58 of those titles at Chicago that had no use at Yale in 1949–53. The

resulting number, approximately 61, could then be compared with the 70 titles at Yale that were not used during either period. (See table 17.)

We hazard this interpretation: If a given rule correctly predicts no use at all during a specified period for 100 titles held in common at two research libraries, the same rule applied at a different research library will average 92 correct predictions if the institutions are similar in general use of research material to Chicago, Yale, California at Berkeley, and Northwestern. Note that there is considerable variation in the figures from which this average was computed, undoubtedly as a result of the sampling process. We therefore accept the average with major reservations. Furthermore, it is impossible to

TABLE 17

Numbers of titles held jointly at pairs of libraries, having zero use in 1954–58, out of groups that had zero use in 1949–53 at the libraries other than Chicago

	Subject	Chicago normalized	Other library	Chicago use normalized as a % of other library's use
Chicago and Yale	Philosophy	61	70	87.14
	Teutonic lang. and lit.	95	102	93.14
	Biology	77	77	100.00
Chicago and Northwestern	Economics	31	29	106.90
	Teutonic lang. and lit.	25	33	75.76
	Physics	31	29	106.90
Chicago and California at Berkeley	Economics	33	39	84.62
	Teutonic lang. and lit.	102	112	91.07
	Biology	34	38	89.47
	Total	489	529	92.44

Overall average = 92.44%.   Mean of means = 92.73%.

This table may be read as follows: Of the titles held jointly by Chicago and Yale in philosophy, there were 61 that had zero use at Chicago in 1954–58 after normalization. These 61 constituted 87.14% of the 70 titles at Yale which had no use in the same period.

employ the figures in the table for comparisons of the strength of subject holdings in pairs of research libraries.

It is important to note that we may not interpret these data as saying that a rule developed at one institution will produce 92 percent as many correct predictions when applied to another collection because from these data we have no notion of how the rule will affect that group of titles which are *not* held in common. Furthermore, the accuracy at the second institution will be directly related to the accuracy of the rule at the institution where the rule was generated.

C. Relation of publication date to use at different libraries for titles held in common

Tables 18, 19, and 20 indicate the extent to which subgroups of jointly held titles that have the same publication date fall into the same categories of use.

Boundaries for publication dates were chosen so as to spread the observations into approximately equal groups.

We need to know whether groups of titles of the same age and in the same language generate similar amounts of reader interest in different research libraries. The question is not answered by whether *individual* titles develop the same amount of use in two libraries; and indeed, important variations in the use of individual titles may be hidden in what appear to be quite similar groups. For example, if a member of the Yale faculty is interested in nineteenth-century German drama and a member of the Chicago faculty, in nineteenth-century German poetry, the use of *individual* titles would show little or no correlation, but the statistics for book use as related to age and language might be identical.

Consequently, we are not interested here in *total* use, but rather in how the total use is distributed by groups of titles.

Our hypothesis is that use is distributed in the same *proportions* among age groups in the several research libraries; for example, it is hypothesized that if California readers use titles published prior to 1904 twice as much as Chicago readers do, California readers will also use titles published after 1933 twice as much as do Chicago readers.

In testing this hypothesis we must decide which predicted variable measure of use we shall employ to compare two research libraries. In this section, *proportion of titles used* from a group is perhaps freest from gross distortion caused by fads and therefore refers most closely to the quantity of interest to us. However, we provide data for all three of the predicted variables.

The conclusions to be drawn from these data will be discussed after the next section, since the results of both this section and the next bear upon the same question.

D. Relation of publication date to use at different libraries for titles not held in common

The above analysis dealt only with titles held by both libraries, although rules to identify books for storage would have to apply to all titles. Therefore, if Yale titles not held by Chicago are quite different in number or kind from Chicago titles not held by Yale, the rules may lead to error. We might expect, however, that titles held in common are used more than those held by only one of the two libraries.[4] If rules are developed for the Chicago collection and Northwestern holds substantially fewer older titles in physics, we might expect that the old titles that Northwestern might store in physics on the basis of

the Chicago functions would be recalled, on the average, more often than they are at Chicago. For such reasons we compared the use of entire collections at Chicago and other libraries, thereby also determining in which directions our comparison samples were biased and whether the biases were similar in the various libraries. (See appendix G for data on that bias.)

Systematic samples of holdings and use were taken at Northwestern and California in the same subject areas as the comparative samples and using the same sampling and data collection procedures described in chapter 1. The samples taken at California were stratified by age; the samples taken at Northwestern were not.

In the tabulations for the random samples for Chicago and California in tables 18 to 20, attention is called to the statistics of use (expressed in terms of three measures) and of *number in group*. The two sets of statistics were developed from different but related samples. To reduce sampling error for average use as much as possible, we took stratified samples, either in addition to the original samples or as the original samples. In this way we increased the number of observations in the books of earlier publication date and improved our estimates of mean use. We used all the observations together from stratified and nonstratified samples to calculate the average use, 0–5 use, and proportion of titles used for the various groups. However, since in the stratified samples we fixed the distribution by age for our convenience, these samples are not an appropriate source for estimating the relative numbers of titles in each age group. Therefore we used the data from the random samples for this purpose, and it is the source of the *number in group* figures.

We first compared distributions of holdings by publication date (see chapter 3, fig. 9), which gave some indication

---

[4] And indeed, that is very much the case. See appendix G.

TABLE 18

A comparison of the effect of publication date on the use of joint-holdings samples at Yale and the University of Chicago in 1954-58

	Total Sample				Published before 1904					Published 1904–33					Published 1934–53				
	No. in sample	Mean use	Mean use 0–5	Proportion used	No. in group	% of total sample	Mean use	Mean use 0–5	Proportion used	No. in group	% of total sample	Mean use	Mean use 0–5	Proportion used	No. in group	% of total sample	Mean use	Mean use 0–5	Proportion used
PHILOSOPHY																			
University of Chicago	226	3.00	1.33	0.48	72	31.86	4.50	1.13	0.42	93	41.15	2.43	1.18	0.41	61	26.99	4.82	1.79	0.61
Yale		5.10	1.65	0.50			4.16	1.50	0.45			4.55	1.37	0.41			6.99	2.26	0.40
Ratio: Chicago/Yale		0.59	0.81	0.96			1.08	0.75	0.93			0.53	0.86	1.00			0.69	0.79	1.53
TEUTONIC LANGUAGES AND LITERATURES																			
University of Chicago	198	1.36	0.83	0.31	60	30.30	1.50	0.75	0.23	85	42.93	1.14	0.65	0.31	53	26.77	1.43	1.17	0.41
Yale		1.20	0.79	0.33			1.00	0.68	0.28			1.00	0.62	0.32			1.44	1.13	0.40
Ratio: Chicago/Yale		1.13	1.05	0.94			1.50	1.10	0.82			1.14	1.05	0.97			0.99	1.04	1.03
BIOLOGY																			
University of Chicago	186	3.24	1.30	0.40	55	29.57	0.29	0.27	0.14	68	36.56	2.41	1.22	0.38	63	33.87	6.68	2.11	0.56
Yale		1.04	1.18	1.21			0.94	0.49	0.22			2.21	1.01	0.32			6.01	1.96	0.44
Ratio: Chicago/Yale		1.04	1.10	1.21			0.31	0.55	0.64			1.09	1.21	1.19			1.11	1.08	1.27

TABLE 19

A comparison of the effect of publication date on use at Northwestern and the University of Chicago

	Total Sample				Published before 1904					Published 1904–33					Published 1934–53				
	No. in sample	Mean use	Mean use 0–5	Proportion used	No. in group	% of total sample	Mean use	Mean use 0–5	Proportion used	No. in group	% of total sample	Mean use	Mean use 0–5	Proportion used	No. in group	% of total sample	Mean use	Mean use 0–5	Proportion used
ECONOMICS JOINT-HOLDINGS SAMPLE																			
University of Chicago	102	2.96	1.17	0.44	21	20.6	0.62	0.62	0.38	40	39.2	1.33	0.40	0.23	41	40.2	5.76	2.20	0.68
NW. Univ.		1.32	0.98	0.43			0.52	0.52	0.29			0.83	0.68	0.40			2.22	1.51	0.54
Ratio: Chicago/NW.		2.24	1.91	1.02			1.18	1.18	1.33			1.61	0.64	0.56			2.59	1.45	1.27
ECONOMICS RANDOM SYSTEMATIC SAMPLES																			
University of Chicago					201	24.8	0.29	0.22	0.14	342	42.2	0.61	0.32	0.18	268	33.1	2.47	1.17	0.42
NW. Univ.					53	15.4	0.23	0.23	0.11	145	42.2	0.82	0.70	0.36	146	42.4	1.81	1.45	0.53
Ratio: Chicago/NW.					3.79		1.30	0.97	1.26	2.36		0.75	0.45	0.50	1.84		1.36	0.81	0.79
TEUTONIC LANGUAGES AND LITERATURES JOINT-HOLDINGS SAMPLE																			
University of Chicago	99	2.05	1.12	0.36	36	36.4	2.28	0.97	0.28	40	40.4	2.25	1.15	0.38	23	23.2	1.35	1.30	0.48
NW. Univ.		1.03	0.59	0.23			1.81	0.64	0.19			0.53	0.48	0.20			0.70	0.70	0.35
Ratio: Chicago/NW.		1.99	1.91	1.57			1.26	1.52	1.43			4.29	2.42	1.88			1.94	1.87	1.37

TABLE 19—Continued

	Total Sample				Published before 1904					Published 1904–33					Published 1934–53				
	No. in sample	Mean use	Mean use 0–5	Proportion used	No. in group	% of total sample	Mean use	Mean use 0–5	Proportion used	No. in group	% of total sample	Mean use	Mean use 0–5	Proportion used	No. in group	% of total sample	Mean use	Mean use 0–5	Proportion used
TEUTONIC LANGUAGES AND LITERATURES RANDOM SYSTEMATIC SAMPLES																			
University of Chicago					345	41.5	0.94	0.39	0.16	325	39.1	0.74	0.47	0.43	161	19.4	4.41	0.82	0.31
NW. Univ.					252	36.5	0.37	0.33	0.17	260	37.6	0.51	0.40	0.21	179	25.9	0.97	0.63	0.26
Ratio: Chicago/NW.					1.37		2.54	1.91	0.95	1.25		1.44	1.17	2.09	0.90		4.54	1.31	1.16
PHYSICS JOINT-HOLDINGS SAMPLE																			
University of Chicago	97	9.86	2.39	0.71	17	17.5	3.53	1.29	0.35			6.42	1.94	0.67	47	48.5	14.62	3.11	0.87
NW. Univ.		3.34	1.71	0.50			1.29	0.77	0.29	33	34.0	2.33	1.27	0.42			4.79	2.36	0.64
Ratio: Chicago/NW.		2.95	1.40	1.41			2.59	1.69	1.20			2.75	1.52	1.57			3.05	1.32	1.37
PHYSICS RANDOM SYSTEMATIC SAMPLES																			
University of Chicago					82	22.8	0.49	0.34	0.18	134	37.2	2.02	0.73	0.29	144	40.0	5.79	1.69	0.556
NW. Univ.					67	24.7	0.39	0.36	0.19	110	40.6	1.35	1.03	0.42	94	34.7	3.35	2.02	0.64
Ratio: Chicago/NW.					1.22		1.26	0.94	0.91	1.22		1.50	0.71	0.69	1.53		1.73	0.84	0.87

TABLE 20

A comparison of the effect of publication date on use at the University of California at Berkeley and the University of Chicago

	Total Sample				Published before 1904					Published 1904–33					Published 1934–53				
	No. in sample	Mean use	Mean use 0–5	Propor-tion used	No. in group	% of total sample	Mean use	Mean use 0–5	Propor-tion used	No. in group	% of total sample	Mean use	Mean use 0–5	Propor-tion used	No. in group	% of total sample	Mean use	Mean use 0–5	Propor-tion used
ECONOMICS JOINT-HOLDINGS SAMPLE																			
University of Chicago	163	2.15	0.99	0.39	30	18.4	0.40	0.40	0.27	72	44.2	0.97	0.46	0.24	61	37.4	4.39	1.92	0.64
U. of Calif.		5.18	1.83	0.56			1.20	1.17	0.40			3.18	1.33	0.49			9.66	2.75	0.72
Ratio: Chicago / Calif.		0.42	0.54	0.70			0.33	0.34	0.67			0.31	0.34	0.49			0.46	0.70	0.89
ECONOMICS RANDOM SYSTEMATIC SAMPLES																			
University of Chicago					201	24.8	0.29	0.22	0.14	342	42.1	0.61	0.32	0.18	268	33.0	2.47	1.17	0.42
U. of Calif.					48	13.5	0.94	0.64	0.24	180	50.7	0.84	0.66	0.27	127	35.8	1.28	0.87	0.29
Ratio: Chicago / Calif.							0.31	0.39	0.59			0.73	0.48	0.68			1.92	1.34	1.42
TEUTONIC LANGUAGES AND LITERATURES JOINT-HOLDINGS SAMPLE																			
University of Chicago	235	1.36	0.75	0.29	90	38.3	1.28	0.66	0.20	86	36.6	1.71	0.77	0.38	59	25.1	0.98	0.88	0.34
U. of Calif.		1.91	1.26	0.42			1.71	0.97	0.36			2.05	1.34	0.47			2.02	1.58	0.48
Ratio: Chicago / Calif.		0.71	0.60	0.68			0.75	0.68	0.56			0.84	0.57	0.83			0.49	0.56	0.71

TABLE 20—*Continued*

	Total Sample				Published before 1904					Published 1904–33					Published 1934–53				
	No. in sample	Mean use	Mean use 0–5	Proportion used	No. in group	% of total sample	Mean use	Mean use 0–5	Proportion used	No. in group	% of total sample	Mean use	Mean use 0–5	Proportion used	No. in group	% of total sample	Mean use	Mean use 0–5	Proportion used
TEUTONIC LANGUAGES AND LITERATURES RANDOM SYSTEMATIC SAMPLES																			
University of Chicago		3.54	1.39	0.45	345	41.5	0.94	0.39	0.16	325	39.1	0.74	0.47	0.43	161	19.4	4.41	0.82	0.31
U. of Calif.		5.01	2.05	0.58	222	30.0	1.14	0.84	0.32	229	30.9	1.47	1.10	0.37	289	39.1	5.64	2.01	0.63
Ratio: Chicago/Calif.	198	0.71	0.68	0.78			0.83	0.47	0.49			0.50	0.43	1.18			0.78	0.41	0.49
BIOLOGY JOINT-HOLDINGS SAMPLE																			
University of Chicago							0.39	0.39	0.23			2.53	1.33	0.46			8.08	2.52	0.67
U. of Calif.							1.95	1.11	0.44			5.15	1.83	0.50			7.98	3.28	0.82
Ratio: Chicago/Calif.					62	31.3	0.20	0.35	0.52	76	38.4	0.49	0.73	0.92	60	30.3	1.01	0.77	0.82
BIOLOGY RANDOM SYSTEMATIC SAMPLES																			
University of Chicago					144	36.8	0.29	0.27	0.14	139	35.5	1.07	0.66	0.25	108	27.6	5.56	1.92	0.54
U. of Calif.					159	33.6	1.30	0.89	0.32	176	37.2	2.40	0.99	0.35	138	29.2	3.72	2.07	0.59
Ratio: Chicago/Calif.							0.22	0.30	0.45			0.45	0.66	0.71			1.49	0.93	0.91

TABLE 21

Results of basing the rule for storage on use as a function
of publication date and language

	Cumulative % of titles to be stored taken in increasing order of predicted use at Chicago	Number of titles that would be stored	Number of those stored that would be used once or more in 1954–58	Percent of those stored that would be used once or more in 1954–58	Number of uses generated by this group	Proportion of uses generated by this group to uses generated by entire sample in percent
Teutonic languages and literatures:						
Chicago	25	208	18	9	184	23
Northwestern	25	173	25	14	64	16
California	25	185	38	21	118	14
Economics:						
Chicago	25	203	25	12	31	3
Northwestern	25	86	8	9	19	5
California	25	89	24	27	55	5

of the considerable variation from library to library. If there is considerable difference between libraries, any library wishing to determine how many books to store under a given rule must either base the rule on its own data or make the judgment that the distribution of its holdings is similar to the Chicago pattern. The latter, however, is not likely to be the case. Northwestern, for example, holds about the same number of titles in economics published in 1934–53 as published in 1904–33 (146 to 146), whereas California holds considerably more for the earlier period and Chicago holds considerably more for the later period.

Looking at the data on use predicted from age for both the joint holdings and the systematic samples (tables 18–20), we see that the *relative* amounts of use in pairs of libraries varies considerably both among subject areas and among publication date groups within a subject area.

It is evident that the comparative data on use and holdings are relevant to fu-ture preservation efforts, cooperative storage plans, and cooperative acquisition schemes. The data may also be of considerable value to students of communication processes who are interested in the extent to which reading interests in various parts of the scholarly world are similar.

E. Comparison of the effect of the same storage rule at different research libraries

The material in sections B through D does not allow us to deduce the effect of a given rule developed for Chicago, when the rule is employed at another library. To do so we must test the rules themselves.

Table 21 provides results for a single rule: use in relation to publication date plus language (function 4). The effect of the rule can be compared for economics and Teutonic languages and literatures at three institutions.

The results given in table 21 were obtained by ranking the groups of titles in the samples at California and Northwestern in the same order as that used at Chicago. We then designated for storage the bottom 25 percent of each of the ranked distributions in each subject area (for example, economics at California) and examined that 25 percent to determine the effect.

The only statistic with which we can properly compare the three institutions is the *percentage* of use accounted for by the stored titles to the use by the entire sample, as shown in the last column of table 21. We would not necessarily expect this statistic to vary with amount of library patronage. The results for the three institutions are strikingly similar when we consider the possible effects of sampling error and differences in collections. The general conclusion is that if libraries of different sizes and populations put similar rules into effect, the proportion of uses generated by the titles sent to storage to the uses generated by the entire group would be a similar percentage in each such library. This assumes that the libraries in question and their uses are similar to the institutions analyzed here.

These results do *not* remove the effect of different patterns of holdings by publication date. The similarity appears *despite* the evident differences in such patterns and is the more striking for that reason. If account was taken of the differences in holdings, the same rule would result in different numbers of titles sent to storage in the different institutions.

Since most libraries have records of past use available for monographs, they could employ a rule that included past use as a predictor variable. Assuming independence of use from one time period to another, the longer the period of prior use considered, the more accurate such a rule will be. Furthermore, it is un-

doubtedly true that as the period of time considered becomes sufficiently long, the results for individual titles will become more and more alike at different institutions. This relationship does not depend upon the special characteristics of a subcollection unless there is a major reversal in the demand for books of a particular kind, a phenomenon which there is no reason to anticipate.

On the other hand, results for groups of titles in terms of numbers sent to storage, will still depend very much upon the total use for the library. To illustrate: For two titles at different libraries, neither of which has been used for the past 25 years, the probability of being used in the next five years is quite similar, though the probability may be slightly greater at the library that has the larger patronage. On the other hand, if the rule is simply to send to storage titles that have not been used for 25 years, a larger proportion of any subject area will almost surely be sent to storage in the library that has fewer readers in that area.

F. Summary and conclusions

1. There is considerable similarity in reading interests of scholars at different institutions. For low-use titles held by a pair of libraries, past use at one institution predicts *almost* as well for the future at another institution as it does for the original institution. But because of the differences in holdings, it is not possible to employ this finding directly to produce rules to identify titles for storage.

2. Despite the apparent similarity in reading interests, there appear to be substantial similarities and substantial differences in the composition of collections, and these differences are not explained simply by size.

3. Both in the jointly held samples and in the random systematic samples, the distributions of use of titles by publication date show considerable similarity among the various predicted measures of use. But the differences, perhaps due to sampling error in many cases, are great enough to make it impossible to deduce the effects of the same storage rule at various institutions from the data alone.

4. A rule based on publication date plus language (function 4), employing an ordering of titles by increasing order of predicted use at the University of Chicago, and applied at the Berkeley campus of the University of California and at Northwestern University, produced quite similar results at the three institutions in terms of the *percentage* of use represented by the 25 percent of the titles selected for storage to the use by the entire sample.

5. Differences in the holdings of research libraries by publication date would make it necessary to survey a collection before predicting the number of titles that would be removed from storage with a given rule developed at Chicago.

6. On the basis of strongly persuasive logical evidence, if a research library other than Chicago employed rules based on time periods since last use, with the time period observed taking values up to 25 years, the library might expect results quite like those at the University of Chicago for the probability of a particular title's being used in a specified period of future time.

5

Decline in the use of monograph titles due to obsolescence

A. Problem and background

It is important in planning for the future growth of both working and storage library collections to know how much books decrease in use as they get older. The principal study of obsolescence rates is that of Gosnell,[1] who examined several lists of recommended holdings for college libraries and based his measure of obsolescence upon the number of titles recommended from each time period. In a study based on data of this kind, shifts of scholarly interests and variations in world publishing rates and the objectives of the editors of the lists could all combine in various ways to mask "true" rates of obsolescence.

Figures 10a–10c illustrate the difference in conclusions about obsolescence rates that an investigator might reach by taking account, or not taking account, of the numbers of titles held by a library for various publication date periods. These figures were developed from our survey of current circulation records. For

the period December 11, 1959, to January 15, 1960, we collected data on every book circulated from the library system, excluding reserve use. We then examined the data for three subject areas: biology, Teutonic languages and literatures, and philosophy. Our observation units were the *titles* circulated. The number of titles circulated during the various periods constitute the *numerators* for the solid bars in figures 10a–10c, and they constitute the *whole numbers* for the open bars. The denominators for the solid bars are *relative*[2] estimates of the numbers of titles that the library held for each publication date period, based upon the survey described in chapter 3.

The solid bars give us correct *relative* estimates of the amount of use of titles in the various groups during the period of the analysis. However, we can tell nothing about *absolute* use from these current-circulation materials, since the amount of use is a function of the length of time in which data were collected,

[1] Charles F. Gosnell, "The Rate of Obsolescence in College Book Collections, as Determined by an Analysis of Three Select Lists of Books for College Libraries" (Ph.D. diss., New York University, 1943).

[2] It is not possible to express these estimates as percentages that add to 100 percent because we have omitted pre-1894 publications from this portion of the study. The numbers shown also indicate the sample size.

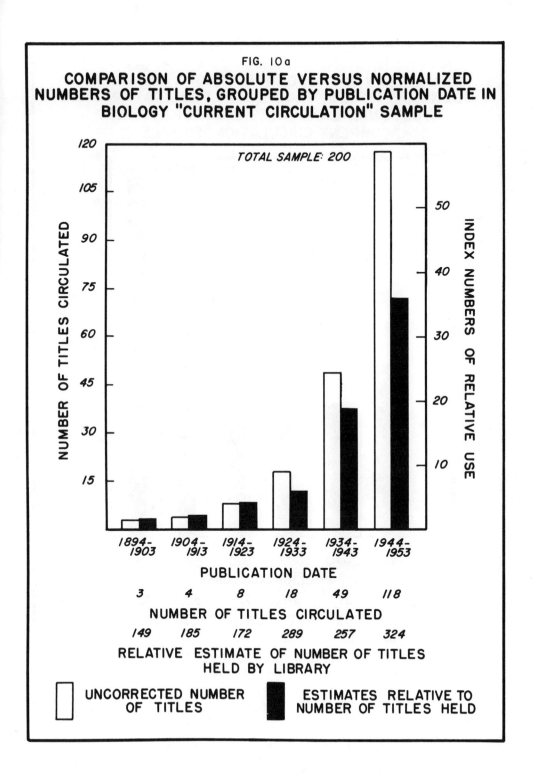

FIG. 10a

COMPARISON OF ABSOLUTE VERSUS NORMALIZED NUMBERS OF TITLES, GROUPED BY PUBLICATION DATE IN BIOLOGY "CURRENT CIRCULATION" SAMPLE

TOTAL SAMPLE: 200

NUMBER OF TITLES CIRCULATED

INDEX NUMBERS OF RELATIVE USE

1894–1903	1904–1913	1914–1923	1924–1933	1934–1943	1944–1953

PUBLICATION DATE

| 3 | 4 | 8 | 18 | 49 | 118 |

NUMBER OF TITLES CIRCULATED

| 149 | 185 | 172 | 289 | 257 | 324 |

RELATIVE ESTIMATE OF NUMBER OF TITLES HELD BY LIBRARY

☐ UNCORRECTED NUMBER OF TITLES   ■ ESTIMATES RELATIVE TO NUMBER OF TITLES HELD

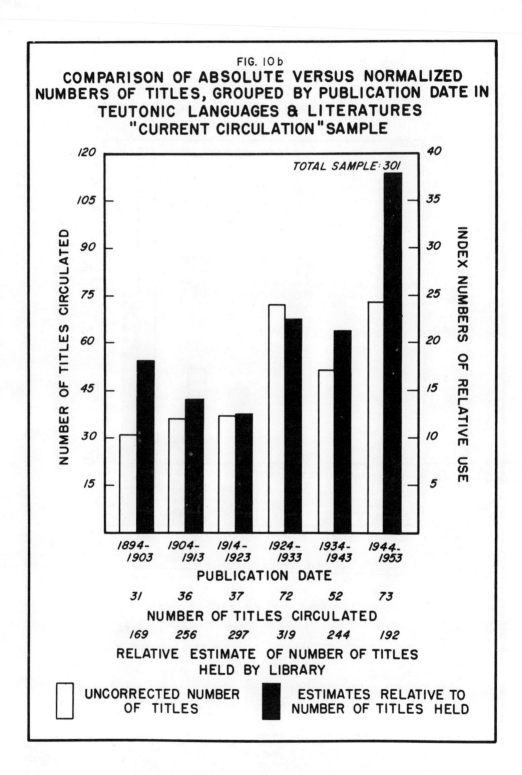

FIG. 10 b

COMPARISON OF ABSOLUTE VERSUS NORMALIZED
NUMBERS OF TITLES, GROUPED BY PUBLICATION DATE IN
TEUTONIC LANGUAGES & LITERATURES
"CURRENT CIRCULATION" SAMPLE

TOTAL SAMPLE: 301

NUMBER OF TITLES CIRCULATED

INDEX NUMBERS OF RELATIVE USE

1894-1903	1904-1913	1914-1923	1924-1933	1934-1943	1944-1953

PUBLICATION DATE

31	36	37	72	52	73

NUMBER OF TITLES CIRCULATED

169	256	297	319	244	192

RELATIVE ESTIMATE OF NUMBER OF TITLES
HELD BY LIBRARY

☐ UNCORRECTED NUMBER
OF TITLES

■ ESTIMATES RELATIVE TO
NUMBER OF TITLES HELD

70

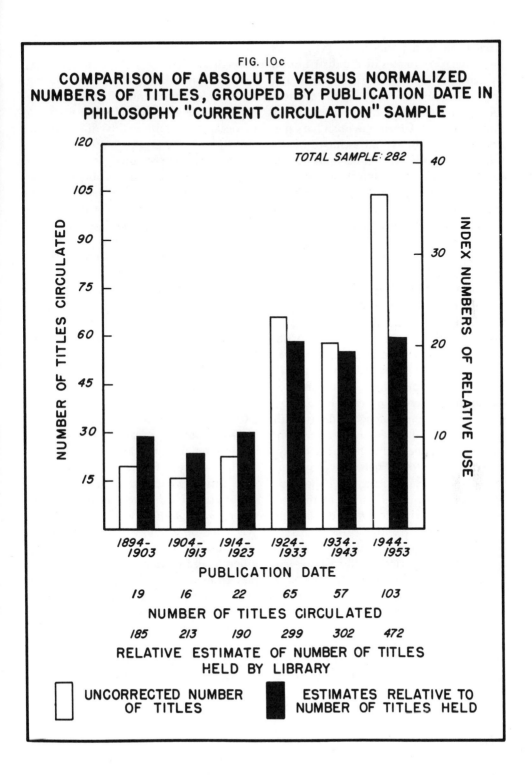

FIG. 10c

COMPARISON OF ABSOLUTE VERSUS NORMALIZED
NUMBERS OF TITLES, GROUPED BY PUBLICATION DATE IN
PHILOSOPHY "CURRENT CIRCULATION" SAMPLE

TOTAL SAMPLE: 282

NUMBER OF TITLES CIRCULATED

INDEX NUMBERS OF RELATIVE USE

PUBLICATION DATE	1894–1903	1904–1913	1914–1923	1924–1933	1934–1943	1944–1953
NUMBER OF TITLES CIRCULATED	19	16	22	65	57	103
RELATIVE ESTIMATE OF NUMBER OF TITLES HELD BY LIBRARY	185	213	190	299	302	472

☐ UNCORRECTED NUMBER
OF TITLES

■ ESTIMATES RELATIVE TO
NUMBER OF TITLES HELD

71

circulation loan periods, etc. The open bars give us estimates of the distribution by date of the titles actually used and are analogous to the Gosnell method. The reader will note that in the biology and philosophy figures the open bars suggest a much more rapid estimate of obsolescence in use with time than do the solid bars. The Teutonic languages figures show the effect of the drop in holdings in the last period. It is evident that there *is* a basic obsolescence effect in operation, but its regularity and slope are not readily apparent.

B. Comparison of use of groups of titles of different ages

Our previous methodology suggests that we look at individual titles to observe the possible decrease in use over the time that they have been in the library. An exponential function has served to represent other natural and social science phenomena of decay with age and it would seem natural to consider the hypothesis that book use decays exponentially, too. There are, however, several obstacles to testing this hypothesis by fitting exponential curves to the record of use over time for *individual* titles:

1. For most titles—those that are used once in five years or less—the data are too sparse (for the period of 50 years or less for which there are records).

2. There have been major changes in university population which would affect the use of titles.

3. Changes in circulation rules and procedures preclude an accurate and consistent record of use in the University of Chicago library and most other libraries over the entire period since the turn of the century.

For these reasons it seems more appropriate to look at the use of *groups* of titles, taken together on one basis or

another, over periods of time short enough so that obstacles 2 and 3 above will be minimized. It is worth noting, however, that if individual books decayed in use exponentially but each *rate* of decay was considerably different, the statistics for the groups would not necessarily appear exponential.

We first approach the problem by considering the differences between the mean use of two or more groups of titles in the same observation period. Two examples are (1) the proportion used in 1954–58 of the titles published before 1920 or (2) the proportion used of the titles published in each decade of the past two hundred years. It is crucial to keep in mind the underlying assumption that the nature of titles of each of the periods being considered is the same as the nature of the titles in the other periods. The assumption means that titles published in 1930 were as valuable in 1954–58 as titles published in 1925 were in 1949–53. But we already know that this assumption does not always hold.

The first set of data to be examined with this approach is the most general: it consists of *all observed titles in all monograph samples* we have collected. We make no attempt to assess the varying influence upon these results of the different size samples, or the lack of samples from some subject areas of the library (though we shall list the components of the sample).

Table 22 gives a detailed breakdown of the areas from which these titles were drawn; the overall sample consists of 9,508 titles. Figure 11 charts the relationship of publication date to our three predicted measures of use.

Next we look at the subgroups for the humanities, the natural sciences, and the social sciences. Figures 12a, 12b, and 12c show presentations similar to figure 11.

TABLE 22

Composition of monograph samples

	No. of titles	Subjects	Library of Congress classification	Nonstratified titles only	Stratified and nonstratified titles (total)
Humanities	4,955	General, foreign, and Latin American History	D, DB–DX (except DE, DF, and DS), F	1,147	2,026
		Philosophy	B–BJ (except BF)	424	628
		Romance lang. and literatures	PC, PQ	197	620
		Teutonic lang. and literatures	PD, PF, PT	830	1,002
		American and Eng. lit.	PN, PS PE, PR	417	677
Natural sciences	2,083	Physics	QC	360	605
		Natural hist. and biology	QH–QR	391	703
		Gen. science, chemistry, and geology	Q, QD, QE		774
Social sciences	2,470	Economics	HB–HJ	811	1,062
		Anthropology and sociology	GF–GT HM–HT	373	753
		Political science	JA–JX, HX		655

The makeup of the groups is shown in table 22. Chapter 3 has presented similar data in tabular form for each individual subject area.

We look at charts of the relationship of age to use at other libraries to corroborate our findings at the University of Chicago library. Figures 13a–13c and 14a–14c show the results of samples taken at the University of Chicago, Northwestern University, and the University of California at Berkeley. The patterns are generally similar for the three libraries, though the Teutonic languages and literatures sample curve for the University of California is even flatter over time

than is that for the University of Chicago sample.

It is tempting to draw the immediate inference from the data that after titles become 60 or 70 years old, the likelihood of their being used stabilizes. Note that we do not know and cannot determine from these data whether the flattening out occurs because of characteristics of scholars' interest or because of the nature of the books available within the library. It may well be, for example, that books 40 or more years old in libraries that have built their collections largely in the twentieth century represent a more selective acquisition than is applied to contemporary materials.

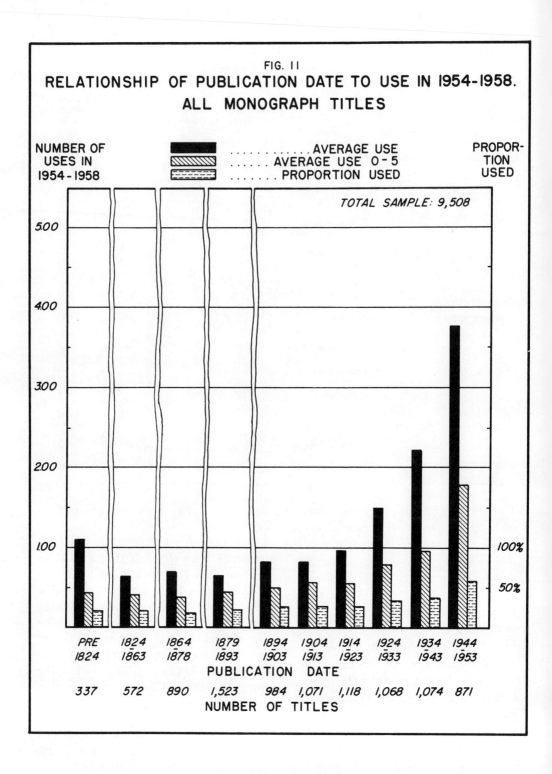

FIG. II

RELATIONSHIP OF PUBLICATION DATE TO USE IN 1954-1958.
ALL MONOGRAPH TITLES

NUMBER OF
USES IN
1954-1958

.... AVERAGE USE
...... AVERAGE USE 0-5
.... PROPORTION USED

PROPOR-
TION
USED

TOTAL SAMPLE: 9,508

5.00

4.00

3.00

2.00

1.00

100%

50%

| PRE | 1824 | 1864 | 1879 | 1894 | 1904 | 1914 | 1924 | 1934 | 1944 |
| 1824 | 1863 | 1878 | 1893 | 1903 | 1913 | 1923 | 1933 | 1943 | 1953 |

PUBLICATION DATE

| 337 | 572 | 890 | 1,523 | 984 | 1,071 | 1,118 | 1,068 | 1,074 | 871 |

NUMBER OF TITLES

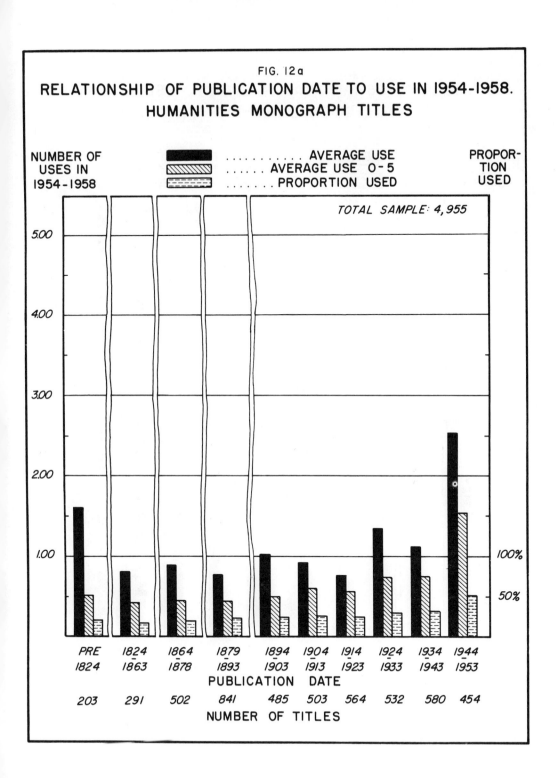

FIG. 12a

RELATIONSHIP OF PUBLICATION DATE TO USE IN 1954-1958.
HUMANITIES MONOGRAPH TITLES

NUMBER OF
USES IN
1954-1958

.... AVERAGE USE
...... AVERAGE USE 0-5
...... PROPORTION USED

PROPOR-
TION
USED

TOTAL SAMPLE: 4,955

5.00

4.00

3.00

2.00

1.00

100%

50%

| PRE 1824 | 1824 1863 | 1864 1878 | 1879 1893 | 1894 1903 | 1904 1913 | 1914 1923 | 1924 1933 | 1934 1943 | 1944 1953 |

PUBLICATION DATE

| 203 | 291 | 502 | 841 | 485 | 503 | 564 | 532 | 580 | 454 |

NUMBER OF TITLES

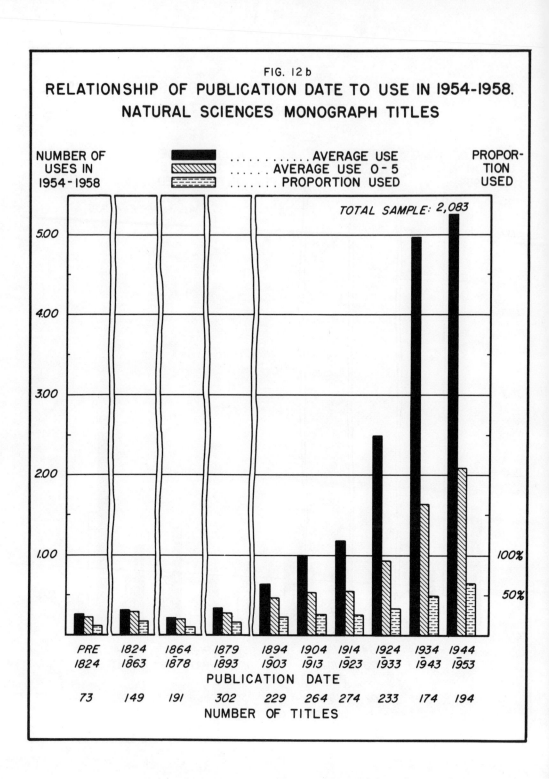

FIG. 12 b

RELATIONSHIP OF PUBLICATION DATE TO USE IN 1954-1958.
NATURAL SCIENCES MONOGRAPH TITLES

NUMBER OF USES IN 1954-1958

·············· AVERAGE USE
······· AVERAGE USE 0-5
······· PROPORTION USED

PROPORTION USED

TOTAL SAMPLE: 2,083

5.00

4.00

3.00

2.00

1.00

100%

50%

| PRE 1824 | 1824 1863 | 1864 1878 | 1879 1893 | 1894 1903 | 1904 1913 | 1914 1923 | 1924 1933 | 1934 1943 | 1944 1953 |

PUBLICATION DATE

| 73 | 149 | 191 | 302 | 229 | 264 | 274 | 233 | 174 | 194 |

NUMBER OF TITLES

76

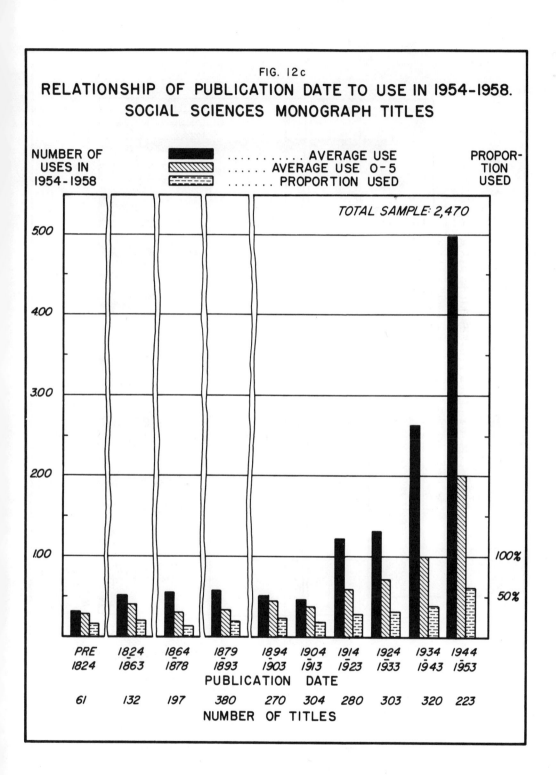

FIG. 12c

RELATIONSHIP OF PUBLICATION DATE TO USE IN 1954-1958.
SOCIAL SCIENCES MONOGRAPH TITLES

NUMBER OF USES IN 1954-1958

. . . . AVERAGE USE
. . . . . . AVERAGE USE 0-5
. . . . PROPORTION USED

PROPOR-TION USED

TOTAL SAMPLE: 2,470

500
400
300
200
100

100%
50%

| PRE 1824 | 1824 1863 | 1864 1878 | 1879 1893 | 1894 1903 | 1904 1913 | 1914 1923 | 1924 1933 | 1934 1943 | 1944 1953 |

PUBLICATION DATE

| 61 | 132 | 197 | 380 | 270 | 304 | 280 | 303 | 320 | 223 |

NUMBER OF TITLES

77

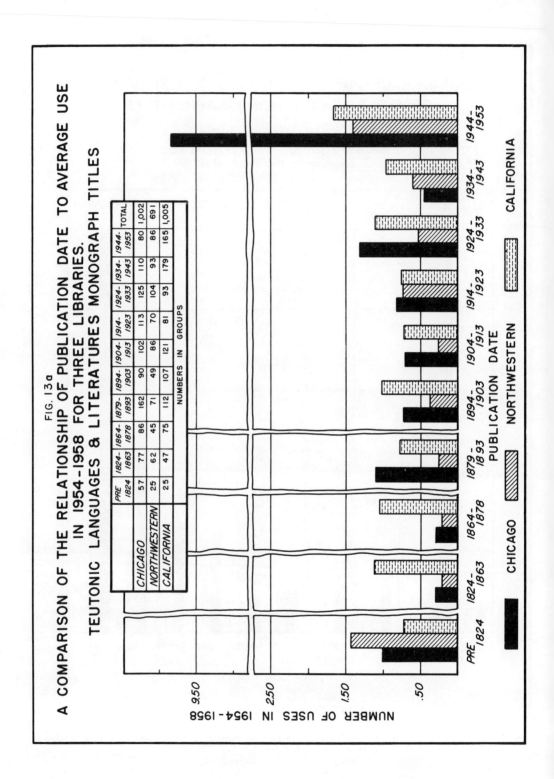

FIG. 13a

A COMPARISON OF THE RELATIONSHIP OF PUBLICATION DATE TO AVERAGE USE IN 1954-1958 FOR THREE LIBRARIES.

TEUTONIC LANGUAGES & LITERATURES MONOGRAPH TITLES

	PRE 1824	1824- 1863	1864- 1878	1879- 1893	1894- 1903	1904- 1913	1914- 1923	1924- 1933	1934- 1943	1944- 1953	TOTAL
CHICAGO	57	77	86	162	90	102	113	125	110	80	1,002
NORTHWESTERN	25	62	45	71	49	86	70	104	93	86	691
CALIFORNIA	25	47	75	112	107	121	81	93	179	165	1,005

NUMBERS IN GROUPS

NUMBER OF USES IN 1954-1958

9.50 2.50 1.50 .50

PRE 1824 1824- 1863 1864- 1878 1879- 1893 1894- 1903 1904- 1913 1914- 1923 1924- 1933 1934- 1943 1944- 1953

PUBLICATION DATE

CHICAGO NORTHWESTERN CALIFORNIA

78

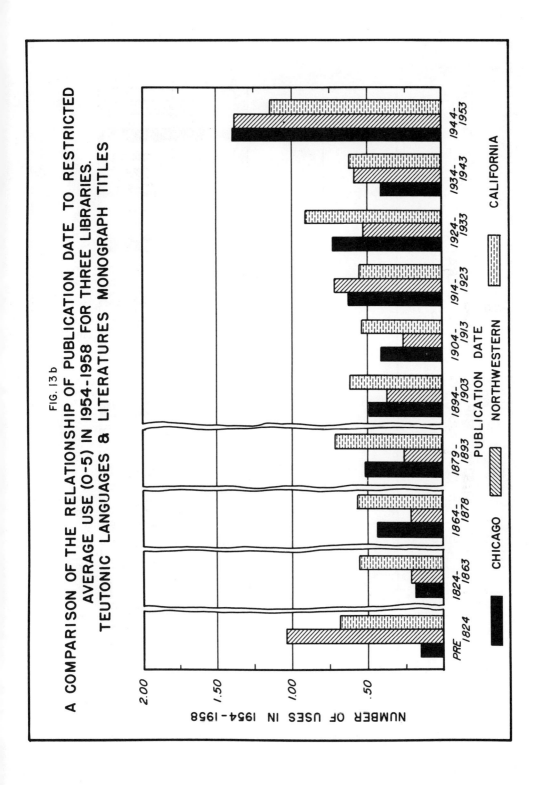

FIG. 13 b

A COMPARISON OF THE RELATIONSHIP OF PUBLICATION DATE TO RESTRICTED AVERAGE USE (0-5) IN 1954-1958 FOR THREE LIBRARIES. TEUTONIC LANGUAGES & LITERATURES MONOGRAPH TITLES

79

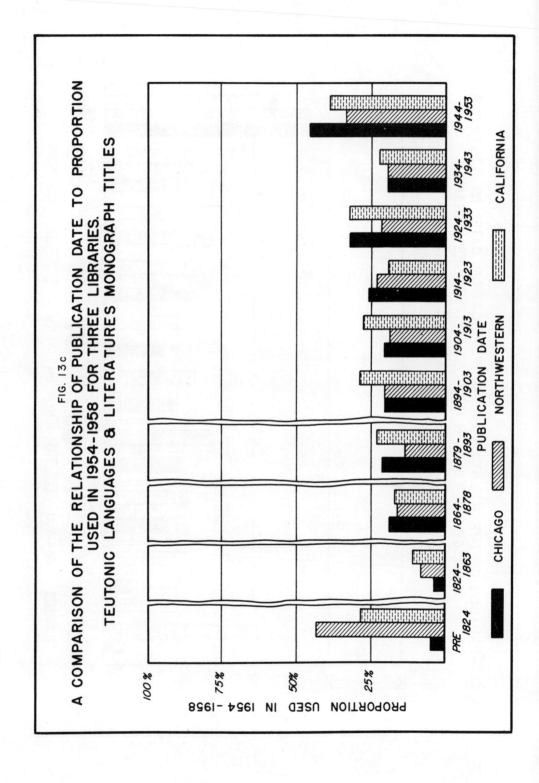

FIG. 13c

A COMPARISON OF THE RELATIONSHIP OF PUBLICATION DATE TO PROPORTION USED IN 1954-1958 FOR THREE LIBRARIES.
TEUTONIC LANGUAGES & LITERATURES MONOGRAPH TITLES

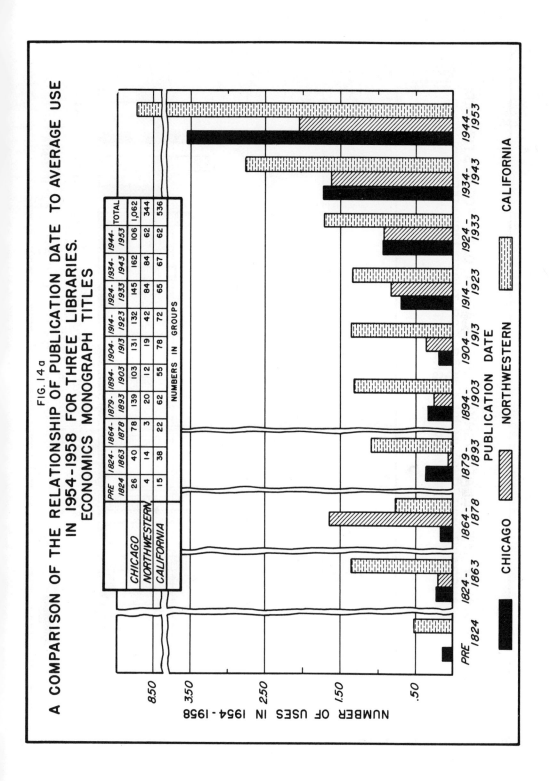

FIG. 14 a

A COMPARISON OF THE RELATIONSHIP OF PUBLICATION DATE TO AVERAGE USE IN 1954-1958 FOR THREE LIBRARIES. ECONOMICS MONOGRAPH TITLES

	PRE 1824	1824- 1863	1864- 1878	1879- 1893	1894- 1903	1904- 1913	1914- 1923	1924- 1933	1934- 1943	1944- 1953	TOTAL
CHICAGO	26	40	78	139	103	131	132	145	162	106	1,062
NORTHWESTERN	4	14	3	20	12	19	42	84	84	62	344
CALIFORNIA	15	38	22	62	55	78	72	65	67	62	536

NUMBERS IN GROUPS

CHICAGO   NORTHWESTERN   CALIFORNIA

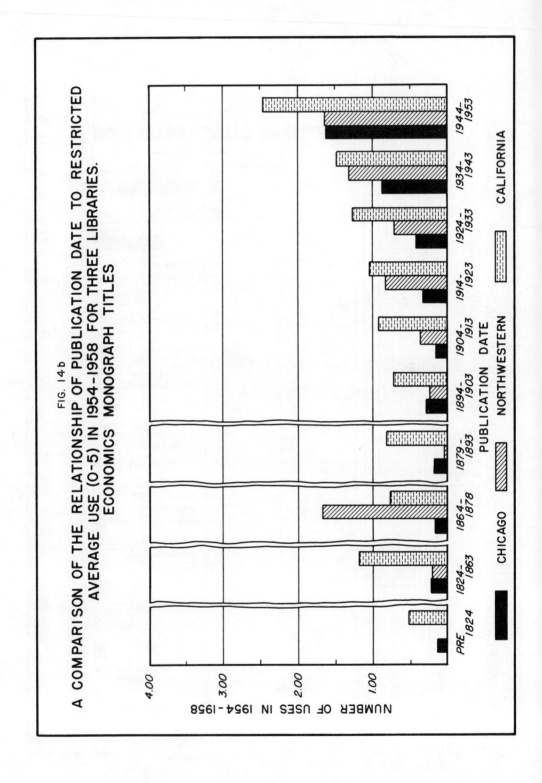

FIG. 14 b

A COMPARISON OF THE RELATIONSHIP OF PUBLICATION DATE TO RESTRICTED AVERAGE USE (0-5) IN 1954-1958 FOR THREE LIBRARIES. ECONOMICS MONOGRAPH TITLES

NUMBER OF USES IN 1954-1958

PUBLICATION DATE

CHICAGO   NORTHWESTERN   CALIFORNIA

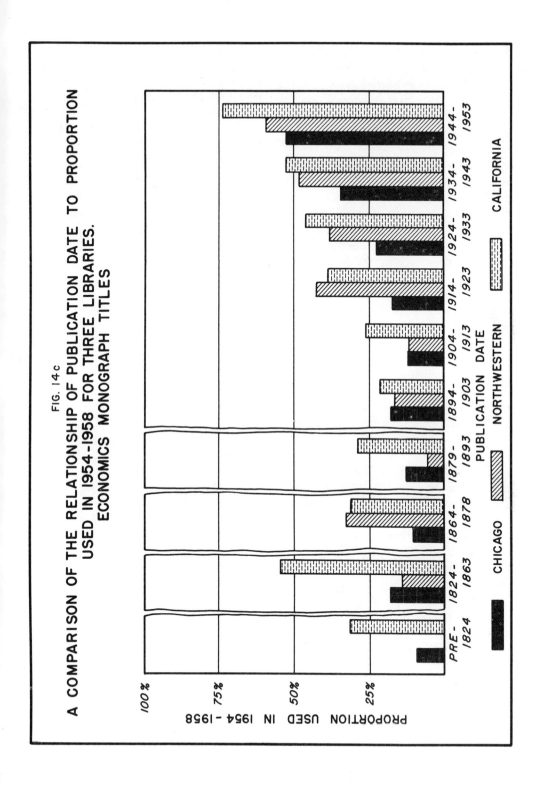

FIG. 14 c

A COMPARISON OF THE RELATIONSHIP OF PUBLICATION DATE TO PROPORTION
USED IN 1954-1958 FOR THREE LIBRARIES.
ECONOMICS MONOGRAPH TITLES

CHICAGO   NORTHWESTERN   CALIFORNIA

PUBLICATION DATE

PROPORTION USED IN 1954-1958

C. Comparison of use of individual titles in two time periods

By a different technique each group of titles is set up as its own control and the behavior of each group is examined in two contiguous time periods. The question is then asked: how does does a group of titles published, for example, in 1934–43 behave in 1949–53 versus 1954–58?

This technique runs headlong into population change problems. The group may show less use in the later period because *all* the titles in the library were used less, perhaps because there were fewer people on campus. We may be able to surmount this obstacle by normalizing the behavior of the sample as a whole.[3]

It is important to note the rationale of the normalizing process. We considered that use during the period 1949–53 of the sample of titles acquired before 1949 is in direct relation to the use of the universe of titles in those five years. If we then *add* to the sample those titles acquired in 1949–53, the use of the *augmented sample* in 1954–58 would be in direct relation to the use of the *augmented universe* in that period. The augmentation is necessary to avoid the influence of a change in *total* use which can be caused at least partly by obsolescence.[4]

If the sample was used x percent more or y percent less in the later period, we assumed that each group in the sample, if it had not obsolesced, would also have been used the same x percent more or y percent less than in the previous period. We could then compare a group's actual performance against the normalized figure.[5]

The normalization was accomplished

by taking the total use of the sample for the period 1949–53 and dividing it by the total use of the sample for the period 1954–58. To give an actual example, the normalization factor for the humanities average-use table (table 24) was calculated as follows:

Total use 1949–53   = 3,036
Total use 1954–58   = 2,786
Normalization factor = 3,036 ÷ 2,786 = 1.090

In other words, use in 1949–53 was 109 percent of use in 1954–58.

We dealt only with those titles that were acquired before 1949 so that we had two full five-year periods for obser-

[4] The number of books in a library increases from year to year, and assuming a constant total use of the library, each book *on the average* would have to be used less. However, a book is used less primarily because it becomes superseded by new books rather than because there are more books. The "dilution" effect must be quite small. Consider a collection of two million books and a fixed university population. The addition of 50,-000 books would reduce average use by only $2\frac{1}{2}$ percent per year if that was the only factor, and we know from data presented later in this chapter that books decline in average use much faster, at least at first. It seems reasonable to assume that people tend to go to new books mostly because they are new, and as a consequence they tend to go less often to older books.

[5] Titles for which we *estimated* use are obviously not appropriate for this test, and so we removed them from the sample. It would be difficult to determine whether removing them biased our obsolescence estimates in significant ways. We indicate the numbers of books removed because some part of their use was estimated. There are two more loose ends in this procedure: (a) It takes no account of the use contributed to the total use in 1949–53 by titles acquired after 1948, or of the use contributed to the total use in 1954–58 by titles acquired after 1953. It is probably fair to assume that the absolute sizes of the two omitted contributions would be approximately the same. If the difference between the *totals* is relatively small, adding equal quantities to the two totals will not affect the normalizing ratio significantly. (b) Some titles are included in the 1954–58 observations but not in the 1949–53 observations. Removing them from the sample does not alter the drop-off rates in any significant fashion; in other words, the late accessions do not behave very differently in this context from titles that were acquired earlier.

[3] Normalizing with regard to total library circulation is another possible approach to this problem.

vation. Again we employed all three measures of use because of the various advantages they offer.

Table 23 shows the rate of decay after normalizing all titles taken together. Tables 24–26 show the rate of decay for the humanities, the natural sciences, and the social sciences. These data suggest that, contrary to the impression given by figures 12a–12c, decay in use does *not* cease at a discernible moment in the career of a title. Furthermore, the data for the natural sciences suggest that the rate of decay is a constant percentage (exponential) function. The rate of decay is given for five-year periods. A reasonable approximation of the one-year rate may be derived by dividing the five-year rate by five.

There is an apparent reversal of the obsolescence trends in occasional time periods for the various indexes in the social sciences and the humanities. Why they show less regularity than the natural sciences is not obvious, but the fact that some of the irregularities occur in different periods in the different indexes *for the same broad subject groups* suggests that sampling error is the likely cause. Putting very different subject areas together in broad groupings may also be partly responsible.

When we look at total use, the decay rate—for reasons that are not clear—seems to be inversely related to the age of titles in the social sciences and in the humanities.

In all three subsamples of titles published in 1944–48 the absolute, unnormalized proportion of titles used goes *up* from 1949–53 to 1954–58 further than any other group, although the *total* use index does not show the same invariable effect. If we measure popularity by total number of uses, then popularity begins to decline quite soon after publication. But the likelihood that the title will have utility for a given reader takes some time to hit a maximum. We might hypothesize that the most used books gain immediate acceptance because of intensive oral and other publicity, while the less used books take some time to have their importance recognized. We must keep in mind that the observations from which these data were generated are a biased sample (in that they exclude the very high use titles); we might consider that the materials they represent are the backbone of a *research* library.

It is our belief that the inferences derived from this procedure are much more believable than are those from the procedure specified earlier in section B. We feel that if obsolescence is an operational question for a library, these are the more relevant estimates. At the same time, we wish to emphasize that this question is one for which unqualified conclusions are extraordinarily difficult to draw, and great caution must be exercised in using the results pending further study and observation.

D. Relationship of obsolescence to popularity

We have presented data concerning differences in rates of obsolescence for different subjects and for titles of different ages. It is also possible that there are differences in obsolescence rates between highly used books, very little used books, and books of medium use. A study by Ernst and Shaffer[6] purported to demonstrate a fitting of Poisson functions to books of three degrees of popularity, and it was stated therein that popular books fall off in use faster than less popular books.

[6] Martin L. Ernst and Bertram Shaffer, "A Survey of Circulation Characteristics of Some General Library Books" (unpublished study, Massachusetts Institute of Technology, Cambridge, Mass., 1954).

TABLE 23

Decay in the use of nonestimated titles in all subject areas together[a]

Total Sample = 8,108 (1949–53) and 8,458 (1954–58)

Publication date period	No. of titles observed 1949–53	Mean use 1949–53	No. of titles observed 1954–58	Mean use 1954–58	Normalized mean use 1954–58	Decay in normalized use between periods	Drop-off as a percent of 1949–53
			AVERAGE USE INDEX				
Pre-1864	814	0.38	843	0.34	0.29	0.09	23.4%
1864–78	819	0.36	837	0.31	0.27	0.09	25.5%
1879–93	1,399	0.44	1,434	0.36	0.32	0.13	28.7%
1894–1903	901	0.67	914	0.48	0.42	0.25	37.4%
1904–13	955	0.64	990	0.46	0.40	0.24	37.0%
1914–23	1,040	0.67	1,056	0.56	0.49	0.18	26.7%
1924–33	954	1.10	985	0.87	0.76	0.34	31.2%
1934–43	931	1.25	982	0.95	0.83	0.42	33.8%
1944–48	295	2.77	417	1.25	1.09	1.68	60.6%

Normalization factor=0.87

Publication date period	No. of titles observed 1949–53	Mean use 1949–53	No. of titles observed 1954–58	Mean use 1954–58	Normalized mean use 1954–58	Decay in normalized use between periods	Drop-off as a percent of 1949–53
			AVERAGE USE 0–5 INDEX				
Pre-1864	814	0.35	843	0.28	0.26	0.09	25.4%
1864–78	819	0.32	837	0.26	0.23	0.08	25.7%
1879–93	1,399	0.37	1,434	0.32	0.29	0.08	21.1%
1894–1903	901	0.48	914	0.38	0.35	0.14	28.4%
1904–13	955	0.47	990	0.36	0.33	0.15	30.6%
1914–23	1,040	0.55	1,056	0.41	0.37	0.18	32.6%
1923–33	954	0.90	985	0.48	0.44	0.46	51.2%
1934–43	931	1.00	982	0.69	0.63	0.37	37.3%
1944–48	295	1.76	417	1.15	1.05	0.72	40.7%

Normalization factor=0.91

Publication date period	No. of titles observed 1949–53	Mean use 1949–53	No. of titles observed 1954–58	Mean use 1954–58	Normalized mean use 1954–58	Decay in normalized use between periods	Drop-off as a percent of 1949–53
			PROPORTION USED INDEX				
Pre-1864	814	0.18	843	0.17[b]	0.15[b]	0.03[b]	14.7%
1864–78	819	0.18	837	0.15	0.13	0.05	27.7%
1879–93	1,399	0.20	1,434	0.18	0.17	0.03	17.1%
1894–1903	901	0.26	914	0.22	0.20	0.06	23.1%
1904–13	955	0.23	990	0.20	1.19	0.04	18.5%
1914–23	1,040	0.26	1,056	0.23	0.21	0.05	20.2%
1924–33	954	0.37	985	0.28	0.26	0.11	30.2%
1934–43	931	0.38	982	0.32	0.29	0.10	24.8%
1944–48	295	0.42	417	0.45	0.41	0.01	1.9%

Normalization factor=0.91

[a] Stratified samples are included, as the figures are those for all nonestimated titles published before 1948.

[b] This column designates *proportion used* rather than mean use.

TABLE 24

Decay in the use of all nonestimated titles in the humanities
Total Sample = 4,218 (1949–53) and 4,418 (1954–58)

Publication date period	No. of titles observed 1949–53	Mean use 1949–53	No. of titles observed 1954–58	Mean use 1954–58	Normalized mean use 1954–58	Decay in normalized use between periods	Drop-off as a percent of 1949–53
			AVERAGE USE INDEX				
Pre-1864	434	0.46	452	0.41	0.44	0.02	3.7%
1864–78	458	0.44	466	0.37	0.40	0.05	10.2%
1879–93	761	0.49	778	0.41	0.45	0.05	9.2%
1894–1903	435	0.57	441	0.40	0.44	0.13	22.8%
1904–13	442	0.69	461	0.55	0.60	0.09	12.4%
1914–23	525	0.71	533	0.52	0.57	0.15	20.4%
1924–33	478	0.89	494	0.63	0.69	0.20	22.1%
1934–43	516	0.91	549	0.64	0.70	0.21	23.1%
1944–48	169	2.60	244	1.40	1.53	1.08	41.3%

Normalization factor = 1.09

			AVERAGE USE 0–5 INDEX				
Pre-1864	434	0.40	452	0.35	0.37	0.03	7.2%
1864–78	458	0.35	466	0.33	0.35	0.01	1.7%
1879–93	761	0.43	778	0.39	0.41	0.03	5.8%
1894–1903	435	0.50	441	0.38	0.40	0.10	20.2%
1904–13	442	0.55	461	0.44	0.47	0.08	15.2%
1914–23	525	0.55	533	0.44	0.46	0.08	15.7%
1924–33	478	0.80	494	0.57	0.60	0.20	25.5%
1934–43	516	0.80	549	0.60	0.63	0.17	21.4%
1944–48	169	1.73	244	1.03	1.08	0.65	37.4%

Normalization factor = 1.06

			PROPORTION USED INDEX				
Pre-1864	434	0.18	452	0.18[a]	0.15[a]	0.02[a]	13.1%
1864–78	458	0.22	466	0.19	0.16	0.06	25.8%
1879–93	761	0.22	778	0.21	0.18	0.05	20.1%
1894–1903	435	0.27	441	0.21	0.18	0.09	33.2%
1904–13	442	0.26	461	0.24	0.20	0.06	22.5%
1914–23	525	0.26	533	0.23	0.20	0.06	22.4%
1924–33	478	0.35	494	0.29	0.25	0.11	30.0%
1934–43	516	0.33	549	0.30	0.26	0.07	22.2%
1944–48	169	0.41	244	0.41	0.36	0.05	13.2%

Normalization factor = 0.86

[a] This column designates *proportion used* rather than mean use.

TABLE 25

Decay in the use of all nonestimated titles in the natural sciences
Total Sample = 1,780 (1949–53) and 1,818 (1954–58)

Publication date period	No. of titles observed 1949–53	Mean use 1949–53	No. of titles observed 1954–58	Mean use 1954–58	Normalized mean use 1954–58	Decay in normalized use between periods	Drop-off as a percent of 1949–53
			AVERAGE USE INDEX				
Pre-1864	207	0.22	208	0.17	0.16	0.05	24.4%
1864–78	183	0.20	183	0.14	0.14	0.06	29.9%
1879–93	286	0.26	287	0.20	0.20	0.07	25.1%
1894–1903	213	0.55	213	0.45	0.44	0.11	20.2%
1904–13	242	0.73	243	0.57	0.55	0.17	23.8%
1914–23	257	0.68	259	0.43	0.41	0.26	38.8%
1924–33	202	1.48	207	1.01	0.98	0.50	33.6%
1934–43	132	1.40	139	1.04	1.02	0.39	27.5%
1944–48	58	2.10	79	2.27	2.21	−0.11	− 5.0%

Normalization factor=0.98

			AVERAGE USE 0–5 INDEX				
Pre-1864	207	0.22	208	0.17	0.17	0.04	20.2%
1864–78	183	0.20	183	0.14	0.14	0.06	27.9%
1879–93	286	0.26	287	0.20	0.21	0.05	20.5%
1894–1903	213	0.48	213	0.39	0.40	0.08	16.7%
1904–13	242	0.38	243	0.31	0.32	0.06	14.9%
1914–23	257	0.62	259	0.39	0.40	0.21	34.3%
1924–33	202	1.00	207	0.65	0.67	0.32	32.6%
1934–43	132	1.26	139	0.94	0.98	0.28	10.9%
1944–48	58	1.48	79	1.48	1.54	−0.05	− 3.6%

Normalization factor=1.04

			PROPORTION USED INDEX				
Pre-1864	207	0.17	208	1.13[a]	0.11[a]	0.07[a]	37.9%
1864–78	183	0.14	183	0.08	0.06	0.07	53.3%
1879–93	286	0.15	287	0.19	0.16	−0.01	− 4.0%
1894–1903	213	0.23	213	0.21	0.17	0.05	24.0%
1904–13	242	0.19	243	0.19	0.15	0.03	17.3%
1914–23	257	0.27	259	0.21	0.18	0.09	33.8%
1924–33	202	0.39	207	0.27	0.22	0.17	42.7%
1934–43	132	0.50	139	0.37	0.30	0.20	39.9%
1944–48	58	0.66	79	0.54	0.45	0.21	31.5%

Normalization factor=0.83

[a] This column designates *proportion used* rather than mean use.

TABLE 26

Decay in the use of all nonestimated titles in the social sciences
Total Sample = 2,110 (1949–53) and 2,222 (1954–58)

Publication date period	No. of titles observed 1949–53	Mean use 1949–53	No. of titles observed 1954–58	Mean use 1954–58	Normalized mean use 1954–58	Decay in normalized use between periods	Drop-off as a percent of 1949–53
			AVERAGE USE INDEX				
Pre-1864	173	0.38	183	0.25	0.36	0.02	5.6%
1864–78	178	0.32	188	0.20	0.29	0.03	8.8%
1879–93	352	0.49	369	0.37	0.54	−0.05	−10.3%
1894–1903	253	0.53	260	0.40	0.58	−0.05	− 9.4%
1904–13	271	0.47	286	0.29	0.42	0.05	10.7%
1914–23	258	0.58	264	0.46	0.64	−0.06	−10.7%
1924–33	274	1.21	284	0.61	0.89	0.32	26.7%
1934–43	283	1.79	294	0.92	1.33	0.46	25.7%
1944–48	68	3.74	94	1.49	2.15	1.58	42.4%

Normalization factor = 1.45

			AVERAGE USE 0–5 INDEX				
Pre-1864	173	0.36	183	0.25	0.31	0.05	14.8%
1864–78	178	0.32	188	0.20	0.25	0.07	22.5%
1879–93	352	0.32	369	0.28	0.36	−0.03	− 9.6%
1894–1903	253	0.46	260	0.38	0.48	−0.03	− 5.5%
1904–13	271	0.43	286	0.27	0.34	0.09	20.4%
1914–23	258	0.50	264	0.38	0.47	0.03	5.6%
1924–33	274	1.00	284	0.58	0.73	0.27	27.4%
1934–43	283	1.19	294	0.75	0.94	0.25	20.6%
1944–48	68	2.09	94	1.20	1.51	0.58	27.5%

Normalization factor = 1.26

			PROPORTION USED INDEX				
Pre-1864	173	0.19	183	0.19[a]	0.20[a]	−0.01[a]	− 7.0%
1864–78	178	0.15	188	0.11	0.12	0.03	19.5%
1879–93	352	0.18	369	0.18	0.20	−0.01	− 7.1%
1894–1903	253	0.25	260	0.23	0.24	0.00	1.2%
1904–13	271	0.21	286	0.16	0.18	0.03	15.0%
1914–23	258	0.27	264	0.25	0.26	0.01	2.2%
1924–33	274	0.38	284	0.29	0.31	0.07	18.8%
1934–43	283	0.42	294	0.33	0.35	0.07	17.1%
1944–48	68	0.47	94	0.48	0.51	−0.04	− 9.4%

Normalization factor = 1.07

[a] This column designates *proportion used* rather than mean use.

TABLE 27

Change in use from 1953–55 to 1954–58 as a function of use in 1950–52
for all nonestimated single-book titles

Use in 1950–52	Number of Observations	Mean use 1953–55	Difference between mean use in 1953–55 and 1956–58 as a % of mean use in 1953–55
0	5,319	0.102	+ 2.9%
1	653	0.440	− 3.0%
2	190	0.874	− 9.7%
3–4	46	1.462	−16.1%
5–12	119	2.043	−31.9%

Unfortunately, the results of that study seem to be confounded by the regression phenomenon: just as the tallest group of fathers will have more sons shorter than themselves (closer to average height) than any other group of fathers, so the highest-use group of books in any short period of time must apparently decrease in use toward their mean. We must question the specific parameters suggested in the Massachusetts Institute of Technology study because the curves were fitted to points that included the first period use, which was also the criterion for sorting the books into the three popularity groups. However, our computations on their data, excluding the first time period, indicate that there is *at least a mild effect* in the direction they suggest (that is, more popular books become obsolescent faster).

To verify this effect with a sample from our data, we grouped the nonestimated, one book unit to a title[7] observations from all our monograph samples. We then separated groups of titles on the basis of use in 1950–52 and observed the change in use of the various popularity

[7] The rationale for excluding estimated-use titles is obvious. But the bias goes to the heart of the problem since it eliminates many of the most popular books, a category we intend to employ for comparison. Only single-book titles were included because of the difficulty of summarizing multiple-book titles on the IBM equipment. With this procedure our conclusions about the *direction* of the effect should be free of possible bias.

groups from 1953–55 to 1956–58. The relevant statistic is the percentage loss of use from period to period found by dividing the difference in mean use from 1953–55 to 1956–58 by the mean use in 1953–55.

For the titles that had *zero* use from 1950–52, there was actually a *gain* in use from 1953–55 to 1956–58. We may attribute this effect to a combination of little obsolescence and a rise in the total use of the library. The data for all groups are given in table 27 and support the unequivocal conclusion that the more highly used a title, the greater the *percentage* by which its use is expected to drop in succeeding time periods.

Interesting as the problem is, and satisfactory as our results are, we believe that the relative obsolescence of popular and unpopular books is not a matter of prime importance to the library contemplating a storage program because the popular or heavily used books are obviously not candidates for storage. And there is no evidence to support the view that once the period of heavy use has ended, these books would be used at rates appreciably different from all the other seldom used books that are the heart of a research library.

E. Summary of findings about obsolescence

1. Because of the lack of adjustments for changes in the book publication rate

over the years, or for differences in holdings of libraries by various publication date periods, previous studies may have overestimated the rate at which the use of books drops off.

2. Together, the evidence from the two lines of investigation (sections B and C) suggests that (a) the rate of use of titles continues to decrease indefinitely with the age of the title; and (b) the older a group of holdings is, the more valuable, in terms of use, is the *average* book in the group. The latter conclusion is not immediately obvious from the data, but it is the only plausible theory that will reconcile the various sets of data. The argument for this theory goes as follows:

a. The average use in 1954–58 of different groups of books published prior to 1893 appears *not* to be a function of their ages. (See figure 12.) For example, *very, very old* books (more than 100 years) are not used less than *very old* books (between 70 and 100 years old). If use is our indicator of value, *very, very old* books were at least as valuable in 1954–58 as were *very old* books.

b. The average use of *all* books, however, appears to be in a continuous decline. (See table 23.) Again, if use is our indicator of value, *very very old* books were less valuable in 1954–58 than in previous periods of time.

c. Books that were *very, very old* in 1954–58 were more valuable when they were *very old* than the books that were *very old* in 1954–58. The probable reasons for this apparent decline in relative value are numerous and complex. Among them may be a tendency for the library to be more selective with works published prior to the beginning of the collection than with works published contemporaneously with the library's existence. Another possible cause is the steadily growing recognition that schol-

ars require a fuller printed record of the past in order to understand and reconstruct it. We do not think we can pursue this line of speculation further without more detailed data.

3. We measure decline in use by the ratio of (a) the difference between the use in two time periods to (b) the use in the earlier time period. Except for titles published in the most recent period, this measure is quite constant for titles of various ages in the natural sciences. The measure decreases with increasing age in the social sciences and in the humanities. The numerical estimates depend upon the index of use chosen.

4. In its simplest form the concept for stabilizing the size of a working research collection demands that groups of books by age decrease in use by the same *absolute* amount each year. Our results suggest that the rate of decay is much closer to a constant *percentage* each year or —even worse for the stabilization principle—that the percentage may tend to *decrease* over time. It is also relevant to recall that the rate of input for most subjects at present is much greater than was the rate of input twenty or thirty years ago, a simple arithmetical proposition that militates against the stabilization concept, except at the cost of putting an increasing percentage of total use into storage.

5. The drop in use of all books in a subject area may be seen as the natural outgrowth of adding more books. Circulation figures suggest (although we have not studied the problem rigorously) that the *number of books read per capita* may remain roughly constant even though the number of books in the collection increases.

If the number of circulations per capita remains roughly constant, we must assume one of two effects or, more likely, a combination of the two: (a)

We may assume that a newly acquired volume will simply be used in place of some other book already in the collection. This *replacement* effect may not take place all at once but over a reasonable period of time. The mean use of books for the entire collection would, of course, drop even though the number of books used and the distribution of use among them remained the same. (b) On the other hand we may assume that the newly acquired volume takes away some but not all of the use from other books. The effect would be to *dilute* the total use over a larger and larger universe. The mean use per volume would also decline, but the distribution of use would gradually change. We are inclined to believe that both phenomena are likely to occur side by side with significant differences in extent according to subject field. The latter effect suggests also the perfectly reasonable assumption that a larger collection is likely to offer readers books that will more closely match their exact needs. It does this, of course, at the expense of ascending costs of acquiring and housing the growing collection.

We may employ this theory to give us an idea of the requirements and possibilities of book storage plans. If we deal with the simplified case of a subject group such as the natural sciences, where the decay among all books appears to be much the same, we can employ the various sets of data discussed in chapters 2 and 3 to estimate the number of identifiable books that would have less than some arbitrary amount of predicted use at a future time. For example, if a library knows the distribution of its books by *number of years since last use,* it could estimate (a) how many of those books would be used in the next ten years directly from the prediction function

employed and (b) from the rate of *dilution,* how much the expected use of that group of books would drop by the end of ten years. From the two estimates could then be predicted the number of books that would have less than perhaps 0.01 probability of being used in a single year at the point in time ten years away.

The reader must observe four cautions when considering the statements just made:

a. If a university is willing to pay the increasing cost of supplying more pieces and more exacting or better matching pieces of information by maintaining ever larger collections, the level of predicted use that would be employed to identify books for storage would decrease over time.

b. Our data suggest that in at least two of the three broad subject areas the dilution caused by new acquisitions affects *new* books more than *old* books. We would hazard that this also means that dilution affects *heavily used* books by a greater *percentage* than it affects lightly used books. It would be good practice to adjust any set of calculations to reflect this phenomenon.

c. Predicting on the basis of the data contained in this section of the study is risky at best. Certainly there is loss of accuracy in employing data from one subject area to predict for another subject area that we have not studied. Furthermore, it is necessary to interpolate, extrapolate, smooth curves by eye, and generally manipulate the observed data in order to come up with any prediction. The aid of a trained statistician may be essential in preparing a policy program based upon such data as these.

d. By the declining use measure, popular titles decline in use more than do unpopular titles.

6

The development of functions to identify serial volumes for storage

A. Purpose of the chapter

The purpose of investigating serials was the same as in the study of monographs: to develop a satisfactory method of selecting a predetermined proportion of serial volumes for storage. The criteria for evaluating the methods are the number of volumes recalled from storage for circulation and lost browsing use of the stored volumes.

B. Serials as compared to monographs

1. Definition

We define *serial* as "a related sequence of publications issued at regular or irregular intervals, with some scheme of consecutive numbering, and intended to be continued indefinitely." In doubtful cases we examined the number of contributing authors since serials generally contain articles by several persons.

The definition would include periodicals, journals, newspapers, and some monograph series. We arbitrarily excluded newspapers, and we excluded most monograph series because their individual volumes are related to one another only through the system of numbering and sometimes a common call

number. In this study, the volumes of a monograph series were handled individually using the techniques developed for monographs.

2. The "family" quality of serials

The most important characteristic of serials is their nature as families of volumes whose use patterns are related to one another. The strength of this relationship determines whether it is more useful to view serials solely in terms of the connected sequences they form or as groups of volumes having relatively independent use patterns.[1]

Table 28 demonstrates the "family" quality by examining the relation between the use of successive pairs of volumes in our full-length (explained below) serial samples in biology and in Teutonic languages and literatures. The first volume and the second volume in a serial run were considered as one pair. The second volume and the third volume were another pair, and so on. Each volume, then, entered into two pairs of volumes. If used volumes tended to be scattered randomly through serials, then the tendency

[1] The same question arises for multivolume monograph titles, which comprise only a small fraction of all monographs.

TABLE 28

Comparative use of successive serial volumes
(Taken from full-length serial samples)

	2nd volume in pair has no use	2nd volume in pair has some use
3,026 Successive pairs of biology serial volumes dated 1954 and earlier; use during 1955–59		
	Cell A	Cell B
1st volume in pair has no use	1,800	330
	Cell C	Cell D
1st volume in pair has some use	309	587
750 Successive pairs of Teutonic languages and literatures serial volumes dated 1954 and earlier; use during 1955–59		
	Cell A	Cell B
1st volume in pair has no use	646	38
	Cell C	Cell D
2nd volume in pair has some use	36	30

would be for cell D of each table to bear the same proportion to cell B or cell C that cell B or cell C bears to cell A. Since the ratio of cell D to either cell B or C is relatively high, we conclude that the used volumes are *not* randomly distributed through serials.

3. The serial volume as an anthology

Another difference between serials and monographs is that most serial volumes are collections of several short articles that may act independently in drawing readers to the volume. Because of the brevity of articles, there may be more browsing and unrecorded use of serials than of monographs.

Many libraries restrict at least the more heavily used serials to the reading room. Therefore, they do not have data from which to develop functions based on past use. However, because serial volumes form collections of several relatively independent articles, their use patterns might be more alike from li-

brary to library than is the case with monographs. If functions requiring knowledge of past use to predict future use are clearly superior to other types, as they were for monographs, then a library that has such records—as does the University of Chicago—might develop these functions and provide other libraries with a list of stored serial volumes.

C. Description of the serials collection

1. Numbers of titles and volumes

In 1961 there were an estimated 20,000 serial titles being currently received and over 64,000 serial titles, open and closed, held in the University of Chicago. Records on acquisitions and judgments of the library staff indicated that there were about as many serial volumes in the library as there were monograph volumes.[2]

[2] These results come from two independent systematic samples of shelf list cards, one of 25 half-

TABLE 29

Distribution of bound volumes per serial title for biology, philosophy, economics,
and Teutonic languages and literatures at the University of Chicago
(Taken from the samples of full-length serials, including
all volumes dated[a] 1959 or earlier)

No. of bound volumes	Number of serial titles			
	Biology	Philosophy	Economics	Teutonic languages and literatures
5–10	29	16	20	20
11–15	19	9	7	8
16–20	11	9	3	5
21–25	12	4	3	5
26–30	7	4	3	1
31–35	7	1	4	2
36–40	3	2	2	4
41–45	5	3	3	2
46–50	1	1	0	1
Over 50	16	8	5	0
Total	110	57	50	48

[a] See appendix C for definition of the publication date of a serial volume.

Since Chicago had approximately 2,000,-000 volumes, we may assume that about 1,000,000 of these were serials. This estimate is related to the precision of other estimates: We want to predict with some confidence the number of serial volumes that a function will select for storage, because if the error is greater than a few percent, we can err by 50,000 volumes or more. Also, the size of the serials collection is large enough to indicate that detailed study of serial volume storage can be valuable.

2. Variation in distribution of bulk among fields

If there actually were 1,000,000 serial volumes and, say, 65,000 to 70,000 titles, the average is 15 volumes per serial title. A distribution of the size of serial titles in terms of volumes is given for the fields of biology, philosophy, economics, and

drawers, and one of 50 quarter-drawers of cards. "Open" serials are those that are currently being published; "closed" titles have ceased publication.

Teutonic languages and literatures in table 29. These figures include multiple copies, counted as part of the bulk in our investigation. Table 30 shows the mean number of bound volumes per title dated 1954 and earlier for each of these fields.

3. Effect of unbound material

We cannot learn much about the use of unbound serial materials in the University of Chicago library because of the absence of records of past use. However, if unbound material represents an appreciable portion of a collection, it will affect any storage policy. Judgments of library staff members indicated that 5 to 10 percent of the serial collection in the stacks of Harper Library, the central unit in the University of Chicago library system, was unbound. In most departmental libraries, the bulk of unbound material was generally less, and perhaps negligible. However, in the business and economics library, a collection in excess of 140,000

TABLE 30

Mean number of bound volumes dated 1954 and earlier per serial title
(Data taken from full-length serial samples
at the University of Chicago)

Field	Mean number of volumes per serial	Number of serial titles in sample
Biology...........................	30.85	106
Philosophy........................	26.38	50
Economics.........................	24.13	46
Teutonic languages and literatures	16.39	44

volumes, the unbound materials probably exceeded 10 percent.

This fraction will vary from library to library, depending on past and present budgets and binding policies, and it is difficult to generalize. Unbound material probably has less use than bound material, since librarians tend to choose higher-use material for binding. Browsing use is lower for unbound materials, since it often takes considerable effort to ascertain what a box or folio contains. The amount of unbound material affects the error in estimating the fraction of bound serial volumes that would be removed by any particular policy.

4. Effect of differences in binding practices

Different libraries may not bind the same issues of a serial in one volume. For example, one library may bind ten consecutive numbers together and another may bind only eight. Thus, the second library may have 25 percent more volumes in its run of the serial. Also, some libraries may have more or less of the serial unbound or hold different portions of it, or more or fewer copies. If the volumes are bound differently, but the same portion of the serial is held, the number of volumes will appear to be less, though the bulk is clearly the same.

D. Generation of functions and storage rules

This section discusses types of procedures or functions for predicting future use of serials, desirable properties of functions, and the relation of these factors to sampling. A full description of the details of sampling procedure will be found in a later section.

1. Two basic assumptions

We assume that libraries prefer to store only consecutive volumes in the early portion of a serial. This keeps record changing simple, since only one notation—say the date of the latest volume stored—would have to be made on a serial record card.

We also assume as we did for monographs that the older the book is, the lower its use tends to be. Thus, we seek a procedure for selecting a continuous run of volumes from each serial from the oldest toward the newest, the length of that run to be determined by functions of whatever characteristics we can find that predict future use.

2. Classes of functions distingushed

Two classes of functions are those that depend only on demographic characteristics,[3] and those that depend on past use also. Functions based on demographic characteristics will lead to the same decision about volumes having identical characteristics, so that the larger the spread of use among such volumes, the less successful these demographic characteristic functions will be.

The question, then, is whether a function of past use as well as of demographic characteristics would be superior to a function based on demographic characteristics alone. In the case of monographs, past use materially aided prediction, so it seems likely that it would do the same for serial volumes. Furthermore, the "family" quality of serials suggests that past use may be an even more valuable predictor.

3. Two approaches to deriving rules for serial storage

One method of deriving rules for serial storage is to study the volumes individually, without attending to their connection with each other within a serial title. The other approach is to study each volume in conjunction with all the other volumes constituting that serial. Both methods can take past-use data into account, but such data probably can better be employed under the latter approach.

4. Desirable properties of functions

The functions we choose should send books to storage that would be withdrawn a minimum number of times. They should (a) yield fairly quick and precise estimates of the percentage of volumes to be stored and the mean use of these volumes, (b) be easy to apply,

and (c) minimize the number of characteristics to be observed and the number of decisions to be made at the shelf.

E. Variables

1. Demographic characteristics defined and enumerated

We define demographic characteristics of a bound serial volume as those that can be measured or observed or determined unambiguously by a relatively untrained person and can usually be ascertained from the shelf list card. This excludes judgments about the content or merit of the volume. Selection methods based on statistically determined functions are expected to be carried out as clerical tasks.

Publication date: This is unique for a given *volume,* the date of the latest material included in the volume. Accession date is not useful for serials because it usually is the same as the publication date.

Language

Number of volumes: This is the number of physical book units of the serial held in the University of Chicago collection, excluding multiple copies.[4] The hypothesis is that a serial published often, regularly, and for a long time is probably well known and esteemed by scholars. Presumably, its endurance and size are indicative of readership.

Subject area: The broad general discipline to which the serial's articles are relevant is indicated by the Library of Congress classification. We investigated the development of decision functions *within* subject areas, that is, considering data from only one subject area at a time. As with monographs, we presume that the distribution of use patterns may differ among subject areas.

Number of libraries holding the serial: Taken from the *Union List of Serials,* this is the number of research libraries in the United States that reported holding the se-

---

[3] Demographic characteristics include publication date, language, and length of serial run—characteristics of a volume that can be measured independently of its use.

[4] For certain procedures we include multiple copies, as explained later in section G, "Developing and applying functions."

rial, a reflection of the apparent extent of general interest in it.

Terminated or nonterminated: A terminated serial is either no longer published or no longer received in the University of Chicago library.

2. Past use

Our definition of past use of a volume is similar to that described for monographs in chapter 1.

F. Sampling

1. Two approaches

We sampled from the universe of serial volumes in two ways: (a) by taking a random sample of volumes, and (b) by taking a random sample of serial titles including every volume of every title chosen. The former is called a *random systematic* sample, the latter a *full-length* sample.

2. Sample universe

There were several possible universes for sampling serial titles for full-length samples. One of these was the shelf list. Sampling from it has the drawback that the number of cards for serial titles is small (perhaps 8 percent of the total), and these cards are highly concentrated because the Library of Congress classification system groups together most of the serials in a given subject area. For instance, QC 1 contains the bulk of all the physics serials, and nothing but serials.

A second possible universe could have been the serials listed in bibliographies. These lists suffer from two defects: (a) some bibliographies would list serials that the University of Chicago does not hold, and vice versa, and (b) bibliographies, generally, would not have the same limits for inclusion as does the Library of Congress classification, so that some of the books in a list of physics serials might be included under chemistry in the Library of Congress classification, and vice versa.

A third possible universe for sampling serial titles, and the one which we employed for the full-length sample, was the shelves themselves. The procedure will be described later.

3. Procedure for sampling random volumes

For our random systematic sample of the volumes in the collection the procedure was as follows: (a) Make an approximate manual count of the number of serial volumes in the subject area being studied. (b) Find the interval such that, if every "nth" volume were chosen, the sample size would be approximately 400. (c) Beginning at one end of the subject area classification system, count off "n" volumes on the shelves, excluding volumes published after 1953. (Duplicate copies were not counted in the interval.) (d) Within each interval select one volume randomly using a set of random numbers. If the selected volume was acquired after 1953, the next volume was chosen in the physics sample. For other areas in the case of acquisition past 1953 the interval was skipped entirely. (e) Collect the data for all copies of the volumes chosen. (f) Take a similar sample from among the serial volumes charged out at the time in each departmental library.

For the systematic sample of serial volumes, we gathered the same kind of data that were collected for monograph volumes (see chapter 2 and appendix A), as well as the number of unique volumes held (excluding multiple copies), and the number of libraries in the *Union List of Serials* holding any of the serial.

4. Procedure for the full-length serial sample

The random selection was accomplished by numbering the shelves in the subject area being sampled, then selecting the shelves from a table of random numbers. Data were collected only for

TABLE 31

Results of a storage policy for serials based on a function of publication date

Subject	Cumulative % of volumes to be stored taken in increasing order of predicted use	Mean use in 1955–59 of volumes classified for storage as of 1954	Mean use in 1955–59 of volumes not classified for storage as of 1954
Teutonic languages and literatures[a]	25%	.11	.14
	35%	.11	.14
	50%	.10	.17
Biology[a]	25%	.09	1.29
	35%	.12	1.46
	50%	.22	1.76
Philosophy[a]	25%	.38	1.69
	35%	.39	1.89
	50%	.49	2.24

The data for this table were taken from the full-length serial samples.
[a] Sample sizes are as in table 30.

serials whose *first volumes* were on the chosen shelves.

G. Developing and applying functions

1. Functions based on demographic characteristics

An example of a simple, one-characteristic function would be one based only on the publication date of the volume. Since we have evidence that older volumes are used less than newer ones, we might select for storage the oldest volumes in the library. The efficiency of this technique depends on how steeply mean use rises as age decreases (cf. figures 15a–15c). Table 31 presents the results of selecting the oldest 25 percent, 35 percent, and 50 percent of the volumes in three subject areas. The table shows the mean use in the next five years of the sample books that would have been stored and that would not have been stored under this procedure. The results are not very satisfactory either by an absolute standard or by comparison with other functions we derive later in the chapter.

One way of handling several demographic characteristics together would be to combine the variables in a regression equation to predict some measure of use. There are many forms in which the demographic characteristics may be combined in this type of analysis. The only way to judge the merits of a particular form is to analyze a set of data with it and then evaluate the results. We tried several regression equations using data from the random volumes samples. The results of only one were satisfactory.

This complicated function employed various transformations of *language, publication date, terminated versus nonterminated, number of unique volumes in the serial,* and *number of libraries in the Union List of Serials holding the serial.* The variable predicted was "0," "1," or "2" if the volume had that number of uses, "3" if there were 3 to 5 uses, and "6" if there had been 6 or more uses in 1954–58.

Regression functions were developed for biology and philosophy, and were set to select for storage the 25 percent of

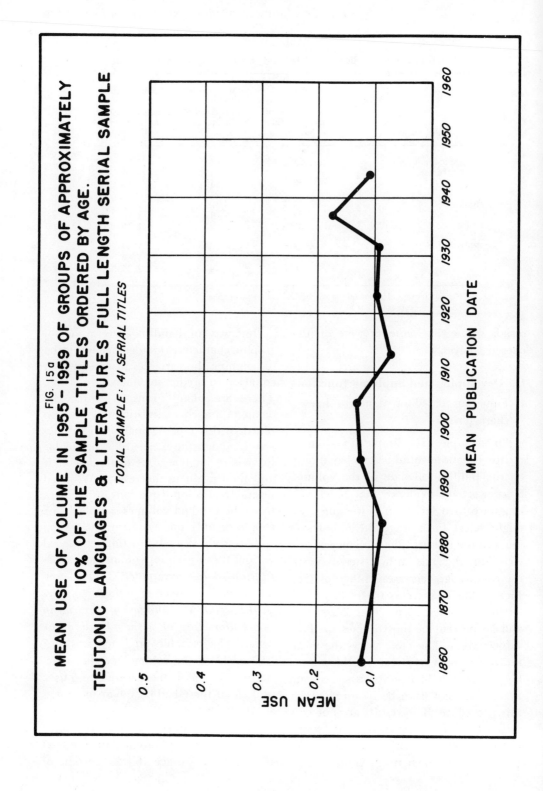

FIG. 15 a

MEAN USE OF VOLUME IN 1955 - 1959 OF GROUPS OF APPROXIMATELY
10% OF THE SAMPLE TITLES ORDERED BY AGE.
TEUTONIC LANGUAGES & LITERATURES FULL LENGTH SERIAL SAMPLE

TOTAL SAMPLE: 41 SERIAL TITLES

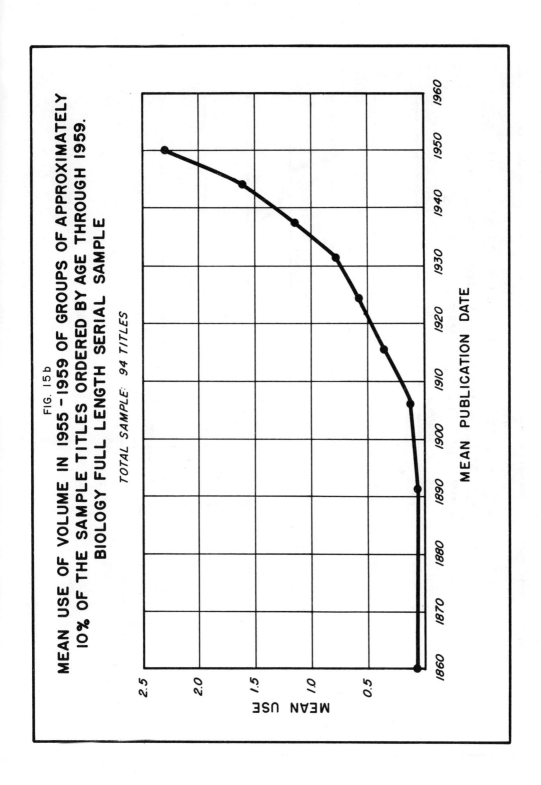

FIG. 15 b

MEAN USE OF VOLUME IN 1955 - 1959 OF GROUPS OF APPROXIMATELY
10% OF THE SAMPLE TITLES ORDERED BY AGE THROUGH 1959.
BIOLOGY FULL LENGTH SERIAL SAMPLE

TOTAL SAMPLE: 94 TITLES

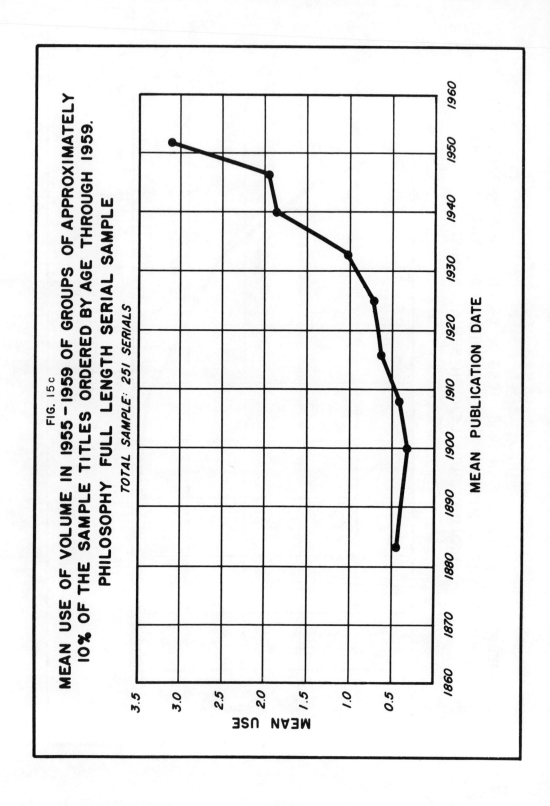

FIG. 15c

MEAN USE OF VOLUME IN 1955 – 1959 OF GROUPS OF APPROXIMATELY 10% OF THE SAMPLE TITLES ORDERED BY AGE THROUGH 1959. PHILOSOPHY FULL LENGTH SERIAL SAMPLE

TOTAL SAMPLE: 251 SERIALS

the sample with the lowest predicted future use. The results are shown below:

	Biology	Philosophy
Estimated percent of volumes that would have been stored	18%	34%
Estimated percent of stored volumes that would have been used in the following five years, 1955–59	11%	16%
Estimated mean use in 1955–59 of volumes that would have been stored	.12	.19
Estimated mean use in 1955–59 of volumes that would not have been stored	2.0	2.0

These functions appear fairly effective in terms of the use that the books would generate while in storage. The average biology volume stored would be used on the average once in 45 years, and the average philosophy volume would be used once in 30 years. There was considerable variability in the results achieved in terms of the proportion of books that would have been stored. The functions were expected to take 25 percent of the universe, but the biology function actually would have taken an estimated 18 percent and the philosophy function actually would have taken an estimated 34 percent. These percentages are within the range of expected normal variation.

If a library has no records of the past use of serials and does not wish to use storage lists generated at other libraries, it might use functions like those described above. However, the creation of such functions would be laborious and difficult, and there is considerable doubt that they would be useful in humanistic disciplines.

2. Functions depending upon the "family" quality of serials: a priori rules

In these functions, *total use in a given five-year period* was employed. The ap-

proach was to write arbitrary selection rules, apply them to the data, and study their effects. The rules were arbitrary in that they were not predesigned to cut a specified percentage of volumes from the collection, nor were they derived from statistical analysis of the data. They were based on the assumptions that (a) as we progress from the earliest volume to the latest, the expected use of the volumes tends to increase, and (b) the use of adjacent volumes within serials is correlated.

The general form of the rules was: Examine the total-use data in a serial for a five-year period, volume by volume, starting with the earliest volume and moving forward until the first occurrence of some specified amount of use. Store all volumes older than this critical volume or cluster of volumes and keep the remainder. The use data from the next five years was used to evaluate the results of the procedure. The rules were devised from data for 1950–54 and tested on data for 1955–59.

Three a priori rules were tried. *Rule 1:* Find the earliest volume used in 1950–54. Count back five volumes and take all earlier volumes to storage. Store no volume published in 1941 or thereafter. If rule indicates fewer than five volumes for storage, send none. If rule indicates that fewer than five volumes are to remain, send those volumes also. *Rule 2:* Store all volumes earlier than the earliest volume showing use in 1950–54 but store or keep at least five volumes. *Rule 3:* Store all volumes older than either the earliest volume showing two uses in 1950–54, or the earlier volume of a pair of volumes used in 1950–54 and published within five years of each other, whichever applies first. Store or keep at least five volumes. For example, suppose that all volumes of a particular serial dated before 1940 showed no use in 1950–

TABLE 32

Summary of the results of three serial rules applied on the basis of 1950–54 data
and tested on 1955–59 use data

Subject	1 Estimated % of physical serial volumes that would be stored	2 Estimated % of volumes stored that would be used in 1955–59	3 Estimated mean use 1955–59 of volumes stored	4 Estimated mean use in 1955–59 of volumes not stored	5 Estimated % of 1955–59 use of stored volumes to total use of all serial volumes 1955–59
	RESULTS OF RULE 1				
Biology, n = 106 titles	17.43	3.86	0.04	1.2	0.71
Teu. lang. and lit., n = 44 titles	44.66	1.55	0.02	0.24	5.26
Econ., n = 46 titles	48.38	2.23	0.02	1.02	2.15
Phil., n = 50 titles	12.85	6.17	0.07	1.55	0.64
Am. lit., n = 23 titles	34.88	6.19	0.08	0.53	7.44
	RESULTS OF RULE 2				
Biology	23.67	5.04	0.06	1.29	1.41
Teu. lang. and lit.	57.28	2.91	0.03	0.27	13.68
Economics	56.94	3.96	0.05	1.19	5.62
Philosophy	20.62	7.69	0.08	1.77	1.23
Am. literature	44.44	6.94	0.08	0.61	9.92
	RESULTS OF RULE 3				
Biology	32.35	7.28	0.09	1.4	2.79
Teu. lang. and lit.	63.38	5.03	0.06	0.25	29.47
Economics	61.17	3.68	0.05	1.32	5.79
Philosophy	26.25	9.97	0.15	1.78	2.81
Am. literature	57.41	5.91	0.07	0.78	10.74

54 except for the volumes dated 1920, 1930, and 1933. The rule directs that all volumes dated before 1930 be stored, provided there are at least five of them, unless the 1920 volume showed two or more uses in the given five-year period, in which case all volumes before 1920 would be stored.

Table 32 summarizes the results of these three rules applied to samples from several subject areas. The rules select a different proportion from the various fields and vary within fields, too. The proportion selected with any given rule depends on the overall use of the serial collection in a field and on the distribution of use among older and newer serials.

The amount of variation from field to field suggests that a librarian must either (a) be willing to specify a level of use below which he wishes to send serial volumes to storage and then *accept* the results, or (b) make preliminary surveys of each field. Columns 2 and 3 in table 32 measure the effects of the rules in terms of the absolute amount of use that the stored volumes would generate.

TABLE 33

Comparison of results of a priori rules versus storage by age alone for serials

(Taken from tables 31 and 32)

Subject	% of volumes stored by age only	Mean use of volumes stored by age only 1955–59	Closest % of volumes stored by a priori rules based on 1950–54 data	Mean use of volumes stored by a priori rules 1955–59	Mean use in 1955–59 of volumes not classified for storage as of 1954 under a priori rules	Mean use of volumes not stored by age only 1955–59
Teutonic lang. and literatures...........	50	0.10	57.28	0.03	1.42	0.17
Biology...............	25	0.09	23.67	0.06	1.29	1.29
Philosophy............	25	0.38	26.25	0.15	1.69	1.69

There is an inverse relationship between the proportion stored and the amount of use, explained by the fact that when all serial volumes in a subject area are used lightly this will cause both a high proportion to be stored and stored volumes to be used lightly. Indeed, the "high proportion stored–low absolute use" areas show a high relative proportion of use by nonstored volumes (column 4).

The three rules differ in the proportions they would send to storage, but all of them seem to be quite satisfactory. The volumes that they designate for storage are used far less than are the volumes that would be kept in conventional housing. (See column 4 in table 32.) The probability of the average book in the store group being withdrawn in a given year ranges from approximately once in 300 years (Teutonic languages, rule 1) to approximately once in 50 years (philosophy, rule 3).

3. Comparison of methods

Tables 33 and 34 compare the results of the various functions. Both tables in-dicate that the a priori rules are superior to those derived from demographic characteristics of serials.

H. Summary

Several sets of rules were developed for separating serials into groups for storage on the basis of predicted future use. The rules that seem best are based on system of surveying each serial title from the oldest volume onward, until one reaches volumes showing the specified amount of use. These rules separate out large numbers of volumes that will show a relatively small amount of use in future years.

The proportion of serials selected by a given rule varies widely among subject areas, and it would probably be necessary to survey each subject area to implement any policy decision about the proportion of serials to be stored.

Although the average use of many serial publications appears to be quite low, the selection procedures described may lead to storage decisions that will either confuse

TABLE 34

Comparison of results of a priori rules versus demographic characteristics rules for serials
(Taken from table 32)

Subject	Est. % of volumes that would have been stored by demographic characteristics function; standard error of est.	Est. mean use in 1955–59 of volumes that would have been stored by demographic characteristics function	Estimated mean use in 1955–59 of volumes that would have been stored by a priori rules	Estimated mean use in 1955–59 of volumes that would not have been stored by a priori rules	Closest % of volumes that would have been stored by a priori rules
Biology............	18.97	0.12	0.04	1.20	17.43
Philosophy.........	34.01	0.19	0.15	1.97	26.25

or mislead the reader with respect to an institution's true resources, or require him to consult serial or other records rather routinely for older serial publications. A library may wish to avoid this situation by leaving either a larger amount of little-used serial material in conventional book stacks, or by transferring to storage some materials that it would otherwise leave, in order to utilize simple rules such as "most serials published before 18—— are in storage."

7

Browsing and nonrecorded use

A. A discussion of types of use and their relationship to one another

In libraries with open stacks, some portion of the use of books consists of browsing. Since books in storage cannot be used in this way, it is important to know something about the extent of browsing that takes place.

The definitions which we will employ in this chapter are as follows: *Recorded use* is the use of books that leads to a circulation charge. (See the discussion on the unit of use in chapter 1, section C2 for those entries which were not counted as full uses.) *Nonrecorded use* is the use of books that does not result in an entry on the book cards, because the book is used in a book stack, an open shelf reading room, etc.[1] *Browsing* is the use of books that are not brought to readers by messenger. Substantially all nonrecorded use is browsing. But some browsing *is* recorded, when readers decide to charge books out after examining them in book stacks. *Total use* is the sum of nonrecorded and recorded use; it is also the sum of (a) browsing minus that part of recorded use

[1] Browsing in the University of Chicago's biology library is less than might be expected, primarily because of the physical arrangements.

that results from browsing and (b) recorded use. It is from this equation that we can estimate nonrecorded use.

Some books appear to have more nonrecorded use in proportion to recorded use than others for two probable causes: (a) There will be differences in the circulation rules among departmental libraries within a single library system. We may expect that if all else is equal, in a departmental library with completely open stacks there will be more nonrecorded use than in a library that limits access to its stacks. (b) There will be differences in the relationship of recorded to nonrecorded use between one subject area and another, and between different kinds of materials, notably monographs and serials. We can hypothesize that the shorter the reading time for a given work or the more diverse its contents, the less likely it is to be withdrawn. For example, if a reader is interested in scanning one short article in a large serial volume, he might not bother to withdraw the book. Dictionaries are a good example of books unlikely to be withdrawn; the information they contain is diverse, and use is normally brief.

Novels, by contrast, are likely to be withdrawn.

The elements and quantities that we seek to understand concern the relationship between browsing and recorded use for groups of books. We would like to determine whether there is a systematic relationship between the two kinds of use; if the relationship is systematic, what the proportions are for browsing and recorded use; what percentage of the browsing is judged valuable by the browser; and finally, whether the proportion is similar for groups of books in different subjects.

With knowledge about the quantities, we could predict how much browsing is likely to be lost if a book is removed to storage. We shall therefore attempt to examine the relationships between these quantities for different subject areas, and for monographs as distinguished from serials. Within each group, defined by subject matter and form, we shall try to find out whether there is some constant relationship.

B. Procedure

1. Difficulties in finding a unit of measurement

In studying nonrecorded use it is difficult to define an unambiguous unit of behavior that can be counted as *use*. For instance, counting books left on reading tables would be likely to underestimate the total because many books are used in the stacks and then replaced by the readers. If observers were to follow readers, they would almost surely affect reading behavior.

There does not seem to be a satisfactory mechanical or electronic method of describing browsing. The number of readers is sufficiently small and stack areas sufficiently large to make motion pictures or closed circuit TV impractical. Furthermore, it would be difficult through such techniques to tell which books were used.

Another possible measure is a *touched* book. Except for touches that occur only because the title cannot be determined from the outside of the book, all touches have some meaning to the reader, no matter how slight. If we were willing to accept fortuitous contact in our count, we might have employed substances to indicate that a book had been touched within a given period: infrared dust, beads on top of the book, or unexposed photographic paper inserted between the pages. (The last was tried unsuccessfully.) The other obvious all-or-nothing techniques do not allow us to determine how *many* times a book was touched within a given period. But to determine the value of browsing, we must also separate the contacts into categories of value. We must also determine which contacts would not have taken place under a different library organizational plan.[2]

2. Technique adopted

The technique that we employed was to place a brief questionnaire, reproduced in figure 16, in each book that was part of a title in our sample of mono-

[2] A student in the Graduate Library School, Alice Bowen, undertook an investigation that employed a "diary" technique. The procedure was to present readers, chosen at random, with questionnaires at some random time during their stay in the stacks. The reader then provided information about the next four books he touched. The results are given in: "Nonrecorded Use of Books and Browsing in the Stacks of a Research Library" (M.A. thesis, the University of Chicago Graduate Library School, 1961).

The Library of Congress retained Herner and Company to study this question by interviewing readers in the LC book stack: Saul Herner, "A Pilot Study of the Use of the Stacks of the Library of Congress" (unpublished, Washington, D.C.: Herner & Co., 1960).

PLEASE READ OTHER SIDE

Not to be filled in by reader

Title No. _____

Call Number _____

Shelf Number _____

Date Placed in Book _____

Date Sheet Returned _____

Book brought to check-out desk by reader?   Yes ☐ No ☐

Book brought to check-out desk by messenger?   Yes ☐ No ☐

```
FRONT OF
QUESTIONNAIRE
```

THE PEN is to aid you in filling out this brief questionnaire. We would like you to keep it as token payment for the moment of your time that it takes to help us improve the service of the Library

It is extremely important that every person who picks up this book fills out the questionnaire. Please drop the completed form into the box at the entrance to the library

A. How did you happen to pick up this book? Check one.

☐ 1. Found it via the card catalog

☐ 2. Came to the stacks looking for a work of this general nature

☐ 3. Looked for this particular book but without the call number

☐ 4. Picked it up through casual browsing

B. How will you use this book? Check one or more.

☐ 1. Check the book out of the Library

☐ 2. Carry it to a desk and read it there

☐ 3. Note the title for future reference

☐ 4. Examine a specific passage in the volume

☐ 5. Skim through it while standing up

☐ 6. Merely glance at the title page

```
BACK OF
QUESTIONNAIRE
```

Your department or school affiliation (or "none") _____

Your status (undergraduate, staff, visitor, etc.) _____

THANK YOU   The Library Use Study, Harper   E 43

Fig. 16.—Questionnaire form first used in browsing analysis

graphs and serials in the physics and general history (QC and D in the Library of Congress classification) subject areas, the first two sampled.[3] The questionnaire requested that every reader who picked up the book, no matter how brief his reading of it, fill out the questionnaire, describing how he found the book and the use to which he expected to put it. The reader was then asked to deposit the questionnaire in a box at the entrance to the stacks.

After some experience with the questionnaire in figure 16, a new one was designed, adding a direct question about the value of the use that the book provided. The revised questionnaire is shown in appendix D. To obtain information about multiple uses during the base period (October 18, 1959, to April 17, 1960), a new questionnaire was placed in the book within two days of the return of an original questionnaire.

The questionnaires were arranged around the pages of the book in such a manner that it was impossible to open the book without disturbing the questionnaire, and the questionnaires were not visible unless the book was actually removed from the shelf. Half of the questionnaires, in alternate books, were taped to ball-point pens that provided a writing instrument and a token reward.

3. Problems of response

In any questionnaire survey, there arises the question of how many people do not answer the questionnaire at all, and, of those who do, how many answer it honestly. The

[3] Questionnaires were also placed in all other books that fell into monograph samples, but because the length of time between sampling and the expected end of the study was not much more than six months, used questionnaires were not replaced, and these materials will not be considered here.

motivation for answering untruthfully can probably be discounted with one exception: An unknown number of users of any university library will have strong feelings about the desirability and importance of browsing and the possible threat to browsing that a use study might imply. Such individuals might, in consequence, have given inflated value judgments on the utility of browsing.

Some readers will not bother to read and answer a questionnaire. The pen questionnaires were an attempt to combat this. This number of questionnaires *with* pens that were returned versus the number *without* pens that were returned hints at the degree of caprice in motivation. It was possible for readers to search out questionnaires that had pens in order to take the pen, but because of the wide scatter of books that had pens in them (perhaps 600 in 10,000 books in each area), and the low value of the pen, this was not likely to be a very profitable activity. The pens were so placed that they could not be seen without a close examination of the book. Table 35 shows that many more "pen" than "no-pen" questionnaires were returned (the expected returns of each were equal), so we may assume that at least as many questionnaires as the difference between the two groups were seen but not returned.

We attempted two checks on the amount of nonresponse: First, in a subsample of 40 economics titles taken from the monograph sample for another purpose, four books had browsing questionnaires missing at the close of the survey, and all had been returned. A random sample of forty more titles had one questionnaire missing, and it had been returned. There might have been questionnaires that were seen by readers but not removed from the book.

Second, in August 1960 we returned to the books in the samples in economics, history, biology, and Teutonic languages and literatures and examined approximately 25 titles in each sample at random. The decision about whether the questionnaire had been disturbed seemed relatively clearcut; it is doubtful that many readers would have observed how the questionnaires were in-

TABLE 35

Browsing questionnaires returned for physics (QC) and history (D)
monographs and serials with and without pens

| | Monographs | | Serials | | |
	With Pens	Without Pens	With Pens	Without Pens	Total
Physics	190	130	218	127	665
History	71	40	38	27	176
Total	261	170	256	154	841

Total with Pens   = 517
Total without Pens = 324

serted and then taken the trouble to replace them in exactly their original position. It would be considerably less trouble to fill out the questionnaire. On the other hand, several groups of books had been shifted by the library staff so that it was difficult to assess whether a disturbance was caused by a reader. Twenty-seven volumes out of this sample of 100 titles gave some evidence of disturbed questionnaires, falling into equal groups of about nine each, disturbed but remaining in the books, missing but not returned, and returned.

C. Findings

Line 1 of table 36 indicates the number of books (not titles) in which browsing questionnaires were placed. These totals exclude some books on reserve for most of the base period, others in restricted shelves, and others charged out at the beginning of the base period and for a long time afterward. Line 2 shows the total number of browsing slips returned and estimates the total number of uses of all kinds during that period. These totals are not immediately comparable between areas and types of books for several reasons, chief among them being the disparity in sample sizes.

We then subtracted the number of uses that were serviced by messenger.

Line 3 shows the total returned less the messenger-serviced uses.

Our basic interest was in the value of the use provided by browsing. To illustrate, a reader might carry a classification number from the catalog to the stacks and examine the book without charging it out. If the stacks were closed he might have ordered that book via messenger. Therefore, the A section of the questionnaire enabled us to identify uses that would have occurred whether or not the book were in open stacks. A check mark in boxes 1 or 3 of section A indicated that the reader would have been able to secure the book under any conditions of storage. On the other hand, boxes 2 and 4 in section A indicate use that might not have occurred if the book were in storage. So we subtracted the uses in boxes 1 and 3 in section A. See line 4.

Some of the browsing use is of value to the reader, some is not. To examine a title and reject it is often essential in a search of the literature, and browsing may be an efficient way of reaching these rejections. Unfortunately, this kind of use cannot be distinguished on our questionnaire from an examination of the book that judged the book useless or

TABLE 36

Analysis of the data from the physics (QC) and history (D) browsing questionnaires

(Returned between October 18, 1959, and April 17, 1960)

	Physics Monographs		History Monographs		Physics Serials		History Serials	
1. Total number of browsing questionnaires placed[a]	574		587		515		413	
2. Total number of browsing questionnaires returned[a]	353		73		301		102	
3. Line 2 less those brought to circulation desk by messenger	340	100%	71	100%	295	100%	98	100%
4. Line 3 less those with affirmative answers to A1 or A3	262	77%	53	75%	88	34%	48	49%
5. Line 4 less those with affirmative answers only to B5 and/or B6. Tight core browsing	135	40%	18	25%	36	12%	18	18%
6. Line 4 less those with affirmative answers only to B6. Loose core browsing	218	64%	34	48%	54	18%	33	34%
7. Number of tight core browsing uses lost — Number of browsing uses lost if all books not used in last 15 years were stored	8	2%	2	3%				
8. Number of loose core browsing uses lost —	19	6%	2	3%				

  [a] Note that the ratio of line 1 to line 2 does *not* indicate the amount of nonresponse. Many of the volumes in which questionnaires were placed were not touched by readers during the survey period, and several successive questionnaires were returned from some volumes.

irrelevant for other reasons, and a check of the contents was not basically required if the needed information could be obtained elsewhere.

Despite the difficulty of separating use into valuable and not valuable, we did so on the basis of the phrases in the questionnaire in two ways: by treating box 6, section B ("Merely glance at the title page") as not valuable; and by also calling box 5, section B ("Skim through it while standing up") not valuable.

Line 4 minus the use in boxes 6 and 5 we referred to as *tight core* browsing. It is shown in line 5 of table 36. Line 4

minus the use in box 6 we refer to as *loose core* browsing. It is shown in line 6 of table 36.[4] Both tight core and loose core use is of value and might not have occurred if the stacks were closed or the book were in storage.

We concerned ourselves with the prob-

  [4] This arbitrary assumption of the value attached to the various responses was roughly validated by inspection of returns of the expanded form of the questionnaire mentioned earlier and shown in appendix D. Practically all responses of "glanced at the title page" were associated with "little or no value," while "skimmed through it" was distributed between "some value" and "little or no value," with the preponderance in the latter category.

TABLE 37

Relation of "valuable" browsing use to recorded use in physics

Line no.	Number of uses in 1949–53	0	1	2	3	4	5	6	7–10	11+
	PHYSICS MONOGRAPHS									
1	Number of titles in group for entire sample, n = 313	189	43	21	8	9	5	7	9	22
2	Total recorded use in 1954–58	64	22	17	18	37	18	36	52	623
3a	Tight core browsing use	21	8	4	5	10	5	7	8	56
b	Loose core browsing use	48	16	5	8	13	8	7	14	79
4a	Tight core browsing use as a % of line 2	33%	36%	24%	28%	27%	28%	19%	15%	9%
b	Loose core browsing use as a % of line 2	75%	73%	29%	44%	35%	44%	19%	27%	13%
	PHYSICS SERIALS									
1	Number of titles in group for entire sample, n = 322	187	51	20	13	9	15	1	12	14
2	Total recorded use in 1954–58	21	35	24	24	20	45	5	58	303
3a	Tight core browsing use	4	4	3	1	1	1	1	2	9
b	Loose core browsing use	6	9	3	1	1	1	1	2	15
4a	Tight core browsing use as a % of line 2	19%	11%	13%	4%	5%	2%	20%	3%	3%
b	Loose core browsing use as a % of line 2	29%	26%	13%	4%	5%	2%	20%	3%	5%

able effect of a book storage program on core browsing. If data were available, and a book storage program were to identify monographs for storage by their recorded use, the number of years since last use would undoubtedly be a critical variable. Under a policy that would lead to storing 25 percent of the monographs in an area, it is unlikely that any title that had shown recorded use in the last fifteen years would be stored. If we make this arbitrary assumption, lines 7 and 8, table 36, show the number of tight and loose core browsing uses that would have been lost under such a monograph storage policy.

Next we looked into the relationship between browsing and recorded use. (It is well to remember that the two are not exclusive, since some recorded use stems from core browsing.) One relevant quality is the proportion, core browsing/recorded use.

First, we separated the titles in the original samples into groups according to their use in 1949–53 (tables 37 and 38, line 1). We then determined the number of recorded uses that these groups of titles

TABLE 38

Relation of "valuable" browsing use to recorded use in history

Line no.	Number of uses in 1949–53	0	1	2	3	4	5	6	7–10	11+
	HISTORY MONOGRAPHS									
1	Number of titles in group for entire sample, n=374	258	56	19	9	7	7	3	9	6
2	Total recorded use in 1954–58	67	26	37	10	26	32	4	37	109
3a	Tight core browsing use	6	4	3	0	2	2	0	0	0
b	Loose core browsing use	9	8	4	3	2	2	0	0	2
4a	Tight core browsing use as a % of line 2	9%	15%	8%	0%	8%	6%	0%	0%	0%
b	Loose core browsing use as a % of line 2	13%	31%	11%	30%	8%	6%	0%	0%	2%
	HISTORY SERIALS									
1	Number of titles in group for entire sample, n=352	245	47	26	10	8	5	2	4	5
2	Total recorded use in 1954–58	20	13	21	19	14	12	8	19	54
3a	Tight core browsing use	4	2	3	1	2	0	0	0	2
b	Loose core browsing use	12	3	4	1	5	0	0	1	2
4a	Tight core browsing use as a % of line 2	20%	15%	14%	5%	14%	0%	0%	0%	4%
b	Loose core browsing use as a % of line 2	60%	23%	19%	5%	36%	0%	0%	5%	4%

showed in 1954–58 (line 2). Next we determined the number of tight and loose core browsing uses of each of the groups of titles in the six month base period of observation. This is shown in lines 3a and 3b. The resulting percentages in lines 4a and 4b are the statistics of interest.

The small number of observations in each cell of the table makes it difficult to draw firm conclusions, but there does seem to be some tendency for low-use books to get proportionally more browsing. In all four samples the "0" group had the highest or second highest percentage figure in line 4a, and the highest percentage in three of the four groups on line 4b. Lines 4a and 4b are not independent of each other, but either result alone would be highly unlikely to occur by chance. And the "1" group is above the median group in all four samples on both lines 4a and 4b. There is no obvious difference between the "0" and the "1" groups, and it may well be that high-use books get less than their share of browsing partly because they are not on the open shelves as much of the time or are quickly identified by the reader as wanted without browsing.

Books that fall into our "0" and "1" classes constitute a tremendous preponderance of the library's holdings; probably more than 70 percent of the collection falls into the former category alone. So we may fairly attend to the browsing among the low-use books only. The evidence suggests that nonrecorded use is roughly proportional to recorded use. This means that storing the books with the least recorded use will also minimize the amount of nonrecorded use lost. It is necessary to take account of the understatement in browsing data resulting from nonresponse.

D. Effect of shelf level upon browsing

As an indication of how seriously or systematically browsers search for material, we attempted to see whether browsing was distributed uniformly through the book collection or showed a concentration at eye level.

Tables 39 and 40 show a simple breakdown of tight core browsing by level of the shelf from which the browsing originated. The tables also show the total number of books (not titles) in the sample on each of those shelves and the number of recorded uses in 1958 from those shelves. (Titles sometimes have books on different shelves and in different departmental libraries.)

The results in tables 39 and 40 appear to indicate a significant *shelf level effect* in the physics monograph collection. Titles on the sixth shelf down (the bottom shelf in most cases) showed considerably less browsing and recorded use. Such an effect was not found among physics serials nor among history mono graphs or serials.

There are several possible explanations for these results: (a) Among physics monographs the sixth shelf is far more often the bottom shelf than is the case with the other three groups. Unfortunately, we did not indicate in our data whether a shelf was the bottom shelf. It could be that the effect would appear for the other groups if we could analyze them in this respect. (b) Because the physics stacks are entirely open, while the "D" history stacks are semiclosed, we would expect a stronger effect on the recorded use indicator among the physics books. (c) Because of the high intercorrelation among volumes of the same serial, a single highly used serial on a lower shelf could alter the entire picture. It would require further analyses to determine to what extent this is the case in the physics serials. (d) We believe that further investigation of this matter may be worthwhile to indicate the character of browsing use.

E. Conclusions

1. Books that develop little recorded use develop little browsing, and books that develop much recorded use develop much browsing, except for the highest-use books, for which extrinsic factors distort the picture.

2. Because of this relationship a storage program that identified books on the basis of predicted recorded use is not likely to alter use patterns substantially.

3. There is considerably more browsing (as measured by the number of touches) than recorded use for books housed in stacks that are open to large segments of the reading population. The relationship may be 3 to 9 times as much browsing as recorded use, depending on the regulations governing stack access and the nature of the subject.

TABLE 39

The effect of shelf level on the use of physics and history monographs

Shelf no.	Total number of book units at shelf level			Tight core browsing use per book in percent			Recorded use in 1958 per book in percent		
	Physics mono.	History mono.	Combined mono.	Physics mono.	History mono.	Combined mono.	Physics mono.	History mono.	Combined mono.
1[a]	89	94	183	54/89 = 61%	13/94 = 14%	67/183 = 37%	21/89 = 24%	8/94 = 9%	29/183 = 16%
2	84	79	163	71/84 = 85%	13/79 = 16%	84/163 = 52%	19/84 = 23%	5/79 = 6%	24/163 = 15%
3	96	90	186	75/96 = 78%	12/90 = 13%	87/186 = 47%	23/96 = 24%	12/90 = 13%	35/186 = 19%
4	92	90	182	54/92 = 59%	11/90 = 12%	65/182 = 36%	35/92 = 38%	2/90 = 2%	37/182 = 20%
5	94	85	179	66/94 = 70%	11/85 = 13%	77/179 = 43%	37/94 = 39%	13/85 = 15%	50/179 = 28%
6	93	68	161	23/93 = 25%	8/68 = 12%	31/161 = 19%	6/93 = 6%	15/68 = 22%	21/161 = 13%
7	6	37	43	2/6 = 33%	5/37 = 14%	7/43 = 16%	1/6 = 17%	7/37 = 19%	8/43 = 19%
8	1	14	15	6/1 = 600%	0/14 = 0%	6/15 = 40%	0/1 = 0%	2/14 = 14%	2/15 = 13%
9	8	0	8	0/8 = 0%	0/0 = 0%	0/8 = 0%	15/8 = 188%	0/0 = 0%	15/8 = 188%

[a] Highest shelf.

TABLE 40

The effect of shelf level on the use of physics and history serials

Shelf no.	Total number of book units at shelf level			Tight core browsing use per book in percent			Recorded use in 1958 per book in percent		
	Physics serials	History serials	Combined serials	Physics serials	History serials	Combined serials	Physics serials	History serials	Combined serials
1[a]	81	35	116	70/81 = 86%	18/35 = 51%	88/116 = 76%	21/81 = 26%	3/35 = 9%	24/116 = 21%
2	105	49	154	70/105 = 67%	18/49 = 37%	88/154 = 57%	32/105 = 30%	10/49 = 20%	42/154 = 27%
3	75	52	127	23/75 = 31%	32/52 = 62%	55/127 = 43%	22/75 = 29%	23/52 = 44%	45/127 = 35%
4	67	42	109	18/67 = 27%	13/42 = 31%	31/109 = 28%	12/67 = 18%	6/42 = 14%	18/109 = 17%
5	88	28	116	68/88 = 77%	9/28 = 32%	77/116 = 66%	42/88 = 48%	2/28 = 7%	44/116 = 38%
6	59	23	82	43/59 = 73%	7/23 = 30%	50/82 = 61%	15/59 = 25%	0/23 = 0%	15/82 = 18%
7	28	22	50	5/28 = 18%	3/22 = 14%	8/50 = 16%	6/28 = 21%	1/22 = 5%	7/50 = 14%
8	11	12	23	4/11 = 36%	2/12 = 17%	6/23 = 26%	4/11 = 36%	0/12 = 0%	4/23 = 17%
9	.	.	.	.....	.....	.....	.....	.....	.....

[a] Highest shelf.

4. The amount of influence on use caused by the shelf level cannot be clearly stated on the basis of our data.

5. These data cannot be safely generalized to other institutions.

The privilege of browsing freely in book stacks is cherished by students and faculty members. There is a satisfaction and an efficiency in examining books directly that cannot be matched through catalogs, reference aids, staff, etc. Furthermore, open browsing permits a serendipity less likely to occur if readers are required to use bibliographies, card catalogs, and other intermediate devices. We see no completely happy solution compatible with removing books for storage. Yet these factors should be noted: (a) For a very long period of time, if not permanently, the great majority of books in most, if not all, research libraries will stay as accessible as they are at present; only a small percentage would go to storage. (b) Those that would go to storage would be very infrequently used.

Expert opinion versus statistical identification in selecting books for storage

A. Background and theory of investigation

Perhaps the ideal method for identifying books for storage would be for scholars to rank the books in their respective subject areas according to current and future value.

The cost of this procedure would be prohibitive. The question then is whether we can approximate that consensus within economically acceptable limits.

Alternatives are to select books for storage (a) by the judgment of one or a few experts,[1] (b) by examining past use of books and/or their characteristics such as language and age that have been statistically related to use and that predict use satisfactorily, or (c) a combination of the two. In this chapter we are concerned almost completely with the first two. We presumed that expert selectors base judgments about the value of books on a number of criteria, of which the probable frequency of use would be only one, whereas objective systems would normally be based solely upon predicted use. The two techniques might be expected therefore to produce different results.

We assumed that if both alternatives can identify low-value books with equal accuracy, or if both are above some arbitrarily selected point of accuracy, the objective technique of selection is preferable because it is likely to be much cheaper. If the objective system, then, is above the required accuracy point, we need not compare it against the expert selector. On the other hand, if the objective system leaves some doubt about the accuracy or satisfaction it will give, it must be tested against the single expert selector to see if the latter will be more satisfactory or accurate. We chose to determine first whether the objective system was superior to the arbitrarily selected standard. The second step was to compare the two methods.

We set an arbitrary standard of satisfaction in terms of the number of books that the objective system (or the expert selector) would store mistakenly, defining "mistakenly" to mean in disagreement with the pooled judgments of several scholars. We did not define the standard in terms of value or importance of a book. The definition of the

[1] Cf. Lee Ash, *Yale's Selective Book Retirement Program* . . . ([Hamden, Conn.]: Archon Books, 1963).

standard was in terms of instructions to scholars that follow below, and the responses to the instructions. We asked whether the consensus of scholars would *object* to the choices made under a mechanical system. If it did, then it would be a "mistake" to store the book.

B. Experimental designs

From our random systematic samples of the subject areas of (a) general science, chemistry, and geology (Q, QD, and QE in the Library of Congress system), (b) economics, (c) American and English literature, and (d) Teutonic languages and literatures, we selected the hundred titles that had the lowest predicted use among the 400 titles in each of the four samples.[2] We assembled on book trucks one copy of the last *used* edition of each title. For each of the four subject areas we asked a separate panel of five University of Chicago faculty members in that field to examine the books. They were not paid for their time and were chosen to provide several areas of experience in the field. Records of past use were removed from the books prior to inspection.

The following instructions were given to the panel members:

It is now generally recognized that sooner or later the growth of large research collections will require that libraries physically distinguish between (a) books likely to be important or useful to regular programs of teaching and research, and (b) books that are marginal, obsolete, or so highly specialized that, even though important, they will be infrequently used.

Assume for the purpose of this experiment that it is necessary for the library to remove

some of the titles from the collection to a storage building somewhere else on campus. These removed books would continue to be available for your use, and it would take 4 to 24 hours to have them brought to a departmental library circulation desk or to your office. But you would be unable to browse and examine the collection in the storage building.

Removal to a second level of accessibility would not be an irreversible decision. Upon discovery that a book important to research was in the storage building, the book would be brought back and housed with the core collection. There is a hidden advantage in storage for some books; it is that they would be safer than in open or semi-open stacks.

Consider that the group of books presented to you has been proposed for storage. Please examine them and, if it seems appropriate to you to do so, please indicate for any of them "I strongly disagree; this book should not be removed to storage." You will not need to be concerned with the problem of weeding out multiple copies or early editions. The books you see will be the principal copy of the work held by the library.

Some panel members asked on what principle they were to select books, and the interviewer referred them back to the instructions and said that the guiding principle must be the scholar's own views about the wisdom for the library and the university of storing that particular book.

After each scholar had completed his task, he was asked to go over the books again, indicating those about which he might have some doubt.

The interests of particular scholars at the University of Chicago might produce low use in a book and allow it to pass into storage despite the fact that the book could be of great interest to future scholars. As a check we arranged for a test using panels of well-known scholars working at institutions other than Chicago. A list of the scholars and a sample list of titles are given in appendix F.

---

[2] Except in the case of science, where we limited the books offered for examination to 43 titles in chemistry proper, and in the case of economics, where the particular rule used for selection produced 171 titles.

To these outside scholars we sent lists containing about 50 of the 100 titles in the lists described above intermixed with 50 more titles, chosen at random from the subgroup in the original sample, that would *not* go to storage under a 25 percent storage policy.[3]

The instructions to the outside scholars were as follows:

It is now generally recognized that unlimited and undifferentiated growth of large research collections cannot continue indefinitely. Sooner or later libraries will be forced to distinguish in their handling methods between those materials likely to be more or less regularly used or consulted and those of marginal value, obsolete, or so highly specialized that, while important, they are likely to be very infrequently used.

Assume, for the purpose of this experiment, that it has become necessary for the library that serves you to remove some of the titles from its collections to a storage building somewhere near the campus. These removed books would continue to be listed in the card catalogs and be available for your use; assume that it would take 4 to 24 hours to have them brought to the general library, a departmental library, or to your office. Since the stored books would probably be arranged by size, you should also assume that you would be unable to browse among the books in the storage building. If it should be found that a book important to research or teaching had been transferred to storage, it could be brought back and rehoused with the "working" collection at any time. There is a hidden advantage in storage for some books; they would be better protected and less likely to be misshelved than those in open or semiopen stacks.

Assume that the list of books presented to you has been proposed for storage. Please examine it and, as it seems appropriate for you to do so, please indicate, 'I strongly disagree;

3 Each of these outside scholars received an honorarium of $25, which seemed necessary to get quick but well-considered responses.

this book should not be removed to storage' or 'I am doubtful about this book.'

Assume that the titles listed are the only copies of the work held by the library in the language indicated. If there is a copy of the work in English in the collections, that will be indicated; in that case, proceed on the assumption that the English edition would remain.

C. Results of the arbitrary standard test

The following discussion refers to, and is summarized in, table 41.

1. Chemistry

Forty-three titles were presented to a five-member panel of the chemistry faculty at the University of Chicago. This group of books was less than half the size of the groups in other subject areas because the subject area that included chemistry also included general science and geology. The least likely to be used 25 percent of the approximately 400 titles included only 43 in chemistry. Of the 43 only one title received an indication of "Do not store," and that title was so marked by two of the five members of the panel. *No* titles received an indication of "Doubtful."

When those 43 titles interspersed with 57 other titles that fell *above* the 25 percent cutting line were submitted to a nine-member panel of outside scholars, eight of the 43 received a single indication of "Do not store." A single member of the panel was responsible for seven of these indications. Another panel member indicated one title. However, there were 18 indications of "Doubtful."

The objective system would appear to be quite satisfactory.

2. Economics

We submitted 171 titles in economics to the five-member Chicago panel.

TABLE 41

Summary of the arbitrary standard test results of expert reactions to titles designated
"store" by objective system under a 25 percent storage plan

Panel	Number of panel members[a]	Number of titles in the sample	Number of "Do not store" indications	Number of titles receiving "Do not store" indications	Possible number of "Do not store" indications	Number of "Doubtful" indications	Number of titles receiving "Doubtful" indications	Number of titles receiving "Do not store" or "Doubtful" indications
Chicago chemistry	5	43	2	1	215	0	0	1
"Outside" chemistry	9	43	8	8	387	18	12	14
Chicago economics	5	171	35	29	855	7	7	34
"Outside" economics	8	62	7	7	496	19	18	24
Chicago American and English literature	4	100	35	29	400	1	1	29
"Outside" American and English literature	9	48	48	39	432	15	14	48
Chicago Teutonic languages and literatures	5	129	83	63	645	12	12	69
"Outside" Teutonic lang. and literatures	7	50	45	36	350	43	31	67

[a] The numbers of "outside" questionnaires sent were: chemistry 11, economics 10, American and English literature 10, Teutonic languages and literatures 8. In all but one case of nonresponse the cause was that the addressee was not reached by the questionnaire because he was out of town.

Twenty-nine of the 171 titles received 35 indications of "Do not store." There were also seven "Doubtful" indications.

On the list of 99 titles sent to the eight-member outside panel were 62 titles that would have been stored by the objective system under a 25 percent storage policy. The panel indicated "Do not store" for seven of the 62 titles, with no title receiving more than one indication. There were 19 "Doubtful" indications. One scholar was responsible for 19 of the 26 "Do not store" and "Doubtful" indications.

In our judgment, the objective system is satisfactory.

3. American and English literature

In a group of 100 titles, the four-member Chicago panel gave 35 "Do not store" indications to 29 titles but only one indication of "Doubtful." The result seems to suggest that we might consider the use of an expert selector. However, there were only six titles that received more than one "Do not store" indication and none of those received more than two. The wide variety of opinion among the experts does not provide a consensus that would serve as well as the objective system.

The nine-member outside panel gave 48 "Do not store" indications for 39 titles from the sample of 48 titles submitted. But we should note that a single expert was responsible for 39 indications, while five others provided among them only two "Do not store" indications and 5 "Doubtful" indications. For those five scholars the objective choices were certainly satisfactory.

4. Teutonic languages and literatures

For 129 titles the panel of five scholars at Chicago gave 83 "Do not store" indications for 63 titles and 12 "Doubtful" indications. Even though 42 of the "Do not store" indications came from a single scholar, the objective system alone is, in the judgment of the panel, not an immediately satisfactory instrument. However, there were only four titles that received more than two "Do not store" indications.

The experience with the outside seven-member panel was similar. There were 45 "Do not store" indications for 36 titles, and 43 "Doubtful" indications for 31 titles. Again there were great variations among scholars, one being responsible for 39 of the 45 "Do not store" indications and three for none of them.

D. Test of the objective system versus the expert scholar

There were great variations in the numbers of books the outside scholars indicated should not be stored. Because we set no limit on such indications it is not possible to compare precisely the efficiency of the objective system and the expert.

Table 42 summarizes the material in this section relating to the University of Chicago panels, and table 43 summarizes the responses of the outside panels.

E. Survey of scholars' attitudes toward storage

As an adjunct to the investigations described in the earlier pages of this chapter, we asked the members of the outside panels of scholars to indicate their attitudes toward a book storage pro-

gram. The questionnaire is reproduced below (figure 17). As was the case for the instructions to the panels, the actual language of the questionnaire must be examined carefully in order to assess the reaction to the questions.

1. Chemistry panel

From the chemistry panel of nine scholars the responses were uniformly sympathetic to a book storage program. Two of the three comments attached:

"Most of the titles are next to worthless."

"I believe it is important that some of the classical works remain . . . accessible. A chance encounter with such a book may be an exciting and valuable experience for the student."

2. Economics panel

The economics panel was also uniformly sympathetic. Excerpts from the comments:

"If the library provides scholars with delivery service within 24 hours at his desk or office or at a convenient place for pickup without queues or complicated signing to do, this would seem incomparably more important than browsing privileges."

"I have marked my general view as 'quite sympathetic' by emphasizing to myself your phrase 'carefully administered,' by minimizing the 'likely' interference of a storage program. It seems to me to be a reasonable compromise with the unattainable ideal of immediate accessibility of all books on any subject . . ."

"Overloading the stacks can make the library a more difficult place to work in . . . There is no perfect method, but because of lack of space our library has stored a considerable number of books. It does not appear to me that we have suffered seriously. In fact, I have had occasion to ask for several such volumes and they were brought to me after a few hours."

TABLE 42

Analysis of the replies received from the scholars on the University of Chicago panels in American and English literature, chemistry, economics, and Teutonic languages and literatures

	Responses to titles that the objective system would have stored	
	"Do not store"	"Doubtful"

AMERICAN AND ENGLISH LITERATURE

Scholar 1..........................	6	1
Scholar 2..........................	13	0
Scholar 3..........................	9	0
Scholar 4..........................	7	0
Titles marked: Once...............	23	1
Twice..............	6	0
Three times.........	0	0
Four times.........	0	0
Five times..........	0	0

Total number of titles the objective system would store = 100

CHEMISTRY

Scholar 1..........................	0	0
Scholar 2..........................	1	0
Scholar 3..........................	0	0
Scholar 4..........................	1	0
Scholar 5..........................	0	0
Titles marked: Once...............	0	0
Twice..............	1	0
Three times.........	0	0
Four times.........	0	0
Five times..........	0	0

Total number of titles the objective system would store = 43

ECONOMICS

Scholar 1..........................	3	0
Scholar 2..........................	7	0
Scholar 3..........................	3	1
Scholar 4..........................	11	5
Scholar 5..........................	8	0
Titles marked: Once...............	24	7
Twice..............	4	0
Three times.........	1	0
Four times.........	0	0
Five times..........	0	0

Total number of titles the objective system would store = 171

TEUTONIC LANGUAGES AND LITERATURES

Scholar 1..........................	21	7
Scholar 2..........................	2	0
Scholar 3..........................	52	0
Scholar 4..........................	4	2
Scholar 5..........................	4	3
Titles marked: Once...............	47	12
Twice..............	12	0
Three times.........	4	0
Four times.........	0	0
Five times..........	0	0

Total number of titles the objective system would store = 129

TABLE 43

Analysis of the replies received from the scholars on the outside panels in American and English literature, chemistry, economics, and Teutonic languages and literatures

	General attitude	Responses to titles that the objective system would have stored		Responses to titles that the mechanical system would *not* have stored	
		"Do not store"	"Doubtful"	"Do not store"	"Doubtful"

AMERICAN AND ENGLISH LITERATURE

Scholar 1	Favorable	4	0	12	0
Scholar 2	Favorable	0	3	6	10
Scholar 3	Favorable	1	0	5	14
Scholar 4	Unfavorable	39	9	41	10
Scholar 5	Favorable	0	2	10	5
Scholar 6	Favorable	1	0	8	3
Scholar 7	Favorable	2	1	2	4
Scholar 8	Favorable	0	0	1	8
Scholar 9	Favorable	3	0	18	0
Titles marked:					
Once		30	13	17	18
Twice		8	1	15	12
Three times		0	0	5	1
Four times		1	0	4	1
Five times		0	0	0	1
Six times		0	0	3	0
Seven times		0	0	1	0

Total number of titles the objective system would store = 48
would not store = 52

CHEMISTRY

Scholar 1	Favorable	7	0	7	4
Scholar 2	Favorable	0	1	4	3
Scholar 3	Favorable	0	1	6	2
Scholar 4	Favorable	1	0	1	4
Scholar 5	Favorable	0	7	1	3
Scholar 6	Favorable	0	3	0	4
Scholar 7	Favorable	0	5	10	6
Scholar 8	Favorable	0	1	1	2
Scholar 9	Favorable	0	0	2	0
Titles marked:					
Once		8	8	9	10
Twice		0	2	4	3
Three times		0	2	2	4
Four times		0	0	1	0
Five times		0	0	1	0

Total number of titles the objective system would store = 43
would not store = 57

TABLE 43—*Continued*

	General attitude	Responses to titles that the objective system would have stored		Responses to titles that the mechanical system would *not* have stored	
		"Do not store"	"Doubtful"	"Do not store"	"Doubtful"
ECONOMICS					
Scholar 1	Favorable	0	0	2	3
Scholar 2	Favorable	0	2	2	5
Scholar 3	Favorable	0	2	0	7
Scholar 4	Favorable	0	0	0	0
Scholar 5	Favorable	1	2	2	5
Scholar 6	Favorable	0	0	0	0
Scholar 7	Favorable	6	13	18	3
Scholar 8	Favorable	0	0	0	3
Titles marked:					
Once		7	17	15	7
Twice		0	1	1	4
Three times		0	0	1	2
Four times		0	0	1	0
Five times		0	0	0	1

Total number of titles the objective system would store   =62
would not store=37

	General attitude	Responses to titles that the objective system would have stored		Responses to titles that the mechanical system would *not* have stored	
TEUTONIC LANGUAGES AND LITERATURES					
Scholar 1	Favorable	33	16	21	28
Scholar 2	Favorable	9	5	28	11
Scholar 3	Favorable	0	0	1	7
Scholar 4	Unfavorable	1	9	2	13
Scholar 5	Favorable	2	6	7	4
Scholar 6	Favorable	0	6	9	7
Scholar 7	Favorable	0	1	0	8
Titles marked:					
Once		28	21	18	18
Twice		7	9	10	13
Three times		1	0	4	10
Four times		0	1	2	1
Five times		0	0	2	0

Total number of titles the objective system would store   =50
would not store=49

"I would be quite sympathetic ... particularly if books can be delivered to the user on 24 hour notice, as at the New York Public Library."

3. American and English literature panel

Among the nine scholars in American and English literature all except one checked the "quite sympathetic" box, and he checked "very likely interfere." In addition, several of the panel volunteered written statements, of which the following are excerpts:

"If books could be secured within 24 hours, some such scheme as you envisage would not interfere with serious research or teaching."

"I vote for a storage program with a slight reservation. I believe that such storage programs are inevitable in most cases, but undesirable where they can be avoided."

"I enclose the questionnaire with the inevitable doubts and misgivings. But my participation in the work of library committees at

THE UNIVERSITY OF CHICAGO

CHICAGO 37 · ILLINOIS

THE UNIVERSITY LIBRARY

Office of the Director

Mr. Herman H. Fussler
University of Chicago Library
Chicago 37, Illinois

Dear Mr. Fussler:

☐ The list of titles is returned herewith. I would classify my attitude to possible book storage as follows:

☐ I would be quite sympathetic to a carefully administered book storage program and doubt that such a program would interfere appreciably with teaching or research.

☐ I am not certain about the possible effects of such a program.

☐ I believe that a book storage program would be very likely to interfere with teaching or research.

☐ I am unable to participate in your study of the use of research library materials.

Date _____

Fig. 17.—Attitude questionnaire used for outside experts

the University of . . . and the University of . . . has made me an enthusiastic proponent of the kind of weeding out you have in mind. . . . If anything, I should be inclined to revise my list to send more items to storage. We are going to have to come to it, and the longer we hesitate the more difficult we make our own problem."

"There can be no doubt that physical restrictions will force the larger university libraries to remove from accessible stacks and place in semi-storage many seldom used books. Such a removal will naturally provoke some irritation in the eager researcher, but, if the books to be stored are wisely selected, it should prove only an annoyance, certainly no serious handicap. Since the separate storing of certain books seems inevitable, the only question is how the books to be stored should be selected.

"From the list sent me of books being considered for storage, I judge it is at present assumed that the volumes to be stored should be chosen principally, if not wholly, upon the basis of recent calls for them. I question the wisdom of that method of selection. Were the selection made on that basis alone, a scholar using the library could learn what was in storage only by consulting the card catalogue for each volume he wished. That not only would be time-consuming but would certainly encourage irritation. Could not the selection be made on some other *easily remembered* principle so that a reader might know before going to the library whether a particular book would be immediately available or require a wait?"[4]

"I must acknowledge frankly that I found it extremely difficult to establish reasonable criteria for sending books into Limbo (even though accessible) and for retaining others. One man's meat is as always another man's poison. Many of the titles are unknown to me but I evaluated them by their apparent nature. Much useful literary research requires browsing in the stacks among fifth and even

tenth rate novels, poems, etc. For the hard-pressed student and scholar a card catalogue is much too often a graveyard of materials rather than a guide when the work is not quickly accessible. I have found this to be true again and again in my own work as a scholar during the past twenty-three years and have frequently had to compromise with the ideal of scholarly thoroughness because of it.

"In the field of literary study it is almost impossible to generalize what kinds of material may not be promptly needed, for one's study cuts across *all* fields of intellectual activity. This is particularly true of work in intellectual and social history. My own research has required that I range the shelves through art and art history, past and present, many of the sciences, biographies, memoirs, collections of letters of important and unimportant persons, long-forgotten books of nineteenth century publicists, obscure periodicals, etc., etc. One of the great advantages of working in the stacks at the University of Chicago, the Newberry Library, Harvard library, and some of the libraries abroad has been precisely the fact that the books have been within easy reach. Each step that increases the time distance between the scholar and the book is a step lost, and often a book lost. One of the great obstacles to effective research in some European libraries is the time lag of anywhere from two to 25 hours in obtaining books. I have found it costly in time, energy, and research funds. Here at . . . , for want of a new library building, we have been driven, as you probably know, to underground storage. Delays are unavoidable and they always throw a monkey wrench into the efficient pursuit of a line of inquiry. Serials that seem unimportant have a way of suddenly becoming important."

4. Teutonic languages and literatures panel

Of the Teutonic languages and literatures outside panel, all but one of the seven were "quite sympathetic" although several of these men underlined the words "carefully administered." The one wrote that he believed a book storage

---

[4] A catalog arranged by the subject classification of the books in storage, as contemplated by the University of Chicago library, might satisfy part, but not all, of the writer's objection.

program would be *"certain* to interfere with research," and added, in part:

"I spent nine months last year working at Chicago, and was tremendously impressed by some of the Germanics collections in Harper; their comprehensiveness, ordered arrangement, and general accessibility are matched by no other library in which I myself have worked. To separate from these collections some of the less frequently used books would to my mind very largely destroy their usefulness and would greatly handicap future research: I would consider it a basic principle of a great research library that frequently used *and* rarely used books on the same subject be kept together.

"Furthermore it does not seem at all desirable for scholars of one generation to be permitted to decide what books future scholars shall find properly grouped on the shelves and what books they will find only through the catalogue; patterns of research vary greatly from one generation to another, and a second basic principle is surely that the present should handicap the future as little as possible.

"From this point of view I am not even happy about the suggestion of members of the Chicago Germanics department that certain categories of books, such as old translations or old popular fiction, are not even of historical interest and so may be consigned to 'dead storage.' It seems to be that any collection of any kind of book that is large enough to be of some significance in its way should never be broken up—though it may of course justifiably be removed to a separate building to await the day when its turn will come.

"Furthermore it seems to me that since most libraries must be selective, it is permissible for them to refuse to stock certain sorts of book altogether. But if they have a collection which they do not want, let them not break it up, but keep it intact until they can give it away. If only libraries would agree which of the less commonly collected sorts of book they would concentrate on, and then really concentrate, how greatly scholarship would benefit!

"In short let the individual scholar select his library according to his needs, but then give him all the help you can, do not hide the interesting books away!"

Another scholar wrote: ". . . I find myself in agreement with the plan in general . . ."

Still a third said: "We have used this system at . . . for some years and it has worked no great hardships; old and little used serials have been put in storage also . . ."

F. Discussion and conclusions

We have the impression that in all the four widely different areas in which we made our panel survey the objective system more accurately ranks books by probable value than would a *single* scholar in the field. It is also our belief that the objective system is, *prima facie*, a satisfactory selector by any set of standards in chemistry and economics. We would be inclined to extrapolate the results in chemistry and economics to the sciences and social sciences generally with the probable exception of history.

It is clear that there is more resistance to implementing a storage plan in the humanities than in the sciences and economics. This resistance undoubtedly is based in part on the fact that literature in the humanities is approached and used in ways that are often different from the so-called cumulative disciplines. There might have been a somewhat different reaction to serials as candidates for storage; however, chapter 6 showed that the use of serials in Teutonic languages and literatures was much less than is the use of serials in other fields, and relatively much lower than monographs.

It is evident that a storage plan might sensibly cut much more deeply into some areas than others, either on a proportional or on an absolute basis. Such a differential policy might well be the best solution.

Experience with and working knowledge of a well-administered storage plan might allay some of the fears and uncertainties that scholars expressed concerning a storage program. Participants in this study seemed to overlook the fact that books in storage continue to be present in the catalogs. In some disciplines, such as literature, the reader would not be likely to overlook books in storage if he used the catalogs properly. Furthermore, reliance on the classified arrangement of the physical book in place of a proper use of library catalogs or general bibliography may lead to erroneous conclusions about the resources of large research libraries. The classification scheme in *belles lettres* is primarily by author, and one might therefore suppose that the physical contiguity of books would be of less help in promoting discoveries than library catalogs or bibliographies. In fiction and certain other classes of literature the catalog card would also seem to contain most of the information that a reader might glean from a quick examination of the book.

In all disciplines there are instances when a catalog card or bibliographical entry cannot possibly indicate the range or the precise relevance of material contained in a book. On the other hand, proper use of a subject-classified catalog for stored books, the general library catalog, and bibliography would reduce or eliminate the possibility that a reader would overlook the presence of a title that he might have found in a physical survey of the collection. However, the library must recognize that this use or checking of other sources may be both irritating and time consuming to the reader.

The reactions of scholars to a book storage plan must be interpreted in the light of the existing bibliographic alternatives to storage, *and the knowledge readers have of such alternatives.* It seems likely that many readers are unaware of the function that a shelf list may serve in surveying a collection. In postinterview discussions several scholars changed their attitudes when they learned that a catalog of stored books in conventional shelf list order could be available.

One by-product of this questionnaire has been regret on our part that we did not undertake a systematic survey of the reactions of scholars who have worked at institutions that have put storage programs into effect. Such comments of this nature as we did receive suggest that experience with storage programs tends to result in a more favorable view.

9

Transferring books to compact storage

A. Introduction

No matter how accurately books used infrequently might be chosen for storage, a storage program would not be feasible unless the cost of storing books is small compared to the cost of conventional housing. Our main purpose in this chapter, then, is (a) to outline a set of practical procedures for storage and (b) to estimate the costs of transferring books. The procedures and the tests are based on records and procedures at the University of Chicago library.

B. Basic assumptions and conditions

1. The storage collection will be composed of materials that are infrequently used but not necessarily of little value. Materials of extremely doubtful value should be discarded rather than stored.

2. In general, a copy of a title will not be placed in storage when another copy exists in the library system. (In the rare instances when a second copy of a title needs to be laid aside for preservation, this second copy will not be stored compactly.)

3. The storage collection should serve to relieve crowded conditions in departmental libraries as well as the main library.

4. Books in storage will be arranged compactly by size and shelved on their fore edges except for sizes where this is not practical.

5. Storage could take place either inside or outside the main library.

6. The storage collection will be closed to browsers because books will not be arranged by subject.

7. Orders for materials from storage will be channeled through the main circulation department.

8. Catalog records will not be changed; all cards remain in their files.[1]

---

[1] For many reasons it would appear best in a storage operation to leave all catalog records in place for stored materials but show that the materials are in storage rather than in their regular location. The University of Chicago library began doing this but finally abandoned the procedure in favor of simply charging books to storage for the following reasons: (1) the storage of some books will be only temporary, their return to the classified shelves awaiting the completion of a new library building; (2) the cost of manual record changing was greater than anticipated; (3) sufficient clerical help to make accurate changes was not always available when needed; and (4) the library envisages in the future a computer-based

C. Processing the books

1. The books are removed from the shelves by a selection staff who determines from the shelf-list card that the book meets the selection rules in the length of time that it has been in the library and the amount of recorded use. The selected books are taken to a processing area and put on review shelves.

2. A reviewer makes the final decision on what should be returned to the shelf, what should be reviewed for transfer to the rare book room, what should be discarded, and what should go to storage.

3. The books destined for storage are sorted by size on a jib by the processing staff. Except for those more than 12" high the width of the book is measured.

4. The following size groups are based on limited information[2] in the literature

---

circulation and book processing system in which record access and record changes will be much less costly.

The penalties of the present procedure are (1) the inevitable cost in circulation operations of checking in the storage charge file for books not found on the shelf and not charged out, and (2) the cost of a reader's time, especially the reader who uses the central catalog of the library for material shown in the catalog as located in a departmental library, but, in fact, in storage. In a very small departmental library the charge records for books in storage and those charged out in the regular manner might be intermingled without too much difficulty. In large charge files, however, the addition of a substantial number of inactive cards to the regular charge files would add to the costs and difficulty of maintaining an accurate charge file.

In fact, the actual use of stored materials has, in accordance with the findings of the study, been sufficiently infrequent to make the difficulties for readers also relatively infrequent: e.g., in 1966–67, there were requests for 1,661 volumes from a storage collection that contained 148,436 volumes at the beginning of the fiscal year and 206,629 at the end of the year, making the average collection size approximately 177,582 volumes.

[2] J. G. Cox, "Optimum Storage of Library Material" (Ph.D. diss., Purdue University, 1964).

---

on book sizes and on the practices of libraries with storage collections.

Size group	Shelved on fore edges
1	up to 5" wide
2	5"–6" wide
3	6"–7" wide
4	7"–9" wide
	Shelved upright
5	12"–16" in height
	Shelved upright or flat
6	over 16" in height

5. A group of books of one size are processed together and the new storage numbers are assigned in numerical order.

6. Serial stamping machines, one for each size group, are used to put the storage number of the books on the charge cards. The original call number should not be altered or obliterated, either on the verso of the title page or on the spine.

All the volumes of a single title, whether a monograph in two or three volumes or a run of a serial in many volumes, will receive the same storage number. (For the treatment of serial sets see paragraph 9.) This is the same principle as that employed for books on classified shelves—all parts of a set receive the small call number.

7. One charge card is separated and goes to the appropriate charge file; one remains in the book.

8. The books are now in order by size and are ready for shelving in the storage area.

9. Runs of serials which do not contain all that was published are stored separately from other books. They are selved compactly by size but in a place where they can be shifted periodically to consolidate additional parts stored at a later time. When holdings of a title end prior to 1900 and the library has no

expectation of completing the run, it may be stored with monographs and complete serial sets.

The same size groups are used for the separately shelved serials, but the storage number is preceded by an "S." A single charge card with consolidated storage holdings is filed in the charge file—not a charge card for each volume.

When a serial set is split—part going to storage and part remaining on the open shelves—a shelf dummy with the storage information is shelved in place of the volumes removed.

D. Withdrawals from storage

When a stored book is withdrawn and reinstated in the active collection, the withdrawal and transfer is handled by the storage processing staff. If the space vacated is sufficient to warrant refilling, the thickness of the book(s) is recorded. It may be less expensive to leave the space empty and note the vacant number as a supplement to the shelf-list record.

E. Costs of transfer

Transfer costs do not appear large enough to be a serious obstacle to a storage program. Using procedures similar to those outlined above, the clerical time required to carry out these storage processes has been roughly calculated at about 5 to 9 minutes per volume. The shorter period is needed for working in the general library with large subject blocks. When working in smaller areas and in departmental libraries, the time required is approximately doubled.

This estimate does not include (1) discarding unwanted items pulled from the shelves but considered not worth storing, including duplicate copies of items stored;[3] (2) faculty, bibliographers, or professional staff review; (3) the physical transportation of books to a storage stack and their reshelving in that location; or (4) filing the charge cards into a charge file.

[3] Discarding is necessarily a significant cost. However, it is not really attributable to storage, since it represents expenditures that would presumably be made at some time whether or not a storage program was undertaken.

10

The economics of book housing

A. Bases for cost comparisons

1. General assumptions and exclusions

This study was based on two underlying assumptions: (a) The costs of housing a large book collection will be lowered if some fraction of the collection is placed in compact storage. (b) The institution or its library could apply the savings to greater needs of the institution. For libraries that have exhausted conventional bookstack space and are unable for whatever reason to expand, there is no practical alternative to compact storage. It is the libraries or institutions that are able to make a free choice in methods of book housing that we wish to consider in this line of argument.

A complete analysis of the economics of book housing would require us to assign specific dollar values to two quantities not customarily evaluated in these terms: (a) the losses that might result from the inability of the reader to browse, and from possible delays in retrieving stored materials, (b) the benefits or gains to the reader of various uses of the savings from compact storage. For example, the savings might be used to acquire more books than would otherwise be possible. While this alternative may seem illogical to those struggling to accommodate the books they already have, it poses very nicely the issue of institutional objectives. What program will produce the maximum benefit from any given number of dollars? More specifically, if the costs of these two programs were identical, which is likely to be of greater benefit to an institution: (a) "x" books in conventional housing, or (b) "x+y" books with some portion of them in compact storage? The institution's gain from such increased resources would be difficult to measure. (In many institutions savings in capital expenditures could not be converted into operating or book expenditures, but this fact should not obscure the real costs of a particular course of action.)

2. Alternative methods of handling little used books

There are sound reasons for believing that inter-institutional cooperative storage programs, and perhaps other cooperative enterprises, would result in storage costs (or, more precisely, costs of access to very infrequently used materials) well below those for a local storage facility. Such comparisons would involve many additional assumptions, making the conclusions less useful than those for a single institution.

A high proportion of the publications of the first half of the twentieth century may suffer from serious physical disintegration in the second half of the century unless expensive remedial measures are taken. Among the alternatives to chemical treatment of the paper itself may be some form of microreproduction. Obviously a large-scale conversion of books in original format into some form of microfacsimile would reduce space requirements, but the extent of the relief from this source will be far from clear for a long time.

However, there are also good reasons for believing that a storage building kept at a lower temperature than bookstacks might greatly extend the life of books printed on poor paper—a potential benefit of very great value if found to be true.

3. The problem of cost variations with time

While it would be desirable to incorporate some adjustments for future operating cost variations, there is no sound way to do so. Consequently, janitorial services, heat, power, etc., were estimated at a constant rate. Such variations in cost would affect storage and conventional book space in a similar manner, and therefore the *relationship* in the costs for the two kinds of space might be expected to stay approximately the same.

4. Estimates of building capacity in volumes

The number of books that can be accommodated in a square foot of conventional bookstack space varies considerably, as does the number that can be accommodated in compact storage.

We assumed that the conventional book-stack has a working capacity of approximately 15 volumes per square foot.[1] For the compact bookstack, some combination of book sizing, shelving books on edge, narrower range aisles, fewer main aisles, shelving somewhat higher than the usual 7'6", and the elimination of empty shelving, will yield a capacity of 30 volumes or more per square foot, and possibly as much as 60.[2] Cost comparisons were based on area, assuming that both the conventional stack areas and compact stack areas are full at the 15, 30, and 60 volume-per-square-foot levels which were used to suggest the range in the probable costs of book housing.

5. Scheduling transfers of materials to be sent to storage

There is no gain in moving any more books to storage than will reduce operating costs or eliminate the cost of new *conventional* storage space for new accessions. The space left vacant in the conventional bookstack might not be filled for several years by new accessions. The

[1] Louis Kaplan, "The Storage of Library Materials," in *The State of the Library Art,* ed. Ralph R. Shaw (New Brunswick: Rutgers University, Graduate School of Library Service, 1960).

[2] Yale University library has compactly stored an average of 60 volumes per square foot of floor area with a collection of 190,000 volumes. The books are stored on their fore edges in five size groups on standard shelving with 7'6" uprights. The aisle is 20" wide at floor level with 10" base shelves, giving an aisle 24" wide at shelf level with 8" shelves. The range in capacity is from 81 volumes per square foot for the smallest volumes to 32 volumes per square foot for the largest. *Source:* letter from John H. Ottemiller, associate librarian, Yale University library, March 27, 1961. The University of Michigan storage library, with Ames drawer shelving and books filling all available space in the drawers, is designed to accommodate 28.3 vols/sq. ft. including sorting room, delivery entrance, toilets, building corridors, etc., and 38.4 vols/sq. ft. excluding these spaces. *Source:* letter from Frederick H. Wagman, January 23, 1961.

TABLE 44

Expected mean use of economics monographs

Groups of titles ranked by expected use	Approximate number		Expected use per title per year in 1961	Expected use per title per year in 1966	Expected use per title per year in 1976
	Vols.	Titles			
Lowest 25%	21,000	14,000	.0200	.0190	.0170
26–35%	8,400	5,600	.0300	.0285	.0255
36–50%	12,600	8,400	.0500	.0475	.0425

space in the conventional stacks would still have a cost, whether in use or not.

It would seem logical, then, to remove only enough of the collection to make room for new accessions, unless the cost of working with such small lots would be greater than the loss of use and the cost of storage. The only transfer cost that might change appreciably with the lot size is the cost of *selecting* titles. Record changes, within certain limits, are relatively constant. Clearly there must be some free space in the conventional bookstack and it must be as uniformly distributed as possible. The amount of free space required and the amount of shifting will depend upon the methods used for selecting materials for storage.

6. Costs of messenger and paging service

On the whole we believe the costs for circulation from storage are not very different from the costs for conventional stacks. In some respects messenger and paging costs are higher for compactly stored materials outside a main library building, but in other respects are lower. Although it may take a messenger some time to reach a storage building and return, he is usually handling an accumulation of call slips for a four-hour or one-day period; the stored books seldom, if ever, require shifting; and the arrangement of the books should make

identification and reshelving less time-consuming than for conventional bookstacks.

7. Circulation load from storage

The number of items called from storage will obviously depend upon the use characteristics of the material stored, the critical use levels decided upon to govern location in storage or nonstorage areas, the accuracy of the rules used to select materials, and related factors. It is not possible to generalize a situation that would be applicable in these respects to many institutions. However, it is possible to illustrate the nature of the problem. Table 44 indicates expected use rates for certain groups of low-use economics monographs at the University of Chicago. Thus, if a decision were made to transfer to storage the lowest 25 percent in level of use, we assume an average annual use rate of slightly less than .02 per monograph title in 1961. If we assume that there were 1.5 volumes transferred for each title (eliminating duplicate copies and allowing for multivolume monographs), we might expect each volume to be used on the average once every 75 years, or 13.3 uses annually for every 1,000 volumes transferred. If we assume one volume per title, the initial use would be at the annual rate of 20 uses for every 1,000 volumes, or each volume would be used once every

50 years. Other classes of materials are likely to generate either higher or lower rates of use, but the projected circulation under reasonable circumstances seems unlikely to create a very serious cost burden.

B. Cost estimates

1. Primary bases for comparisons

We compared the costs of compact and conventional book housing in two ways. One was to arrive at the total capital required for construction, land, and transfer costs, and the endowment funds required to generate the annual operating and maintenance costs. The other was to arrive at an annual cost figure based on the imputed interest costs for the funds required for capital outlays plus the annual operating expenses. We used a 5 percent rate of interest, approximately the yield a nonprofit institution would expect on current purchases of fixed income securities. We assumed an indefinite occupancy of both kinds of space. The basic computations were per square foot of floor area.

2. Elements entering into the cost computation

We included in our cost comparisons the following elements: (a) land, (b) construction costs of the two types of space, (c) long-term, major maintenance costs, (d) current space operating costs for heat, light, janitorial services, building supplies, etc., and (e) cost of selecting and changing records.

Land. It is evident that site values are subject to extreme variations between urban and nonurban institutions, as well as between central and peripheral sites on any single campus. Furthermore, in a multi-tier stack, site costs, unless very high, become a relatively minor cost element. Nonetheless, the cost is real and

was included at the arbitrary values of $2 per square foot for the conventional bookstack site and $1 per square foot for a noncentral storage site; other values may be easily substituted if desired. The allocation of site costs to bookstack space depends upon the number of stack tiers or levels and the adjustments made in our examples matched the building cost estimates, which were based on four-tier and single-tier bookstack alternatives.

Construction costs. In 1960, construction costs under certain given conditions were estimated by Mr. Wesley V. Pipher, then of the architectural firm of Skidmore, Owings, and Merrill. His analysis is given in appendix M. He estimated that air-conditioned and equipped book storage space, one story high, might come to about $14 a square foot, and in four-tier height to about $16 a square foot. Conventional bookstack space, four tiers high, might cost approximately $20 per square foot. These costs are for stack space only and do not include reading rooms, staff work space, general corridors, land, etc. (Library space has been erected in recent years at both higher and lower costs, as reported in the annual building issues of the *Library Journal.* We did not know any way of reducing the rather sharp variation[3] to a satisfactory common denominator, and therefore it seemed best to use the Skidmore, Owings, and Merrill figures.) We believe the approximate relationship between conventional book space costs

---

[3] The University of Michigan storage library (erected in 1953–54) was constructed at a cost of $23.155 per square foot; the Center for Research Libraries, formerly called the Midwest Inter-Library Center (erected in 1950–51), at a cost of $11.98. The CRL cost, adjusted by the Turner Construction Company index of building construction costs, would have been $16.51 at the end of 1959. Both buildings contain staff, working, or reading facilities that are not required for a purely storage operation.

and storage cost is more useful than trying to arrive at a fixed dollar value for both kinds of space. It should be relatively easy to substitute revised figures based on local estimates in making specific cost calculations.

Space operating costs for book housing, as distinguished from other purposes, are difficult to measure. Data on such costs are not readily available. The Center for Research Libraries in Chicago has records of its space operating costs since its establishment. It occupies a building with a net usable area of 74,940 square feet of which all but 13,200 feet are devoted to compact book storage. The building is air-conditioned and well maintained. Operating costs during 1955–60 averaged $0.21 per square foot annually, including janitorial service, power, light, heat, building supplies, minor repairs to the building and building equipment, and decorating, but excluding administrative overhead and insurance.[4] The building is relatively new, and this figure probably does not reflect adequately the long-range costs of routine building maintenance. The operating cost per square foot for the University of Michigan storage building, including space used for binding but excluding the cost of electricity came to $0.46966 in 1959–60.[5] In the light of these figures, we assumed that a storage building, space operating cost would probably be not less than $0.30 per square foot annually.

It was not possible to get as satisfactory an estimate for the operating costs of conventional bookstack space, separate from other library space. The University

of Chicago estimated that its costs for heat, light, power, janitorial services, equipment maintenance, decorating, building repairs, grounds care, guarding, tools and shops, delivery and trucking, and building and grounds overhead, in buildings that are largely devoted to library purposes, come to $0.75–$0.80 per square foot on a *gross* building area basis without air-conditioning (the cost per net usable square foot might be 15 to 20 percent more). These buildings for the most part are older than the CRL and in all cases include facilities other than bookstacks. The amount of traffic and use is very much heavier, and the buildings are open for very much longer periods of time each week than is the CRL. The costs, like other institutional space costs, appeared to be high in relation to commercial building operating costs in Chicago, which were reported at approximately $0.30–$0.40 a square foot for space that is not air-conditioned. However, at least two adjustments were required. We assumed (a) that the cost of operating or maintaining bookstack space was substantially less than overall library space, and (b) that any new library bookstack would be air-conditioned. One adjustment was up, the other down. While any figure was somewhat arbitrary, it seemed reasonable to conclude from these various figures that maintaining and servicing conventional bookstack space that is open long hours, illuminated day and night, and serving large numbers of readers, would be at least double the cost allowed for storage space and might easily run as much as three time as high; we therefore used $0.60 per square foot. Major building repairs have not been included in either set of figures. Building insurance costs seem low enough to be absorbed in the operating cost estimates.

[4] Data from Mrs. Helen Schmidt, assistant director, CRL, based on auditor's reports; see appendix M.

[5] Data from Mr. Frederick H. Wagman, director, University of Michigan library; see appendix M.

A major repair or building mainte-nance fund is essential for any building intended for indefinite use. We allowed an annual major building maintenance item at a flat rate of 2 percent of the initial construction cost of the space. This appears to be reasonable for a stor-age building; it may be a bit low for a conventional bookstack, but there is no satisfactory way to estimate the probable useful lifetime of such space and the costs of major repairs or rehabilitation.

The costs of transferring materials to storage are primarily those of selection and of record changes. The cost applies only to books already in the library and not to new accessions sent directly to storage.

To transfer a book requires labor of three different kinds:

1. Initial selection of the books for transfer. We assume that this would be done clerically on the basis of statistical rules generated by this study, followed by professional or faculty review. (We exclude the cost of such review.)

2. Altering catalog, circulation, or other records to reflect the new location of the book.

3. Physical transport of the books from the conventional bookstack to stor-age. Only the cost in excess of the normal shifting expense would be applicable, and this, in relation to other costs, does not appear to be important enough to include; over a sufficiently long period the normal shifting cost may be greater than the one-time moving cost.

There were two sources of cost data for items 1 and 2, Yale's selective book retirement program, and the exploratory study by Kenneth Soderland in associa-tion with this investigation. (See chap-ter 9.) Together they suggested $0.25 per *title* as an approximate working figure. The cost per *volume* will be substantially

less. For the University of Chicago li-brary we estimated the number of vol-umes per monograph title, *as defined in this study*, at 1.7. This definition in-cluded duplicate copies, all the editions, and multivolume monographs. The cost of transfer per serial volume obviously depends upon the number of volumes transferred *per title*. In the University of Chicago library we estimated that the number of serial volumes and the num-ber of monograph volumes for the col-lection as a whole were approximately equal. However, distribution is certainly not equal in all subject fields, and the sciences have relatively more serials than do the humanities. Libraries that have different ratios of serial volumes to mono-graph volumes or that have more dupli-cate copies of monographs need to make adjustments for these variations in deter-mining the probable costs of transfer.

We assumed transfers of an equal num-ber of serial volumes and monograph volumes and used the figures as devel-oped in chapter 9 as follows:

Monograph transfer cost per
    volume $0.17
Average serial volume trans-
    fer cost .... $0.10[6]
Average cost, assuming equal
    number of monographs
    and serials, per volume .. $0.135

We treated this cost as a cash outlay, reducing it to a square foot basis by mul-tiplying by the number of volumes per square foot in storage (that is, 30 or 60).

C. Applications of cost elements

The elements used for computing space costs and the results are sum-marized for several different arrange-

[6] Assumes the transfer of at least 6.6 volumes per title. If the minimum number is higher, the cost would be lower.

TABLE 45—The estimated costs of book space under different plans of housing

	Conventional book stack space			Compact storage—plan A			Compact storage—plan B			Compact storage—plan C			Compact storage—plan D		
Assumed vols/sq. ft.	15			30			30			60			60		
Assumed site cost/sq. ft.	$ 2.00			$ 1.00			$ 1.00			$ 1.00			$ 2.00		
No. of stack levels	four			one			four			four			four		
Assumed construction cost/sq. ft.	$20.00			$14.00			$16.00			$16.00			$20.00		
Costs per sq. ft. of book space	Cash outlay per sq. ft.	OR Annual direct & imputed int.[a] costs per sq. ft.	OR Required capital fund per sq. ft.	Cash outlay per sq. ft.	OR Annual direct & imputed int. costs per sq. ft.	OR Required capital fund per sq. ft.	Cash outlay per sq. ft.	OR Annual direct & imputed int. costs per sq. ft.	OR Required capital fund per sq. ft.	Cash outlay per sq. ft.	OR Annual direct & imputed int. costs per sq. ft.	OR Required capital fund per sq. ft.	Cash outlay per sq. ft.	OR Annual direct & imputed int. costs per sq. ft.	OR Required capital fund per sq. ft.
Site cost/sq. ft. of book space	$ 0.50	$ 0.025	$ 0.50	$ 1.00	$ 0.05	$ 1.00	$ 0.25	$ 0.013	$ 0.25	$ 0.25	$ 0.013	$ 0.25	$ 0.50	$ 0.025	$ 0.50
Const. cost of space/sq. ft.	20.00	1.00	20.00	14.00	0.70	14.00	16.00	0.80	16.00	16.00	0.80	16.00	20.00	1.00	20.00
Maint. fund at 2% of const. cost	......	0.40	8.00[a]	......	0.28	5.60	......	0.32	6.40	......	0.32	6.40	......	0.40	8.00
Current operation expense	......	0.60	12.00[a]	......	0.30	6.00	......	0.30	6.00	......	0.30	6.00	......	0.60	12.00
Trans. cost at $0.135/vol. per sq. ft.	4.05	0.20	......	4.05	0.20	4.05	4.05	0.20	4.05	8.10	0.41	8.10	8.10	0.41	8.10
Total	$20.50	$ 2.025	$ 40.50	$19.05	$ 1.53	$ 30.65	$20.30	$ 1.633	$ 32.70	$24.35	$ 1.843	$ 36.75	$28.60	$ 2.435	$ 48.60
Direct cost per vol. per year. OR		$ 0.135			$ 0.051			$ 0.054			$ 0.031			$ 0.041	
Required capital fund per vol. OR Direct cost per yr. for space for 500,000 vols.			$ 2.70			$ 1.02			$ 1.09			$ 0.61			$ 0.81
Direct cost per yr. for space for 500,000 vols.		$67,500			$25,500			$27,222			$15,358			$20,292	
OR Required capital fund for space for 500,000 vols.			$1,350,000			$510,833			$545,000			$306,250			$405,000
Cost for 500,000 vols. as a percentage of conv. space		100%	100%		37.8%	37.8%		40.3%	40.4%		22.8%	22.7%		30.1%	30.0%

[a] All interest costs or yields are on 5 percent basis.

ments in table 45. Based on the elements used in the analysis, and assuming the book space in all examples was filled to estimated capacities (that is, 15, 30, or 60 vols./sq. ft.) we concluded that the space cost per volume per year in a conventional bookstack was approximately $0.135. The capital requirement to house a volume for an indefinite period of time was $2.70. Thus the institution that is adding 60,000 volumes a year to its collection should expect to provide capital funds, or the equivalent in terms of current income, of $162,000 *a year* to house the intake. If the institution goes to the most compact form of storage in our analysis, and uses a four-tier bookstack, the housing cost per volume per year would drop to $0.031 or to approximately 23 percent of the cost of conventional housing (table 45, plan C). For the same rate of annual acquisitions, the annual capital requirement would come to $36,600.

The storage plan outlined under table 45, plan D, using conventional book space for storage, is given to illustrate the point that the major economies in compact storage result from increased book capacity of a square foot of space, rather than from lower construction costs.

D. Discussion and summary

We have outlined methods for computing the costs of conventional and compact book housing, basing the comparisons on the required capital fund or the annual direct costs and imputed interest costs required to meet space operating, major repair, construction, and transfer costs for an indefinite period of time. The cost of housing books is a very substantial part of the true operating cost of a library. Estimates of these costs were derived from a variety of sources, but it is evident that costs of book housing, either conventional or storage, are subject to substantial variations. These result from a combination of local construction costs for library buildings, land costs, and space operating costs. We assumed, however, that for any one institution local variations of this kind were likely to apply in roughly equal proportions both to storage and to conventional book space. If this is true, the *percentage* differences in the costs of housing books conventionally and compactly would not change very much from the present analysis. The cost analyses suggest that a given number of books may be housed compactly for approximately 23 to 40 percent of the cost of housing them in a conventional bookstack, depending upon the particular type of structure, the book density attained, and similar factors.

The basic cost comparisons were limited to storage versus conventional housing within the same institution. Cooperative storage or cooperative microfacsimile programs might produce even greater savings. No allowances were made in the computations for browsing loss or waiting time loss; on the other hand, allowances were not made for the possible benefits of removing marginal and very infrequently used materials from a research collection. The level of savings that will justify embarking upon a storage operation must be determined by each institution for itself, primarily by setting the average frequency of use level required for retaining books in the working research collection.

11

Summary and conclusions

In the introduction certain stresses on the modern research library were mentioned. It may be useful to restate some of them.

1. The vast expansion in the bulk and complexity of recorded knowledge shows no signs of abatement.

2. There is a very substantial expansion in serious educational and research interests.

3. There is a growing recognition that prompt and effective access to recorded knowledge is important and valuable to the efficiency and productivity of both educational and research processes.

4. There have been sharp increases in the costs of library personnel, materials, and space.

These pressures may be strong enough to force some alteration in the traditional relationships between scholarly readers and recorded information. If alterations in accessibility to scholarly materials are likely or inevitable, they should be anticipated and shaped in such a way that the ends of research and education will be helped rather than hindered. Both economic and value judgments are essential in examining these relationships and in subsequently defining scholarly needs and objectives, which the library must meet as efficiently and as completely as it can.

This investigation was designed to answer certain questions in this general context. More specifically, we examined the probable freedom of choice that large research libraries might have in the organization and accessibility of their book collections. As a practical model, we assumed a pattern of book housing in which some portion would be separated and stored compactly. The data in the study are relevant to a variety of other models or patterns of accessibility. There are at least three different considerations that are pertinent to this general issue:

1. Is it possible to predict the probable future use in a typical research library of groups of books with defined characteristics? We believe the answer is a qualified yes. The qualifications are often complex and critical, and the confidence limits of the prediction vary significantly from one subject to another.

2. Are the physical facilities for compact storage of some books likely to be more economical than conventional housing? We are convinced that compact storage can significantly reduce operat-

ing and capital costs, but the actual amounts will depend on the number of books stored and local cost factors. It appears that savings might range from about 60 to 77 percent of the costs for conventional housing.

3. What is gained and what is lost, not only in terms of money but also other values, as a result of adopting a compact storage system? Evaluation must assess scholarly benefits and losses. Judgments will determine, in part, the kinds and the extent of materials that might best be stored. While one might attempt to assign monetary values to the possible losses of book use or the inconveniences of some delay in accessibility, we have not believed it appropriate to do so in this study. In the absence of such objective analyses, final decisions in matters of this kind must be reached by informed and wise judgments.

Such judgments, based on many factors, are not foreign to academic institutions nor to the building and operating of distinguished research collections. In short, one institution may decide that the measurable economic gains of a storage operation are not worth the probable, even if largely unmeasured, losses. Another may decide that the gains from a storage operation when applied to increased book capacity or other library or institutional needs and services are well worth the probable losses. Both institutions, if they have applied suitable criteria and have realistically appraised the gains and losses, could be right. The study has attempted to set forth either relevant data or other criteria in the light of which informed judgments might be made and a variety of policy decisions evolved.

We first accepted the premise that the long-range use of a book was a relevant, although not sole, criterion in any effort

to distinguish between books suitable for storage and those that should be housed conventionally. Our first task was then to find and test suitable methods by which a library might predict the future of its books.

The model underlying the entire study treated books as if each had a random probability of use within a specific time period. It assumed that the amount of use per unit of time varies among books, but that the amount of use during one year does not influence the amount of use in any subsequent year. We tested this model and found that it was satisfactory for our purposes.

In chapters 2 and 3 we investigated methods of predicting future use. We surveyed the books in two widely different subjects: economics and Teutonic languages and literatures. Our sampling unit was the monograph *title*, defined to be all of the copies of a book with almost identical content, written by a single author, published in a single language, and including all copies of all volumes and all editions of the work. We took our sample from the shelf list of the University of Chicago library.

For each title that entered into the sample we collected data on the past circulation use and the objective demographic characteristics, principally the language in which it was written, publication date, and date of accession by the library. Book use as measured by recorded circulation during the five-year period from 1954 to 1958 was the variable we sought to predict in most cases. The demographic characteristics, as well as the amount of use in periods prior to 1954, served as the predictor variables. With respect to the age of books as measured by the publication date and the accession date, our study was cross-sectional rather than longitudinal; that is, we compared the amount of use shown by books of different ages rather than the use shown by the same books during successive stages of their stay in the library.

Our ultimate concern lay with the formulation of functions or rules that could be used to identify little used books for storage. Such rules grew out of the combination of policy decisions about the proportion of books to be sent to storage and statistical regression equations that predict which books will be used least. We investigated the properties of two types of rules to predict book use: informal functions of a few variables whose relationships were determined by inspection of the data; and formal multiple regression functions, in which we used several variables whose relationships were solved by the least-squares regression program of a computer. Because of the high variability of the predicted variable within data matrix cells that had similar objective characteristics, the multiple regression functions were no more efficient than the informal functions for separating books into those that show high use and those that show low use.

A not unexpected though crucial finding was that past use over a sufficiently long period is an excellent and by far the best predictor of future use. Since libraries differ in the amount of recorded data they have available about past use, we evaluated various rules for the situations (a) where a library has reasonably complete records of use, (b) where it has records that extend over the past five years (or where it will postpone its storage program until it has accumulated such records), and (c) where the library has no records of use at all.

For libraries that have no record of past use, rules that take into account both language and publication or accession date are most efficient. To develop the appropriate rule for a given subject area, the procedure is to divide the sample into subsamples by language, and then plot the predicted variable of use against the publication date. To identify the groups of books that would go to storage under a policy decision to transfer some given proportion of the collection, the rule-maker moves along the distribution of predicted use for each of the subsamples, starting with the oldest titles and proceeding until the desired proportion has been taken, while keeping the value of the predicted variable the same for all the language subsamples. The principle involved here is that of keeping the loss of use as nearly equal as possible in the several subsamples, which minimizes the loss of use for the sample as a whole.

Such rules work fairly well for economics and other scientific disciplines. If, for example, 25 percent of the economics collection at the University of Chicago were sent to storage using a rule of language and publication date, only about 3 percent of the total use of the economics collection would be accounted for by these books. The average title in such a stored group would have a probability of being used roughly once in thirty-five years. Complete results may be seen in table 3 of chapter 2. The rules are relatively simple, but their derivation and testing are moderately complex.

For Teutonic languages and literatures and other humanistic disciplines, such rules are much less successful. Even if we consider the best of the rules that do not employ past use (language plus accession date) the results are not very satisfactory. For example, in Teutonic languages and literatures the 25 percent of the collection that would go to storage under such a rule would account for 12 percent of total use, and the average title in the group would be used once every ten years. The complete results may be seen in table 2 of chapter 2.

Where libraries have records of use for five years for individual titles, the results would be better. This would mean that, in addition to the language and publication date specifications, no book would be taken to storage if it had been used in the preceding five years. Under this rule, if the 25 percent of the economics collection with the least predicted use were removed, this portion would be reduced to 2 percent of total use; and in Teutonic languages and literatures, 5 percent. There would also be corresponding decreases in the probability of use of the average volume sent to storage.

The variable of past use is sufficiently powerful that for libraries with 20-year use records the objective characteristics make little further contribution. The past-use variable in this case is measured by the number of years between the last use of the book and the examination for storage. The definition of the variable had a single complication: some books will not have been used at all since acquisition. For the most effective function that we generated, we handled this complication by setting up a separate variable to indicate whether the period of time without use dated from accession or from a prior use. We theorize that books that have *never* been used have far less probable future use than books that have been used.

Such a rule would enable the University of Chicago library to remove 25 percent of both the economics and Teutonic languages and literatures monographs with the expectation that only 1

percent of the total use of those collections would come from the stored books. The average monograph title taken to storage from the economics collection could be expected to be used once in slightly less than a hundred years. The average title taken to storage from the Teutonic languages and literatures collection could be expected to be used once in slightly more than a hundred years.

Furthermore there is little question that the overall effectiveness of any formula for selecting books for storage would be improved considerably if one or more scholars reviewed the titles recommended for storage. Such a review would almost surely be part of any library's storage procedure.

We also surveyed the use of monographs in several other subjects and developed selected rules for each, indicating the specific values of the predictor variables that would lead to best results. The findings confirmed the general conclusions given above with respect to the utility of the various rules.

The accuracy in predicting the effects of a given rule is also important. Two general kinds of predictions are of particular interest: those regarding the number of books that would be taken to storage: and those regarding the number of uses that would be generated by the group of books taken to storage.[1] We discussed the statistical manipulations that would produce estimates of the variability in the two types of predictions. The equations would be the same no matter what particular rule

[1] The librarian of the University of Michigan reports that the use of stored material dropped by approximately 50 percent when the general library bookstacks were opened to all users. The assumption is that users found satisfactory substitutes in the bookstacks that they had not previously located through the card catalog.

was chosen, but would differ depending on what kind of information was required. Generally, satisfactory approximations would be produced with simple binomial confidence limits (chapter 1, p. 00).

In developing the rules, we assumed that books would either continue to have about as much use in the future as they had in the recent past, or, if the amount of use should decline in the future, the use for the stored books would decrease at approximately the same *rate*. For the kinds of prediction that we are concerned about, no harm would be done if this assumption were in error.

However, for planning purposes a librarian will wish to know the rate at which groups of books decrease in use and approach the level at which it is possible to store them. If the removal rate were equal to the rate of input of new accessions, the conventional stack space required could be stabilized without reducing the amount of use. We therefore investigated the rate at which books decline in use in two ways: (a) We looked at records of use during a single time period for groups of books of different ages, and (b) we compared the use in the two five-year periods for the same books. These were the major results:

1. We found obsolescence rates by both methods somewhat lower than those suggested by previous studies based on different techniques.

2. Evidence from the two lines of investigation was apparently contradictory, but we believe the two lines can be reconciled to support the view that the rate of use of titles continues to decrease indefinitely with the age of the title.

3. We measured decline in use by the ratio of the difference of the use in two time periods divided by the use in the earlier time period. Except for titles published in the most recent period, this ratio is quite constant for titles of various ages in the natural sciences. The ratio decreases with increasing age in the social sciences and in the humanities. The numerical estimates depend upon the index of use chosen; that is, proportion used, total used, etc.

In its simplest form, a plan for stabilizing the size of a working research collection would demand that age groups of books would decrease in use by the same absolute amount each year. Our results suggest rather that the rate of decline is closer to a constant percentage each year, or, even worse for the stabilization principle, that the percentage of decline tends to decrease over time. It is also relevant that the acquisition rate for most subjects is now very much greater than it was twenty or thirty years ago—a simple arithmetical proposition that militates against stabilizing the size of a working collection except at the cost of putting into storage books that would produce an increasing percentage of total use.

The implications of our findings about decline in use depend upon a given library's decision about what proportion to store and the amount of information available about past use. Obviously, the higher the use level the library is willing to establish as its cutting point for storage, the larger the number of books that will fall below the cutting point each year. The better the procedure for predicting use, the larger the number of books that the library will be able to identify as falling below the cutting point. The data also suggest that if a librarian concerns himself primarily with the effects of book storage over the next twenty or thirty years, and stores only books with relatively low rates of use, the rate of de-

cline will be so small that he may anticipate little further drop.

All the findings of the study would
be more useful if it could be assumed
that they pertained to research libraries
generally. Chapter 4 investigated how
well some of the results applied at three
other major research libraries—Yale University, Northwestern University, and
the University of California at Berkeley.

We listed some of the potential differences between any two libraries that
might vitiate a priori statements about
the effect of the rules generated at the
University of Chicago if put into action
at the other institutions. Evidence was
collected and presented on the distribution of books by publication date and the
total amount of use at the three selected
libraries.

An examination of the relative amount
of use of the same books at different libraries indicates that there is a considerable similarity in the reading interests
of scholars at different institutions. For
those titles held in common predictions
about future use at one institution
would be quite accurate in predicting
future use of the same books at other
institutions, if the total amount of use
of books at the several institutions is
taken into account. But because of books
not held in common this finding is of little help.

We developed rules based on publication date and language for the University of Chicago and applied them to random samples taken at Berkeley and
at Northwestern. The rules produced
similar results at the three institutions
in terms of the percentage of total use
represented by the lowest 25 percent of
the titles identified for storage. Naturally,
the amount of absolute use of those

groups of books was very different at the
various institutions.

On the other hand, a rule framed at
Chicago giving the particular characteristics of language and age of the group
that should be sent to storage is likely
to produce very different numbers of
books for storage at the various institutions because of the differences in distributions of holdings by language and
age. This problem might be surmounted
by minor surveys taken in advance of a
storage program at the various libraries.

However, if a library has records of
the past use of individual books for 20
years or more, it might well employ rules
developed at the University of Chicago
and expect comparable results in terms
of the probability of a particular title's
being used in a specified future time
period.

In chapter 7 we explored the subject
of browsing and nonrecorded use, and
the relationship to recorded use. The
important question we sought to answer
was how closely recorded use would
serve as a satisfactory index of all use.
Our primary technique was a questionnaire placed in books in our monograph
and serial samples. We found that within subject collections housed under much
the same conditions, nonrecorded use for
groups of books categorized by relatively
low recorded use is roughly proportional
to recorded use. In other words, a group
of books that average one recorded use in
five years will average twice as many nonrecorded uses as will books that average
half a recorded use in five years.

We also found that in some subject
areas and some kinds of stack-access conditions, there is considerably more browsing use than recorded use. Furthermore,
many books are found through browsing

directly rather than by way of catalogs or bibliographical devices.

Serials differ from monographs in relation to storage. The volumes within a serial are interrelated in that a library would not wish to store scattered volumes, although it might be pleased to store the early portion of a long run, or the entire title. Serial volumes also seem to be interrelated in the sense that the use of volumes within the same serial is closer than the amount of use of volumes chosen randomly from other serials. We can therefore employ the volumes within a given serial to help predict the future use of other volumes in the serial. This latter interrelationship was demonstrated experimentally in our investigation.

Our data, described in chapter 6, demonstrated that the most efficacious method of identifying serial volumes for storage is by some type of rule that begins with the oldest volume and selects volumes for storage consecutively until a volume is reached that shows some specified amount of use in a prior period of time, perhaps the previous five years. Such a method will produce better results than will a rule based solely on language and age.

However, many libraries have no data on the previous use of serial volumes because they do not permit serials to circulate outside the library. Such libraries might employ a list of the serial volumes stored at some other library, such as the University of Chicago library, which has maintained records of past use. Or they could set up systems to produce the necessary data within a period of five years.

To test the utility of statistical indexes of recorded use, we conducted a comparison between (a) judgment of scholars about the value of books in their own fields, and (b) judgments made by the objective statistical system, based on the rules described in chapter 2. We found that the variability between scholars was great, both in the number of titles and in the choice of individual volumes they would store. The objective system seems to agree with the consensus of a group of scholars at least as well as a single scholar's judgment would agree with that consensus.

There was also considerable variation by subject in the reaction of scholars to storage plans. In economics and chemistry most experts were willing to send a great deal of material to storage, while in the humanistic disciplines of Teutonic languages and literatures and English and American literature, there was considerable resistance from some scholars though little from others.

The various parts of the investigation convince us that with our rules we may predict the future use of books at least as well as any other method known to us. But such information of itself is not sufficient to provide the ground for rational decisions about the numbers of books that should be sent to storage each year.

Chapter 9 described a set of practical procedures for transferring books to storage, with an analysis of the related bibliographical problems and the costs. A procedure that might well be optimum would produce a current cost of approximately $.17 per monograph volume and $.10 per serial volume transferred to storage (based on labor costs of $1.50 per hour). This cost is sufficiently low that the economics of transfers should not be a barrier to storage programs, if changes on the full set of catalog cards can be avoided.

In chapter 10 we compared the costs of housing books in compact and conventional housing. Costs for book space operation (heat, light, janitorial, and related expenses) were ascertained from a limited number of sources. Construction costs for compact and conventional bookstack space were calculated by an architect using what appeared to be a reasonable set of conditions. Based on his analysis, we used in our computations a cost of $20 a square foot for conventional bookstack space and $14 and $16 a square foot for compact storage space. To these two types of costs were added (a) an allowance of 2 percent per year of the original construction cost to cover maintenance of the building for an indefinite period of time, (b) the costs of the record changing required to move books from conventional to compact storage, and (c) an assumed value for the cost of land. Excluded from the computations were the costs to the user that might result from any delay in access or loss of access to material in storage.

Two methods were used to summarize these costs:

1. The first method was based on a determination of the capital fund required per square foot, in terms of the cash outlay for stack construction, land, and book transfer costs, and the endowment funds required to generate the annual operating and maintenance costs. The cost for conventional housing was found to be $2.70 per volume. Equivalent compact storage costs ranged from $0.61 to $1.09, depending on the type of structure and other factors.

2. An alternative method used to summarize the costs was to determine the annual operating and maintenance cash

outlays and add to this the imputed interest costs on capital expenditures for land, physical structure, and transfer costs. On this annual basis the costs per volume of capacity in conventional housing came to $0.135, while compact storage costs ranged from $0.031 to $0.051.

Substantial variation from these figures may be expected because of local cost differences, but the general relationship in the costs of compact storage as a percentage of conventional storage may stay roughly the same. It is evident in the data used in this analysis that the major economies in compact storage are the result of increasing the book capacity per square foot rather than savings in the construction costs of storage space. The cost estimates for compact storage were based upon assumed capacities of 30 and 60 volumes per square foot, while the costs of conventional space were estimated on the basis of 15 volumes per square foot.

The basic relationships between readers and print and the factors that affect those relationships for good or ill are unquestionably important both to scholarship and to the effective and efficient operation of libraries designed to serve scholarly purposes. This investigation was an effort to increase our understanding of at least some of the important elements affecting these matters. Since the investigation was essentially exploratory, we hope additional studies can be carried out by other investigators to verify, qualify, or extend our conclusions in this and related fields.

Bibliography

Abel, Gene M. "A Study of the Costs of Storing Library Materials." Unpublished paper. Chicago: University of Chicago, 1955.

Burchard, John Ely and others. *Planning the University Library Building*. Princeton: Princeton University Press, 1949.

Bush, G. C., Galliher, H. P., and Morse, P. M. "Attendance and Use of the Science Library at Massachusetts Institute of Technology." *American Documentation*, 7 (1956): 87–109.

Cochran, William G. *Sampling Techniques*. New York: John Wiley, 1953.

Curtis, George A. "A Statistical Study of the Services of the John Crerar Library." Master's thesis, University of Chicago, 1951.

Doherty, Francis X. "The New England Deposit Library." Master's thesis, University of Chicago, 1948.

Ernst, Martin L., and Shaffer, Bertram. "A Survey of Circulation Characteristics of some General Library Books." Unpublished manuscript. Massachusetts Institute of Technology, 1954.

Esterquest, R. T. "Comments on the Article Shelving Books by Size." *A.L.A. Bulletin,* 51 (June, 1957): 437.

Friley, Charles E., and Orr, Robert W. "A Decade of Book Storage at Iowa State College." *College and Research Libraries,* 12 (January, 1951): 7–10+.

Fussler, Herman H. "The Research Library in Transition." In *University of Tennessee Library Lectures,* edited by John H. Dobson. Knoxville: University of Tennessee, 1957.

———. "Characteristics of the Research Literature Used by Chemists and Physicists in the United States." *Library Quarterly,* 19 (January and April, 1949): 19–35, 119–143.

———. "The Problem of Physical Accessibility." In *Bibliographic Organization,* edited by J. Shera and M. Egan. Chicago: University of Chicago Press, 1951.

Gosnell, Charles F. "The Rate of Obsolescence in College Library Book Collections as Determined by an Analysis of Three Select Lists of Books for College Libraries." Ph.D. dissertation, New York University, 1943.

Grieder, Elmer M. "The Effect of Book Storage on Circulation Service." *College and Research Libraries,* 11 (October, 1950): 374–376.

Harrer, G. A. "Relocation, Storage, and Rejection of Materials in the Harvard University Libraries." Unpublished paper. Rutgers University, n.d.

Hill, F. J. "Compact Storage of Books; a Study of Methods and Equipment." *Journal of Documentation,* 11 (December, 1955): 202.

Kaplan, Louis. "Storage of Library Materials." In *The State of the Library Art*, edited by Ralph R. Shaw. New Brunswick, N.J.: Rutgers University, 1960.

Lerner, Abba P. *The Economics of Control: Principles of Welfare Economics.* New York: Macmillan, 1944.

Middleswart, Lilian E. "A Study of Book Use in the University of Chicago Library." Master's thesis, University of Chicago, 1951.

Muller, Robert H. "Compact Storage Equipment: Where To Use It and Where Not." *College and Research Libraries,* 15 (July, 1954): 300–308.

———. "Evaluation of Compact Book Storage Systems." In *Association of College and Reference Libraries Monograph No. 11.* Chicago: ACRL, 1954.

Orne, Jerrold. "Storage and Deposit Libraries." In *The State of the Library Art,* edited by Ralph R. Shaw. New Brunswick, N.J.: Rutgers University, 1960.

Orr, Robert W., and Thompson, Lawrence S. "The Library Storage Building." *Library Journal,* 67 (February 15, 1942): 150–153.

Pigou, A. C. *The Economics of Welfare.* 4th ed. London: Macmillan, 1932.

Quinn, E. W. "Characteristics of the Literature Used by Authors of Books in the Field of Sociology." Master's thesis, University of Chicago, 1951.

Rao, C. Radhakrishna. *Advanced Statistical Methods in Biometric Research.* New York: John Wiley, 1952.

Rider, Fremont. *Compact Book Storage.* New York: Hadham Press, 1949.

———. "Library Cost Accounting." *Library Quarterly,* 6 (October, 1936): 331–381.

Shaw, Ralph R. "Pilot Study in the Use of Scientific Literature by Scientists." Mimeographed. New Brunswick, N.J.: Rutgers University, November 21, 1956. (Has annotated bibliography: "Studies of the Use of Literature in Science and Technology," appendix I.)

Sheniti, Mahmoud. "The University Library and the Scholar: A Study of the Recorded Faculty Use of a Large University Library." Ph.D. dissertation, University of Chicago, 1960.

Simon, Julian L. "Economics of Book Storage Plans for a Large University Library." Ph.D. dissertation, University of Chicago, 1961.

Smith, Hal H. "The Recorded Use of a University Library's Books in Two Areas: Biological and Physical Sciences." Master's thesis, University of Chicago, 1951.

Stevens, Rolland E. "Characteristics of Subject Literatures." In *Association of College and Reference Libraries Monograph No. 6.* Chicago: ACRL, 1953.

Tauber, Maurice. *Technical Services in Libraries.* New York: Columbia University Press, 1954.

Wilson, Louis R., and Tauber, Maurice F. *The University Library.* 2nd ed. New York: Columbia University Press, 1956.

Appendices

A. Procedures and supplementary data for the University of Chicago monograph samples

I. Basic procedure

This section describes the procedures used throughout the monograph survey. There were, however, a few variations from one subject area to another which are given in section II of this appendix.

A. Selecting titles for samples

In both the random systematic and the stratified samples, the procedure began with a systematic marking of shelf-list cards at intervals measured with a ruler. In the random samples the choice card was found by counting three cards back from the card with the ink mark on it. Where the ink mark was spread over more than one card, the card from which the counting started was the last card touched by the ink. This card was not itself counted; the card directly behind it was taken as the first of the cards in the count. The third card back was taken as the actual choice card. Anything occupying the space of a card was counted as though it were an actual card: markers, index, and blank cards.

In the stratified sample, counting also started with the card behind the ink-marked card. Beginning with the fifth card back of the inked card several subsequent cards were then considered for the sample, the exact number varying from area to area as indicated in table A-1.

That a card was considered did not necessarily mean that the title it represented was taken in the sample. The categories dropped from the samples were as follows:

1. Serials. The definition of serial was "a publication issued at regular or irregular intervals with some scheme for consecutive numbering and intended to be continued indefinitely." Most serial cards were readily recognizable by the notation "See serial record." Even when crossed out, this notation served to identify the card, since the crossing out meant only that the serial was no longer being received by the library and that the detail cards had been transferred from the serial record to the shelf list. There were a few cases of cards which, by the definition given above, were serials but had no such identification. Examples of decisions on borderline cases are given in the appendix on several samples (appendix C). Whether or not a volume contained material by several authors was an important secondary consideration.

2. Unbound books. All unbound books were omitted, because they have no use records. Unbound books were indicated on the shelf-list cards by the letters "ub" under the call number and usually had no accession number.

3. Other dropped categories.

a. Books acquired later than 1953 were omitted because they did not have sufficient

151

TABLE A-1

Number of cards considered in each interval in
the stratified samples

Subject	No. of cards
Physics	8
History	6
Economics	5
Anthropology	3
Sociology	6
Philosophy	4
Romance languages and literatures	$4\frac{1}{2}$[a]
Teutonic languages and literatures	3
Biology	4
Foreign history	2
American literature	4
English literature	4
Latin American history	8
Chemistry	5
Political science	6

[a] In this sample four and five cards were taken alternately.

use records for most statistical purposes. There were, however, two exceptions to this rule: (a) In three areas such books were taken—economics, anthropology, and sociology (original random samples); (b) where these books were part of a title of which some other part had been acquired earlier, all parts were taken, no matter what the accession date. This exception will be explained more fully later on.

b. Books in the rare book room, the Yerkes library, or the University College library were not considered in the study. The rationale for this omission is given in chapter 1, section D.

c. Any title that included any book in any special collection other than the three mentioned in (b) above was dropped completely. See chapter 1 for the rationale.

d. Any title for which all the books had been lost or released was necessarily dropped.

e. When the choice card was part of a group of cards for a title, but was not the first card of that group, the entire title was dropped. This meant that if the card in front of the choice card referred to the same title in the same language, the choice card was omitted. This procedure was necessary to insure that each title had an equal probability of entering the sample.

f. Cross reference, index, marker, and blank cards were dropped since they did not refer to definite books in the subject area.

A list was kept of all choice cards that were skipped, giving the call number involved and the reason for skipping the card. In the case of serials and multicard monograph groups, the number of cards and the place of the choice card were included. For example, a card might be the second of a group of three; or the third of three cards for the same serial; or the tenth in a group of thirteen. An analysis of these skip lists is given in table A-2.

In the stratified samples, some titles were dropped in the process of stratification by publication dates grouped into decades. There were different instructions for each area as to the numbers of books to include for each decade. First the publication dates and accession dates were listed for all titles. The governing publication date was the earliest publication date for any book in the title. For example, if there were two editions of the same title, one published in 1880 and one in 1890, the publication date for the title would be recorded as 1880. On the other hand, the accession date selected was that of the latest book acquired for the title concerned. In terms of the previous example, if the 1880 edition was acquired in

TABLE A-2

An analysis of drop lists for the unstratified monograph samples

Subject	Unbound	Acquired after 1953	Serial	Not the first of its title group	In a special collection	In the University College library	All books for the title lost	Cross reference card	Index or marker card	Taken in the previous sample (applies only to resamples)	Total
					Numbers of cards dropped for various reasons						
Physics	31	70	4	91							196
History	25	29	24	93	4	1	1	1	4		182
Economics	58		98	29	6	1		1	2		195
Economics resample	78	106	148	70	10			5	15	8	440
Anthropology	15		19	15	5			4			59a
Sociology	10		17	22	10			2			61
Philosophy	14	74	10	63	14		1	10			186
Romance languages and literatures	8	27	2	31	10	2		13	2		95
Teutonic languages and literatures	11	28	9	54	23			11	7		143
Teutonic languages and literatures resample	16	43	15	71	32			21	13	8	219
Biology	6	46	49	66	5			2	1		175
American literature	31	29	7	41	83			4			195
English literature	21	37	1	84	47	1	1	16	7		215
Foreign history	19	62	18	51	9	1		1	2		163
Latin American history	23	35	18	25	3			1	2		107

ᵃ This includes one card out of place with a DS call number.

1892 and the 1890 edition in 1908, the accession date for the title would be recorded as 1908. These lists of publication dates and accession dates, coded into two-year periods, provided supplementary information as to the composition of the collection in the various subject areas.

In the various sample areas different numbers of books printed in the various decades were taken to supplement the random sample already taken. Table A-3 indicates the number of titles taken from the various publication date groups. Titles to be taken with each group were chosen systematically, with a random start. For example, if one out of every nine titles printed between 1890 and 1899 were to be taken, and the eighth title were chosen, the eighth of every nine titles

printed between 1890 and 1899 would be taken throughout that stratified sample area.

In both the random and the stratified monograph samples, a data sheet was made up for each of the physical books among the selected titles. The procedure for filling in the data sheets was changed in several ways before the procedure described here was evolved. The variations from area to area will be described after the standard procedure is explained.

B. Recording information from the shelf-list cards onto data sheets (see figure A-1)

1. The *call number* was recorded in sufficient detail to identify each book in the stacks.

2. Each *title* was given a different title

TABLE A-3

Number of titles taken from each publication date group
for the various stratified monograph samples

Subject	Number of cards taken in publication date group									
	Pre-1870	1870–79	1880–89	1890–99	1900–09	1910–19	1920–29	1930–39	1940–49	1950–53
Physics	1/3	1/5	all	1/3	1/3	1/3	1/20			
History	1/5	all	all	2/3	2/3		1/20	1/20		
Economics		all	all	all[a]	$\frac{2}{8}$[b] $\frac{1}{10}$[c]	1/10	1/10[d]			
Anthropology	2/3	all	all	1/2	2/3	1/3	1/8	1/8	1/4	
Sociology	1/10	1/4	all	2/3	1/6	1/6	1/15	1/15	1/15	
Philosophy		5/8	all	1/2	1/12	1/12	1/12[d]			
Romance languages and literatures	1/8	all	3/5	3/5	1/3	1/3	1/20	1/20	1/5	
Teutonic languages and literatures		1/2	1/2	1/3	1/5			1/5[f]	1/5	
Biology		all	3/4	3/5	5/10	1/3	1/3[e]			
American literature		all	2/3	1/3	1/8	1/8			1/8	
English literature		all	2/3	1/3	1/8	1/8			1/8	
Foreign history		3/4	4/5	1/2	1/5	1/3	1/10		1/5	all
Latin Am. history		all	all	2/5	1/3	1/4	1/4	1/7	1/6	1/2
Chemistry	2/3	all	all	2/3	2/3	2/3	1/4	1/4	1/5	1/3
Political science	1/3	all	all	3/4	2/3	1/2	1/3	1/4	1/5	1/5

This table may be read as follows: For the Physics stratified sample one out of every 3 titles printed before 1870 was taken, one out of every five titles printed between 1870 and 1879 (inclusive), all titles printed between 1880 and 1889, and so on.

[a] To 1894 only
[b] 1895–1904
[c] 1905–09
[d] 1924 only
[e] To 1924 only
[f] From 1935 only

number (columns 4–7). This method differs from common library classification procedure in that by our definition the title included all related editions of a work.

3. *Edition, volume, and copy* (columns 8–12). These indications served to distinguish between different books within the same title. The numbers in these columns were assigned arbitrarily and did not necessarily correspond to the cataloging edition, volume, or copy numbers of the books involved. A discussion of the rationale behind the procedure is found in chapter 1.

a. *Copy*—a book was considered a copy of another book if the two contained identical material and were printed at the same place, at the same time, and by the same publisher. There were, however, exceptions in that later impressions of the same book, if identical to the first impression, were cataloged by the library on the same card and were, therefore, not distinguishable from books belonging to the earlier impression. Books containing identical material published in the same year but in different countries were considered to be copies.

b. *Volume*—volumes of a title are different physical books containing material that could have been printed in one volume but which, for various practical reasons, had been divided among two or more. Different sections of a volume were considered as the same volume if they formed one book but as different volumes if they formed more than one book. Atlases, for example, were considered as separate volumes when they constituted separate books.

c. *Edition*—the customary usage generally agreed with our system, although, due to the library's cataloging procedures, in some cases different impressions of the same text may have been treated as separate editions. Each edition is cataloged on a separate shelf-list card and has a distinct call number.

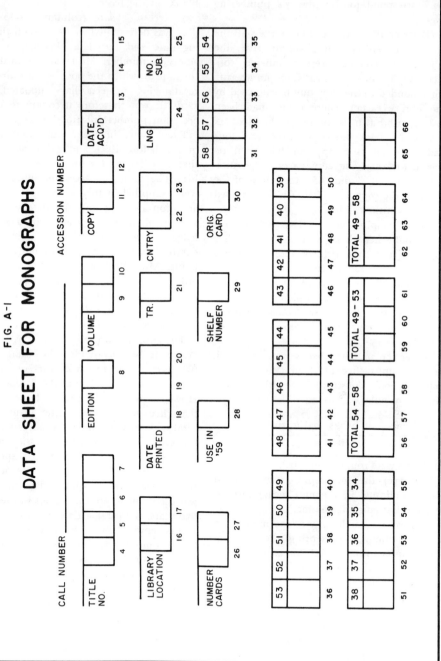

FIG. A-1

DATA SHEET FOR MONOGRAPHS

There were two sets of circumstances in which the numbering of these columns did not correspond to the library's numbering system:

(1) When the library did not possess all the volumes or editions of a certain title, the editions or volumes were numbered consecutively for our purposes. Copy numbering corresponded to the copy numbering used by the library except where copies had been lost or withdrawn. If the library had had six copies of a book but copies three and four had been lost and copy one had been released, the surviving copies would be numbered "01," "02," and "03," regardless of the fact that the copy we called "01" was labeled "copy 2" in the catalog.

(2) Subsampling was used to reduce costs and labor when there were more than five copies of the same title or more than five volumes of the same edition of the title, or more than five editions of the same title. Note that we only subsampled when there were more than five physical books involved at the same level (i.e., editions, volumes, or copies).

Where ten or fewer books were involved, we subsampled five of them. Where more than ten books constituted the title, the following formula was used:

$$\sqrt{\frac{\text{Number of books in the title}}{10}} \times 5$$

Fractions were rounded upward.

Whenever the subsampling was used, it was so indicated in the numbering just before the last edition, volume, or copy taken. This break was made only in the numbering of the columns representing the level at which subsampling had been used. For instance, if random numbers were used to select five copies of a book with eight copies, the last copies taken would all be numbered "06" in columns 11–12; where the subsampling was used to select five of ten editions, the last editions taken would be labeled "Edition 6."

In cases where the choice card referred to a single-book title, these columns were left blank. In all cases of multibook titles all these columns were filled. In no case were some of these columns filled in and some left blank on the basic data sheets.

4. Accession date (columns 13–15). This date was determined by using both the catalog date and the date obtained from the accession number. Most catalog cards have the date on which the book was acquired, but recataloging projects have updated many cards. It was therefore necessary to use the accession number information as well.

Every book in the library that was acquired before 1955, and a few acquired in that year, received a unique accession number. The tables of accession number dates were compiled in two ways: Up to 1928 the accession number and the date each book was acquired were recorded in a series of ledgers. It was relatively easy to collect accurate data on the accession dates up to this point. After 1928, however, the ledger record was discontinued and blocks of accession numbers were assigned to catalogers. Accession number date information from 1928 on was therefore less accurate.

The overall procedure was as follows: When it was available, the catalog date (when it was within five years of the publication date) was taken as the date acquired. However, when there was a lapse of more than five years between the printing and catalog dates for a book, or no catalog date was given on the card, the accession number date was found. If there was a spread of more than five years between the accession number date and the catalog date, the former was used, but where the spread was less than five years, the catalog date was used because it was more likely to be accurate. In practice this meant that for most books acquired before 1915 the accession number date was used, and for most books acquired after 1915 the catalog date was used.

5. Library location (columns 16–17). The code referred to the actual departmental library within the University of Chicago library where the book was located.

6. Publication date (columns 18–20). This was almost always obtainable from the shelf-list card; otherwise it was obtained from the book itself. Occasionally no publication date could be found in the book and it was necessary to date the book from examination of the text.

7. Translation (column 21). This variable was employed to indicate whether the book involved *was* a translation or *had* a translation. For the earlier part of the study the same column served to record "type of publisher" and the "translation" variable was not collected. See section II of this appendix, variations in procedure among areas, for more detail.

8. Country (columns 22–23). This refers to the country in which the book was published.

9. Language (column 24). The language in which the book was written was entered in this column. The only problem arose when two or more languages were involved. Then a special code ("0") was used if the two languages were exactly equivalent—for example, in a dictionary. When the two languages were not exactly equivalent, the code for the one that formed the greater part of the text was used.

10. Number of subjects (column 25). The number of subject headings under which the book was cataloged in the public catalog was usually given on the shelf-list card. Where none was listed, "0" was coded. Listings under title and author were not included in the count.

11. Number of cards (columns 26–27). This column was filled in when the title consisted of more than one book (i.e., when columns 8–12 were filled in), or when a single-book title was represented by two or more contiguous cards. The latter case was rare and was coded specially. In the former and more usual case the number of cards was recorded in ordinary numbers on the first data sheet for the title number, and as "00" on subsequent data sheets for the same title number. The number given was the count of all shelf-list cards for the title-number group. For example, if there were three editions occupying three cards it would be "03"; if ten volumes on one card, "01," and so on.

Note of any lost or discarded books in a title was made in the "remarks" space of the data sheet together with the dates when these events occurred (if given). Books in the title in the rare book room, Yerkes library, or University College were also listed in this space.

The shelf-list data were spot-checked before the sheets were taken to the stacks, except for the work of new people, which was checked in its entirety.

C. Recording data from the physical books

1. Shelf number (column 29). The shelves were numbered from the top down. Empty shelves were not counted, but there were not many.

2. Original card code (column 30). This number refers to the length of a book's life in the library covered by the two charge cards. This datum was determined both from the date of the first entry on the card and also from a consideration of the general condition of the cards. After working with the charge cards for some time, data collectors built up a picture of what cards of different ages tended to look like. There were very few cases in which it was impossible to make a reasonable guess as to the approximate age of the charge cards.

3. Use data (columns 31–55). This information was taken from the charge cards. Ordinarily books had two charge cards, one white and one orange. Under the University of Chicago library system, when a book is charged out the borrower writes his name on the orange card and his name and address on the white card. But the two existing cards do not always show the same number of uses, since the white card is exhausted more rapidly than the orange card, as each entry on it takes up two lines instead of one. Interlibrary loans are recorded only on the white card. Sometimes when books are put on reserve the orange card is used. In some cases books, usually low-use books, have only white cards.

The number of uses for each year for which information was shown on the charge cards was entered in the appropriate column on the data sheet from 1934 to 1958. Uses earlier than 1934 or after 1958 were noted in the "remarks" space. (Column 28 was used to enter the use figure for 1959 for slightly more than half the monograph samples taken.)

Details in the recording of use:

a. Renewals were not counted.

b. Only one use was counted for the same person on any one book unless there was at least a twelve-month lapse between uses, or unless another person used the book in between.

c. Reserve uses were not counted, but a note was made in the "remarks" space of the years when the book was on reserve. Individual reserve uses—which appeared rarely on the charge cards—were not noted.

d. Loans to University of Chicago laboratory collections were not counted as uses.

e. Interlibrary loans were counted, but were also noted in the "remarks" space.

f. Bindery and other institutional entries were not counted as uses, but they were entered in the "remarks" space.

g. Uses in the year in which the book was acquired were not formally recorded, but a note was made of them.

h. When the charge cards were replacements and did not cover the entire period during which the book was in the library, the years not covered were left blank.

D. Missing books

When a book could not be found on the shelf, this fact was noted on the data sheet. If the missing book formed part of a title that had been subsampled, it was replaced in the sample, where possible, by one of the books in the same title which had not been picked. A list was kept of all books that were not on the shelf.

E. Search procedure

1. In the main library (i.e., the library to which the area was block-charged). The books that had not been on the shelf were searched for in the charge-out file. The use data was recorded from the charge cards in this file for those books which were found to be charged out.

When this search failed to find a book, that data sheet was checked against the main shelf list to determine whether information had been correctly collected and whether all location symbols had been interpreted accurately. Books which could not be accounted for by errors in transcription were listed with their titles and authors. This list was given to the library staff so that the books could be traced.

2. In other libraries. In libraries in which only a few blocks in the sample were located, the search procedure was slightly different. The charge-out file was searched first for the books that were not on the shelf, and then the shelf list in the library was checked to see if the book was in it, since there was sometimes a discrepancy between the main shelf list and the various shelf lists in the departmental libraries. Books that could not be found because of this discrepancy between the main and departmental shelf lists probably amounted to three or four in every complete sample. The number was highest when the books in an area were most scattered between different libraries. Science areas tended to show more of this kind of discrepancy because more departmental libraries were involved.

F. Editing, summarizing, and estimation of use

When all the books that could be found had been found and the main search list had produced its results, the data sheets were edited for accuracy. Stray books that turned up later were fitted into the sample if work had not progressed to a stage where additions were not feasible.

Use figures were adjusted in accordance with the following rules:

a. If the book was on reserve, one use was added to any other uses during that year.

b. If a use was undated, the editor assigned to it the most likely year. When the undated use was between two dated uses, it was assigned to the year midway between the two known dates.

c. If one copy or edition had been acquired later than other copies or editions of the same title, the title was credited with its use in its accession year.

d. Where the use data for the last ten years (i.e., 1949–58) was incomplete, the data for that period was estimated. But use was not estimated for any periods between accession and 1949 if the cards were incomplete.

Dummy data sheets ("blow-ups") were made for books that had been skipped by the subsampling process. In that way there would be one IBM card for each physical book in the sample. Average publication and accession number was omitted. Use data for the five-year periods 1949–53 and 1954–58 were calculated by averaging the number of uses for the two periods for all the other book units. Reserve uses were not included in this sum. The "blow-ups" were not credited with use for a period earlier than that in which they were acquired.

The editor recorded the value for "years since last use" in columns 65 and 66. This variable represented the lapsed number of years between 1954 and the last previous use of the book. It was calculated with reference to the year of the last use or to the accession year if the book had not been used at all. The maximum which this variable could attain was "20." Books acquired after 1954 were assigned "00."

Summarizing into the title: Summaries were made for any title that consisted of more than one book. All titles that required summarizing were summarized at all three levels, the exact components of the levels being: at the "77/2" level, a summary contained all the copies of the same book, i.e., the same volume and edition; at the "77/3" level, a summary contained all the volumes of the same edition (this, therefore, involved in some cases summarizing an earlier copy summary); and at the "77/4" level, the summary contained all the editions for a title. At the "77/4" (title) level there was always just one card for each title.

Columns 8–12 of the summaries were filled in in the following way:

Where only one summary was represented by a data sheet, "X" or "XX" was put in the columns for the level at which the summary was being made, i.e., for a "77/2" summary, "XX" in columns 11 and 12; for a "77/3," "XX" in columns 9 and 10, and for a "77/4," "X" in column 8. If, however, more than one summary was represented by one data sheet, "Y" or "YY" was used in the appropriate columns. More than one summary level was made at the same time when two or more levels were exactly the same— as, for example, for a title consisting of two copies of the same book. The "77" numbers were put in the "remarks" space and as many cards as there were "77" figures were made when the cards were punched. The latest date of accession for the books being summarized was used, and the earliest date published. Country of publication was usually the same for all the books involved but when it was not, the conflict was resolved in favor of that country that published the most books read in the United States. Language was always the same for the various books involved. Where there was a discrepancy between the various books in number of subjects, the highest number of subjects was used.

II. Variations in procedure among areas

The area variations are summarized in table A-4. The areas are described in the temporal order in which the samples were taken.

A. Physics (QC)

Physics was the first sample taken, and the method differed somewhat from the standard method that was evolved later. Instead of skipping an interval completely when the choice card was in one of the skip categories, as in the later areas, the card behind it was taken. If that card, too, was in one of the skip categories, the one behind it was taken and so on until a usable title was found.

TABLE A-4

A summary of the area variations for the monograph samples

Sample	Titles acquired after 1953 included	Type publisher collected	Translation variable collected	Title legible recorded	Use in 1959 recorded	Old original card code	New code for single-book titles with more than one card	Use by same man counted	Shelf number recorded	Code in column 3 for University of Chicago theses
Physics		×		×		×		×	×	
History		×		×	×	×		×	×	
Economics	×	×		×		×		×	×	
Anthropology	×	×		×			×	×	×	
Sociology	×	×		×			×	×		
Philosophy		×					×			
Romance languages and literatures					×		×		×	
Teutonic languages and literatures					×		×		×	
Biology					×		×		×	
Foreign history			×		×		×		×	×
American literature			×		×		×		×	×
English literature			×		×		×		×	×
Economics resample			×		×		×		×	×
Teutonic lang. and lit. resample			×		×		×		×	×
Latin American history			×		×		×		×	×
Stratified samples			×		×		×		×	×
Combined stratified and random samples			×		×		×		×	×

This procedure meant that the choice title was not always three cards behind the last ink-marked card.

The edition, volume, and copy numbering (columns 8–12) was on the whole done so that the numbers in these columns did correspond to the actual numbers involved. For example, where the library only had copies 2 and 3 of a title (copy 1 having been lost) these would probably be numbered "02" and "03." This, however, was not always the case, as sometimes the sheets were renumbered at the editing stage so that they were consecutive.

The original card code used in the physics sample was either "1" or "0." "1" was used when the cards covered the period 1949–58 and "0" when they did not. For books ac-quired after 1949 the code "1" was used if the cards covered the time since the book's accession, and "0" when they did not. Use by the same reader was counted whether or not there was a twelve-month gap or another person's use between his two uses. Simple renewals were not counted.

B. History (D)

For the history sample the skip procedure was changed. Intervals were skipped completely when the choice card in one of them was not usable. The numbering of the editions, volumes, and copies became purely arbitrary, the true numbers being written in the call number so that the book could be identified in the stacks.

C. Economics (HB–HJ)

In the economics sample titles acquired after 1953 were included.

D. Anthropology (GF–GT)

The anthropology sample contained about 200 instead of the standard 400 titles. Titles acquired after 1953 were included. The standard original card code was introduced. A new code was introduced for single-book titles with more than one card, employing "OX" and "OY" to distinguish them from multibook titles in which ordinary numbers were used.

E. Sociology (HM–HT)

Sociology was essentially the same as anthropology. There were no changes between the two samples.

F. Philosophy (B–BJ, except BF)

In the philosophy sample several changes were made. Titles acquired after 1953 were no longer included. Shelf number and title legibility information were no longer recorded on the data sheets, although the shelf number was still put on the browsing slips which were placed in the books. A new rule was introduced concerning the counting of the different uses by the same reader: These were not counted unless there were twelve months between the date on which the reader returned the book to the library and the next date on which he took it out, or unless another person used the book between times.

G. Romance languages and literatures (PC and PQ)

In this area the most important change was that the type of publisher was no longer coded and entered on the data sheets. This variable was abandoned for several reasons:

1. It was often difficult to distinguish between the various categories, for example, between an academic institution and a learned society. The name of the publishing house did not necessarily make it clear into which category it should be put.

2. It was impossible to fit some publishers into the code satisfactorily, particularly non-learned societies.

H. Teutonic languages and literatures (PD, PF, and PT)

This area was essentially the same as the Romance language area, except that it was a full-sized sample.

I. Biology (QH–QR)

The data collected in this area were the same as that taken in the two preceding ones. There were, however, certain problems in collecting the data because of the nature of the biology library stacks. The chief difficulty was that most of the time the reader signed the card, even if he only consulted the book in the library reading room. This meant that there were far more names on the cards than there were in other areas where the stacks were not as closed. It was decided that as these within-the-library uses usually appeared only on the orange card and were not usually dated, not to count them at all. It was not always possible, however, to be absolutely certain of the identity of uses, especially when the orange card covered a period which the white card did not.

J. Foreign history (DB–DX, except DE, DF, and DS)

A variable was set up to indicate whether the book was itself a translation of an original which the library either had or did not have, or if there were translations of it in the library. This variable was recorded in the column used earlier for the type of publisher—column 21. A new code was introduced into column 3 to differentiate University of Chicago theses, with an "0." (For areas where the type of publisher had been collected these were generally identified by the "Y" in column 21, since the university library possessed very few other unpublished books.)

K. American literature and English literature (PN and PS; PE and PR)

The variations in these two separate areas will be treated together. Both were half-samples—that is, they contained about 200 titles each. A new method was used to calculate the interval: first, the length necessary to produce 50 equal intervals was calculated, separately for each area, and then eight random starts were taken within the first interval; finally, eight systematic samples of fifty observations each were taken.

L. Economics resample (HB–HJ)

A second full-sized random sample of the economics monographs was taken in the same way as the first sample but using a new random start and an interval of every one and one-half inches. There were no other innovations in the economics resample.

M. Teutonic languages and literatures resample (PD, PF, and PT)

A second full-sized sample was also taken in the Teutonic language area. Here the method used to find the choice cards was different from the method usually employed. About a thousand intervals were created on this basis: A flag was attached to each of the ink marks. A list was made of the numbers of flags in each drawer, and each flag was given a number; there were 959 flags altogether. About 1,000 five-figure random numbers were written on three-by-five cards which were then put in numerical order and duplicates discarded. These numbers were used to locate the actual choice cards. The first three digits of each number referred to a flag, and the last two to a card in that interval. Once the flag had been located in the drawer, cards were counted back from it to find the card and to be used. For example, if the random number is "009 04," the choice card would be the fourth card after the ninth flag. Some numbers had to be discarded because the last two digits were higher than the number of cards in the interval. Once a choice card had been located, a list of titles taken in the first sample was checked to make sure that it had not already been taken.

N. Latin American history (F1140–F9999)

This was a large half-sample containing about 300 titles. The standard procedure was used in data collection.

O. Stratified samples

For all the stratified samples the standard recording procedure was used. The only exception to this was in physics where the first card considered in the sample was one card behind the choice card in the random sample instead of three cards behind the last ink-marked card. In the Romance languages and literatures area enough titles were taken to increase the area to full size (400) as well as the 200 or so that represented the standard size of the stratified sample. In other half-sized areas the stratified sample was also half-sized, i.e., about 100 titles. In one area—Latin American history—the stratified sample produced far too many titles (about 700) and the area had to be reduced in size.

P. Combined stratified and random samples

These samples combined both the stratified and the random samples, so that the final sample was about 600, with roughly equal numbers of titles printed in each decade. The two areas taken were chemistry, for which the distribution of publication dates that had been found in physics was used as a model, and political science for which the various history areas were used as a guide. In the case of chemistry, which included geology and general science as well as chemistry proper, the resulting sample was somewhat too large—containing some 850 titles—but it was used in its entirety. For political science the sample numbered about 1,000 and had to be considerably reduced in size. The main procedure used in the data collection for these two samples was the same as the standard procedure described above.

B. Cutting order for function 4—use as a function of publication date and language for several subject areas

All dates given are inclusive.

1. *Physics (OC)*

Language

Other	To 1913
German	To 1903
French	To 1903
Other	1914–23
German	1904–13
French	1904–13
French	1914–23
German	1914–23
Other	1924–33
English	To 1903
Other	1934–43
French	1924–33
German	1924–33
German	1934–43
English	1904–13
English	1914–23

2. *History (D, DB–DX, except DE, DF, and DS, F 1140–F 9999)*

Language

German	To 1903
Other	To 1903
Other	1904–13
French	To 1903
Other	1914–23
Other	1924–33
French	1904–13
German	1904–13
German	1914–23
Other	1934–43
French	1914–23
German	1924–33
Other	1944–53
French	1924–33
German	1934–43
English	To 1903
English	1904–13

3. *Anthropology and sociology (GF–GT and HM–HT)*

Language

German	To 1903
Other	To 1903
French	To 1903
French	1904–13
German	1904–13
German	1914–23
Other	1904–13
German	1924–33
Other	1914–23
Other	1924–33
Other	1934–43
Other	1944–53
German	1934–43
French	1914–23
English	To 1903
French	1924–33
French	1934–43
French	1944–53
English	1904–13
English	1914–23

4. *Philosophy (B–BJ, except BF)*

Language

German	To 1903
Other	To 1903
Other	1904–13
German	1904–13
Other	1914–23
French	To 1903
Other	1924–33
German	1914–23
Other	1934–43
French	1904–13
German	1924–33
French	1914–23
German	1934–43
Other	1944–53
French	1924–33
French	1934–43
French	1944–53
English	To 1903

4. *Philosophy*—Continued

English	1904–13
German	1944–53
English	1914–23
English	1924–33

5. *Romance languages and literatures (PC and PQ)*

Language

German	To 1923
Other	To 1923
German	1924–53
Other	1924–53
French	To 1903
French	1904–13
French	1914–23
French	1924–33
French	1934–43

6. *Biology (QH–QR)*

Language

German	To 1903
German	1904–13
French	To 1903
Other	To 1903
Other	1904–13
Other	1914–23
Other	1924–33
Other	1934–43
English	To 1903
French	1904–13
English	1904–13
French	1914–23
English	1914–23
German	1914–23
French	1924–33
French	1934–43
English	1924–33
German	1924–33
German	1934–43

7. *American and English literature (PN and PS; PE and PR)*

Language

German	To 1903
Other	To 1903
Other	1904–13
Other	1914–23
Other	1924–33
Other	1934–43
French	To 1903

French	1904–13
French	1914–23
French	1924–33
French	1934–43
German	1904–13
German	1914–23
German	1924–33
German	1934–43
English	To 1903
French	1944–53
Other	1944–53
English	1904–13

8. *Chemistry (Q, QD, and QE)*

Language

Other	To 1903
Other	1904–13
German	To 1903
German	1904–13
French	To 1903
German	1914–23
Other	1914–23
Other	1924–33
Other	1934–43
French	1904–13
German	1924–33
English	To 1903
French	1914–23
French	1924–33
English	1904–13
English	1914–23

9. *Political science (JA–JX and HX)*

Language

Other	To 1903
Other	1904–13
German	To 1903
Other	1914–23
Other	1924–33
Other	1934–43
German	1904–13
French	To 1903
French	1904–13
German	1914–23
French	1914–23
French	1924–33
German	1924–33
Other	1944–53
French	1934–43
English	To 1903
English	1904–13

C. Procedures and supplementary data
for the University of Chicago serial samples

I. Random serial samples

The procedure for the random serial samples was simpler than that for the monograph samples, once a firm definition of what constituted a serial had been determined. The definition used was "publications issued at regular or irregular intervals with some system of consecutive numbering and intended to be continued indefinitely." This definition, though helpful, was not complete. As the study progressed various other criteria were developed: first, that serial volumes were essentially the work of more than one man, and second, that newspapers were not serials as they contained material of purely ephemeral interest. The first of these criteria ruled out both the collected works of one man and, more importantly, sets of monographs by different people on the same or related topics.

The following examples give some idea of how the criteria worked in practice. They also show what other kinds of considerations were relevant in determining whether a certain book was or was not part of a serial.

1. "Belgium, Office du Travail. Salaires et durée du travail dans les industries des métaux au mois d'octobre 1903. (Deuxième partie, Tableaux Statistiques.)" This book was not related to anything else held by the library and must have been acquired as a single book and not because it was part of a serial. It did not, therefore, appear on a shelf with other volumes of the same serial nor was it cataloged as a serial (i.e., it was cataloged in the ordinary monograph form). This book was treated as a collection of statistical data.

2. "English Place-Name Society. Survey of English Place-Names." This was not regarded as a serial because it comprised a series of books on related topics written by different people, not a series of volumes each with articles by different people in them.

3. "The Shakespeare Pictorial, a Monthly Illustrated Chronicle of Events in Shake-

speareland." This was considered not to be a serial because it was in fact a local newspaper which appeared rather irregularly, with news of the Stratford-on-Avon district.

4. "The Boot and Shoe Recorder." This was treated as a serial since it contained some articles of more than temporary interest on general economic topics, as well as information of purely contemporary relevance to the industry.

5. U.S. Emergency Board (Carriers and Employees, Diesel Electric Operators, 1943). Report on "disputes between certain common carriers by rail and certain of their employees respecting the basis of wage rates for firemen of all types of locomotives, the basis of wage rates for all enginemen on Diesel electric locomotives, and the proper manning of Diesel electric and electric locomotives." This was with two other reports on kindred topics by two other similar boards—one appointed in 1942 and the other in 1943. However, each board was separately appointed to report on a specific problem. The "indefinite duration" criterion was not met in this case, and, therefore, the book was regarded as a monograph.

Let us turn now to the actual details of the method. The steps were as follows:

A. Preparing the area

This consisted of locating the serials by going to the library to which the subject was block-charged, examining any book that looked as though it might be a part of a serial, and writing down its call number and the number of volumes in the entire serial. Volumes were only counted roughly at this stage as exact accuracy was not necessary until later. A volume was defined as a book (or books) containing material not found in any other book in the library in exactly the same form. Second copies were therefore not counted in this definition since they contained material identical to that in first copies; they constituted copies of a volume, not volumes in their own right. Index volumes, however, were counted when they constituted separate books since the material they contained was not identical to that in any other book. At this stage anything that looked as though it might be a serial was listed. Doubtful serials were checked in the serial record and in the shelf list.

When the call numbers of all the serials in the main library had been collected, a similar search was made in other libraries where serials might be located. These others were listed in the same way as serials found in the main library. If they were merely second or subsequent copies of a serial in the main library, a note to this effect was made on the list.

Once all the serials had been located and the approximate number of columns counted, the interval for the area was calculated. This was done so that when one out of every "n" volumes was taken, the total sample would be about 400. In making this calculation, allowance had to be made for those volumes that would be dropped from the sample because they were acquired after 1953. This was, however, the only skip category which affected the serial sample. Unbound books were never included in the volume count. The size of the interval (n) varied from subject to subject, ranging from 5 to 45. For the physics serials it was nine volumes; for history, also nine volumes; for Teutonic languages and literatures, five volumes; for philosophy, five volumes (unfortunately owing to a miscalculation this interval did not produce a large enough sample, and so another interval of seven volumes had to be superimposed upon it); and for biology, 45 volumes.

When the interval for the area had been calculated, tables of random numbers were drawn up to determine which particular volume in each interval was to be considered for the sample.

B. Collecting the data

All the data were collected at the same time (either in the stacks or in the charge-

out file) except for the number of libraries in the country holding the serial.

1. Finding the book on the shelf. Working from the list of serial call numbers, the first volume of the first serial was found, and counting started from there. All the volumes of the serial were counted as a check against the total number of volumes that were attributed to it on the list. The first interval was then counted off and the volume indicated by the random numbers was taken from the shelf. For example, suppose in physics, where the interval was nine volumes, the first random number was four; this would mean that the fourth volume of the first nine was the volume to be taken in the sample. Counting was carried over from one interval to the next. To continue with our earlier example, suppose the second random number were two. This would mean including in the sample the second volume in the next interval of nine, or the eleventh volume counting from the beginning of the physics serials. Serials with less than five volumes were not counted in the sample.

If the "choice" volume had more than one copy, all the other copies of it were included in the sample. Volumes acquired after 1953 were not taken. Although the list of serial call numbers compiled in the initial preparation of the area was used as a guide as to where the serials were, it was used critically since in some cases serials had been missed or books were listed as serials when in fact they were not. Corrections to the list were made when they appeared justified.

2. Filling in the data sheets. The data sheets used were similar to the monograph sample data sheets. (See figure C-1.) For a fuller explanation of the various items consult the account of the procedure in appendix A.

a. *Call number and accession number*— The call number included the volume and, when there was one, copy number.

b. *Title number (columns 4–7)*—The title number changed for each volume. Only copies of the same volume had the same title number.

c. *Number of volumes (columns 8–10)*—

FIG. C-I

DATA SHEET FOR SERIALS

CALL NUMBER

ACCESSION NUMBER

TITLE NO. | 4 5 6 7

EDITION | 8 9 10

VOLUME | 11

COPY | 12

DATE ACQ'D | 13 14 15

LIBRARY LOCATION | 16 17

DATE PRINTED | 18 19 20

CNTRY | 22 23

LNG | 24

NO OF LIBRARIES | 25 26 27

USE IN '59 | 28

SHELF NUMBER | 29

ORIG. CARD | 30

S

58	57	56	55	54	53	52	51	50	49	48	47	46	45	44
31	32	33	34	35	36	37	38	39	40	41	42	43	44	45

43	42	41	40	39	38	37	36	35	34	TOTAL 54–58	TOTAL 49–53	TOTAL 49–58
46	47	48	49	50	51	52	53	54	55	56 57 58	59 60 61	62 63 64

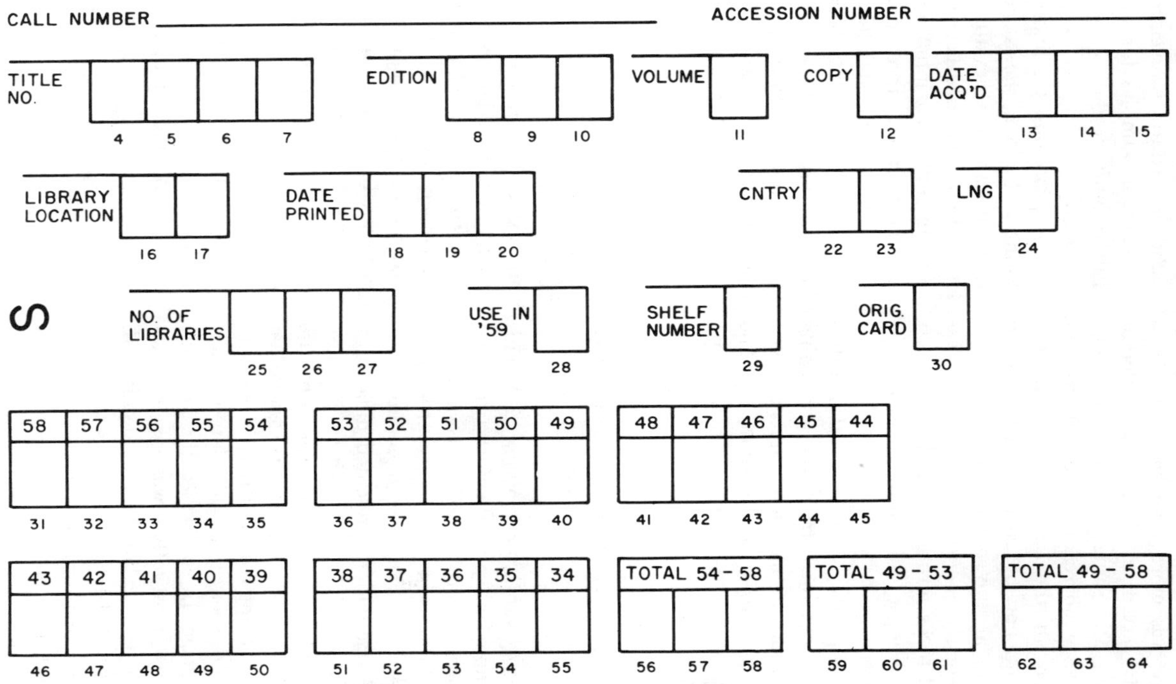

This referred to the total number of volumes in the serial and was, therefore, necessarily the same for all volumes of the same serial.

d. *Copy (column 11)*—This was only filled in if there was more than one copy of a volume. It served to distinguish different books with the same title number. The copies were numbered consecutively as they were taken in the sample. The number usually, but not necessarily, corresponded with the actual copy number.

e. *Terminated (column 12)*—A serial was considered to be terminated unless its latest volume (bound or unbound) was printed in 1955 or later.

f. *Date acquired (columns 13–15)*—Information was obtained from the cataloging date and from the accession number tables.

g. *Library location (columns 16–17)*—The same code was used as in the monograph samples.

h. *Date printed (columns 18–20)*—This information was obtained from the book itself. Care was taken to use the latest date involved when the book contained material printed in more than one year.

i. *Type of publisher (column 21)*—This item was noted only in the first two serial samples (physics and history) and was coded in the same way as in the monograph sample.

j. *Country and language (columns 22–23 and 24)*—These seldom presented difficulties. In some cases serials were written in more than one language. This was especially true of Scandinavian serials, which were often prepared to accept contributions in English, German, and French, in addition to their native language. In such cases, the language that occurred most often was given precedence, or if no one language predominated, the language of the title page was used.

k. *Number of libraries (columns 25–27)*—This was filled in later.

l. *Use in 1959 (column 28)*—Use in 1959 was recorded in this column for all the serial samples except physics and history, where it was used to record whether the title of the book was legible from a foot away or not.

m. *Shelf number, original card code, and use data (columns 29, 30, and 31–55)*—These columns were filled in according to the same rules as those used in the monograph sample. In the physics and history serial samples the same procedure was employed as in the monograph samples for those areas. (For a full account see the section on variations for those areas.)

The procedure for finding the books and filling in the data sheets was repeated in the departmental libraries after all the serials in the main library had been dealt with. There was an added complication in the departmental libraries since some of the serials there were second and subsequent copies of serials that had already been sampled in the main library. For these serials, copies of the volumes that had already been included in the sample were taken. For example, if volumes 3 and 9 of a serial had been taken, these same volumes would be taken again in the departmental library and numbered as "copy 2." In some cases a serial was bound slightly differently in a departmental library, which meant that the exact equivalent of the volume taken in the main library did not exist. For instance, the main library might have a serial bound in two volumes for each year, January to June and July to December, while the departmental library had the same serial bound in three volumes per year. In this case, if the first volume had been taken in the main library, the first and second volumes would be taken in the departmental library to get as exact an equivalence as possible. Most of these problems arose in physics.

C. Sampling the circulation charge file

After all the stack work had been done, a similar sample was taken in the charge files of the main and departmental libraries. The serial list was employed to identify the serial call numbers, and one volume was taken from every interval, counting the charge cards instead of the actual books. Publication date was calculated from the volumes still on the shelf when it could not be readily determined from the charge card.

D. Number of libraries variable

This data was obtained from the *Union List of Serials,* on which each library in the U.S. holding the serial is indicated. The number of libraries holding a serial was counted first in the main list and then in its two supplements. In the supplements, only libraries appearing for the first time were counted. Since many of the lists of libraries were long, they were not actually counted but measured.

There were various legitimate reasons why a serial might not be listed: (1) Government publications are not included in the *Union List of Serials,* an omission that affected quite a lot of serials in economics; (2) even with the supplements, the list only goes up to 1948, omitting all serials begun since that date; and (3) proceedings of international congresses of various learned societies are not included in the list, though these were serials by the criteria of the use study.

E. Editing and summarizing

The method used was almost exactly the same as that used in the monograph samples, though only one summary level—the volume level—was involved. The summaries were all called 77/4s.

II. Full-length serial samples

The first stage in the preparation of these samples was the numbering of all the shelves in the relevant subject area. The shelves in the main library were numbered first, and then those in other libraries where serials were housed. In the subsidiary libraries the number of volumes in an area was usually small enough for it to be possible to assign numbers only to the shelves where serials were known to be. In the main library all shelves for the area were numbered, regardless of whether or not they contained serials. The shelves were measured at the same time as they were numbered so that allowance could be made later, if necessary, for the different lengths involved. For most areas there was a standard length for the shelves, al-though some shelves did not conform to this standard because of the layout of the library. The length measured was the length of the physical shelf and not the length of books on any one shelf. This meant that only one measurement was needed for each shelf range.

Where there was a great discrepancy between the lengths of shelves, allowance was made for this by allotting each group of shelves—a group being made up of all the shelves of the same length in the area in question—the probability of being sampled in proportion to the total length of the area that it represented.

Shelves corresponding to random numbers were found consecutively and the call number of any serial whose first volume was on that shelf was noted. A note was made by the call number if the serial involved had less than five volumes, since such serials were not taken in the sample. Cases of doubtful serials were also noted so that these could be checked later in the serial record. The criteria for determining what was and what was not a serial can be found in the section on the definition of serials. This process of matching random numbers with shelf numbers and noting the call numbers of any serials found was continued until the random numbers were exhausted. Where there was more than one serial starting on the same shelf, more than one call number was noted for that shelf.

The lists of serial call numbers were then taken to the shelf list and checked. Any call numbers that were found not to be those of serials were rejected. The titles of the remaining serials were written down from the shelf list and were checked there and, where necessary, in the serial record, to see whether there were any second copies of them in other libraries. In cases where the stack work revealed more than 50 serials in an area, the list was reduced to about 50 before this shelf list work was done (except for biology). This reduction was effected by using random numbers or dropping every second or third serial depending on the number of serials that had been found.

The completed list of 50 (or so) call numbers constituted the sample for which data was collected. For each book taken in the sample the following information was collected:

1. The volume number of each book, and its copy number where this was appropriate.

2. The print date. Where parts of a serial printed in different years were bound together, the print date taken was that of the latest material printed in the volume.

3. The original card code. The date acquired was determined from the table of accession numbers but was not recorded.

4. The use data. This was recorded in the following groups: before 1935; 1935–39; 1940–44; 1945–49; 1950–54; 1954–59. Interlibrary loans were counted in the use totals and noted in the "remarks" space. Reserve uses were not counted in the use totals but were noted in the "remarks" space. If the same person used a volume twice, with less than a twelve-month gap between his two uses, or if the same person used different volumes of the same set, an indication was made to this effect. Any other notes that seemed necessary were made in the "remarks" space.

For each serial, every bound volume in any of the university libraries, except for the rare book room, the special collections, Yerkes library, and the University College library, was taken, including index volumes and second copies. The charge files for libraries where the serials involved were located were searched and the data collected for volumes that were charged out.

When the data had been collected, the number of other libraries holding each of the serials was found from the *Union List of Serials* (main volume and two supplementary volumes) and written on the top of the data sheets. There was no formal editing process, but the data sheets were all carefully checked for accuracy and legibility.

D. Supplementary data on browsing investigation

This section consists of copies of the original questionnaire (figure D-1) and the revised questionnaire (figure D-2) mentioned in chapter 7, and of the data sheets used for both types of questionnaires (figures D-3 and D-4).

The codes used for "department" and "status" are also given (table D-1). For "department," the code for "division" was used only when no "department" was given; the more detailed classification was preferred to the less detailed. The codes for the other data were either very simple—of the "0" or "1" variety—or were the same as those used in the monograph samples.

A simple code was devised for the column "B Other" to cover questionnaires that had not been completed by ordinary readers or on which readers had written comments. This was as follows:

0 If nothing else added.

1 If found on the floor, a desk, a table, etc.

2 If the book were taken to be put on reserve.

3 If other comments were written on the questionnaire.

4 If the book were taken for interlibrary loan or photoduplication.

THE ORIGINAL QUESTIONNAIRE

PLEASE FILL OUT THIS BRIEF QUESTIONNAIRE. The moment of your time that it takes will help us improve the service of the Library.

It is extremely important that <u>every</u> person who <u>picks up</u> this book fills out the questionnaire. Please drop the completed form into the box at the entrance to the library.

A. How did you happen to pick up this book? Check one.

    ☐ 1. Found it via the card catalog

    ☐ 2. Came to the stacks looking for a work of this <u>general</u> <u>nature</u>

    ☐ 3. Looked for this particular book but without the call number

    ☐ 4. Picked it up through casual browsing

B. How will you use this book? Check one or more.

    ☐ 1. Check the book out of the Library

    ☐ 2. Carry it to a desk and read it there

    ☐ 3. Note the title for future reference

    ☐ 4. Examine a specific passage in the volume

    ☐ 5. Skim through it while standing up

    ☐ 6. Merely glance at the title page

Your department or school affiliation (or "none") _____

Your status (undergraduate, staff, visitor, etc.) _____

       THANK YOU   The Library Use Study, Harper E 43

FIGURE D-2

THE REVISED QUESTIONNAIRE

PLEASE FILL OUT THIS BRIEF QUESTIONNAIRE. The moment of your time that
it takes will help us improve the services of the Library.

It is extremely important that every person who picks up this book fills
out the questionnaire. Please drop the completed form into the box at
the entrance to the Library.

A. What led you to remove this volume from the shelf? Check one.

☐ 1. Found it via the card catalog or serial record

☐ 2. Looked for this particular book or journal (or article in
        the journal) but without specific call number in hand

☐ 3. Came looking for a work of this general nature; used call
        number only to find the general area, if at all

☐ 4. Searched for volume complementary to the one I came for
        and found

☐ 5. Picked it up as a replacement for a book I could not find
        here

☐ 6. Browsing casually; attracted by the title or author's name

☐ 7. Making a systematic survey of the library's holdings in
        this area

B. Where will you use this volume? Check one.

☐ 1. Charge it out of the library

☐ 2. Carry it to a desk and read it there

☐ 3. Read it while standing in the stacks

C. What use will you make of this volume? Check one or more.

☐ 1. Read chapters, articles, or the entire volume

☐ 2. Examine a specific passage (or passages), or tables

☐ 3. Note the title for future reference

☐ 4. Flip through it

☐ 5. Glance at the title page

D. How valuable do you anticipate this volume will be to you?

☐ 1. Considerable value

☐ 2. Some value

☐ 3. Little or no value

The front of this questionnaire is the same as that of the original
questionnaire shown in Figure 16, chapter 7.

172

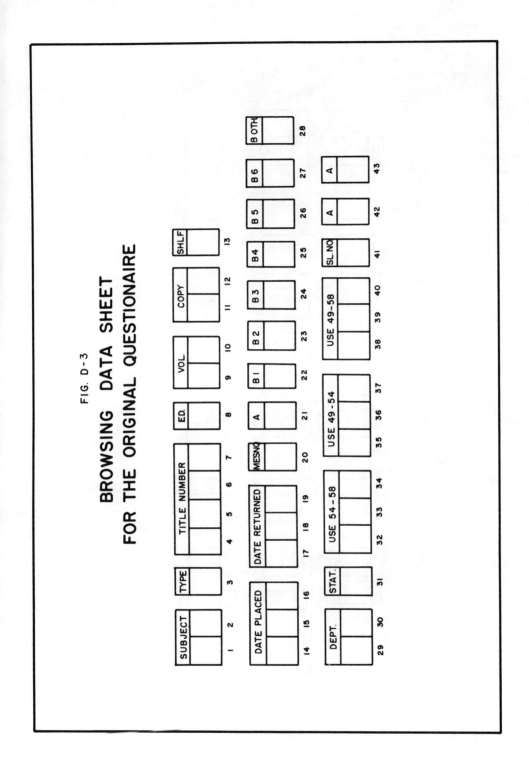

FIG. D-3

BROWSING DATA SHEET
FOR THE ORIGINAL QUESTIONAIRE

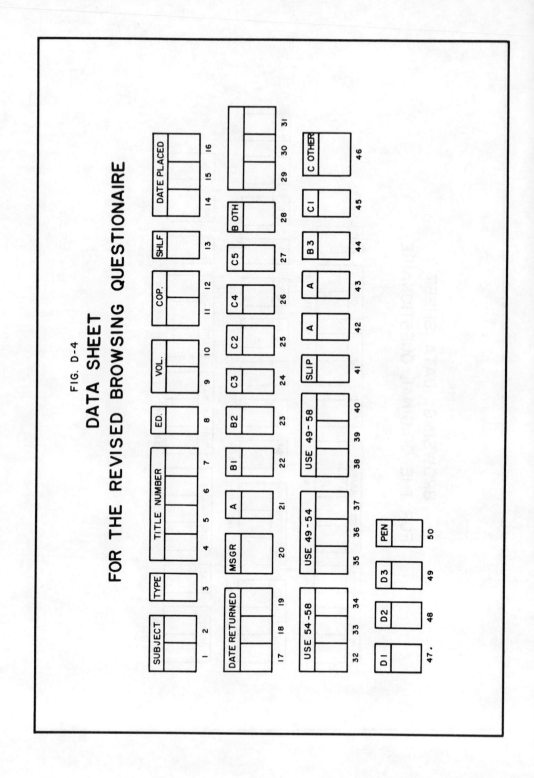

FIG. D-4
DATA SHEET
FOR THE REVISED BROWSING QUESTIONAIRE

174

TABLE D-1

Code for "department" (columns 29–30)

01	Division of Biological Sciences	30	Division of the Social Sciences
02	Biochemistry	31	Anthropology
03	Biophysics	32	Economics
04	Botany	33	Education
05	Mathematical Biology	34	Human Development
06	Medicine (including the Argonne Hospital, Physiology and Anatomy)	35	Political Science
		36	Committee on Social Thought
07	Pathology	37	Sociology (including the Population Center and the Social Service Administration)
08	Zoology	38	International Relations
10	Division of the Humanities		Professional Schools
11	Art	40	School of Business
12	Germanic Languages and Literatures	41	Federated Theological Schools
13	History (including the committee on the History of Culture)	42	Law School
		43	Graduate Library School
14	Romance Languages and Literatures		
15	Music	50	The College
16	Oriental Languages and Civilizations	51	Biological Sciences Sequence (including pre-medical students)
17	Philosophy		
18	English	52	Humanities Sequence (including pre-law students)
19	Linguistics (including Semantics)		
65	Classical Languages and Literatures	53	Physical Sciences Sequence
		54	Social Sciences Sequence
20	Division of the Physical Sciences		
21	Astronomy		Miscellaneous
22	Chemistry	60	Other (unspecified)
23	Geography	61	Encyclopaedia Britannica Research Staff
24	Geology		
25	Mathematics	62	Committee on Ideas and Methods
26	Meteorology (including Cloud Physics Project)	63	Lab. School
		64	Argonne National Laboratory
27	Physics	00	No Department Given
28	Statistics	99	Illegible
29	Fermi Institute		
71	Institute for the Study of Metals		

Code for "status" (column 31)

0	No Status Given	4	Faculty (including Research Associates)
1	Undergraduate Student	5	Staff (including Research Assistants)
2	Graduate Student	6	Visitor
3	College Teaching Staff	9	Illegible

175

E. Supplementary data on the current circulation sample

Figure E-1 shows the sheet on which the data for this sample were recorded. The only respect in which this form differs from the monograph data sheet (see appendix A) is in the columns for the subtitle number (columns 8 and 9), which were assigned arbitrarily to differentiate two or more books belonging to the same title. The use data for these titles were, in fact, never collected.

FIG. E-1

DATA SHEET FOR CURRENT CIRCULATION

CALL NO. _____ LOCATION _____ ACCESS. NO. _____ FILM NO. _____

COMMENTS:

SUBJECT			BK. TYPE		TITLE					SUB-TITLE		
1	2		3		4	5	6	7		8	9	

ACQ. DATE				DATE PRINTED			
13	14	15		18	19	20	

CNTRY			LNG		NO. SUB'T		USE IN '59		ORIG. CARD	
22	23		24		25		28		30	

58	57	56	55	54		53	52	51	50	49		48	47	46	45	44
31	32	33	34	35		36	37	38	39	40		41	42	43	44	45

43	42	41	40	39		38	37	36	35	34		TOTAL 54–58			TOTAL 49–53			TOTAL 49–58		
46	47	48	49	50		51	52	53	54	55		56	57	58	59	60	61	62	63	64

F. Supplementary data on the expert panels

I. Lists of the scholars who formed the panels at the University of Chicago.

II. Lists of the scholars who formed the outside panels.

III. A sample list of titles submitted to the expert panels.

I. Lists of scholars who formed the University of Chicago panels

A. Chemistry
Nathan Sugarman
Robert N. Clayton
Robert A. Clement
Donald Rosenthal
Stuart A. Rice

B. Economics
Theodore W. Schultz
George J. Stigler
Earl J. Hamilton
Bert F. Hoselitz
Carl Finley Christ

C. American and English literature
Ernest Sirluck
Morton Dauwen Zabel
Raven I. McDavid, Jr.
Theodore Silverstein

D. Teutonic languages and literatures
Helena M. Gamer
Gösta Franzén
George J. Metcalf
H. Stefan Schultz
Viola Manderfeld

II. Lists of scholars who formed the outside panels

A. Chemistry
Konrad E. Bloch, Harvard University
George S. Hammond, California Institute of Technology
Frederick R. Jensen, University of California at Berkeley
Herbert A. Laitinen, University of Illinois

Robert S. Livingstone, University of Minnesota
Isadore Perlman, University of California at Berkeley
George C. Pimental, University of California at Berkeley
Walter H. Stockmayer, Massachusetts Institute of Technology
Francis G. A. Stone, Harvard University

B. Economics
Robert M. Solow, Massachusetts Institute of Technology
Moses Abramovitz, Stanford University
Joe S. Bain, University of California at Berkeley
Jacob Viner, Princeton University
Jacob Marschak, Yale University
R. S. Howey, University of Kansas
Philip Taft, Brown University
Ralph W. Hidy, Harvard University

C. American and English literature
Perry G. E. Miller, Harvard University
Henry N. Smith, University of California at Berkeley
Robert E. Spiller, University of Pennsylvania
Ernest Samuels, Northwestern University
A. H. Marckwardt, University of Michigan
René Wellek, Yale University
Robert W. Rogers, University of Illinois
James L. Clifford, Columbia University
Baldwin Maxwell, University of Iowa

D. Teutonic languages and literatures
Wolfgang Fleischauer, Ohio State University
Liselotte Dieckmann, Washington University
Walter A. Reichart, University of Michigan
H. D. Sacker, University College, London
K. J. Northcott, University of Sheffield
Paul Schach, University of Nebraska
Walter G. Johnson, University of Washington

III. Sample list of titles in American and English literature

The numbers by each title on the sample list of titles shown here were for administrative convenience and did not appear on the lists actually submitted to the outside panels. Titles 1 to 48 inclusive were the titles also submitted to the panel at the University of Chicago. The rest of the titles would not have been stored under the storage plan hypothesized. Another group of titles, similar to titles 1–48, were given to the University of Chicago panel to make a total of 100.

USE STUDY

Sample list of titles in American and English literature

Do not store this title	Am doubtful about this title	
____	____	49. Flores, Angel, ed. Literature and Marxism; a controversy by Soviet critics. New York: Critics group, 1938.
____	____	1. Rahn, Fritz. Die Aesthetik des Wortes. Urach: Inaug.-diss., 1928.
____	____	50. Scott, F. N. The Principles of Style. Ann Arbor: Register Publishing Company, 1890.
____	____	51. Balukhatyi, Sergei Dmitrievich. Russkie pisateli o literature (XVIII–XX VV.), otryvki iz pisem, dnevnikov, statei, zapisnykh, knizhek . . . Leningrad: Sovetskii pisatel, 1939.
____	____	2. Shaylor, Joseph. Some favourite books and their authors. London: G. Richards, 1901.
____	____	52. Ceriello, Gustavo Rodolfo . . . Saggi di varia letteratura. Milano: Ceschina, 1943.
____	____	53. Gielen, Josephus Johannes. De Wandelende Jood in volkskunde en Letterkunde. Amsterdam: De Spieghel, 1931.
____	____	3. Turyn, Iwau, ed. and tr. Zar nachtigall; Märchen aus der Ukraine. Leipzig: Wiener graphische Werkstätte, 1922.
____	____	54. Sauer, Julia Lina. Radio roads to reading; library book talks broadcast to girls and boys, ed. by J. Sauer . . . New York: The H. W. Wilson Company, 1939.
____	____	55. Howells, William Dean. The Quality of mercy; a novel. New York: Harper & Brothers, 1891.
____	____	56. Williams, Alfred Mason, Studies in folksong and popular poetry. London: E. Stock, 1895.
____	____	57. Zabel, Eugen. Zur modernen Dramaturgie. 3 v. Oldenburg: Schulzesche Hofbuchhandlung und Hofbuchdr., 1903–05.
____	____	58. Engel, Johann Jakob. Practical illustrations of rhetorical gesture and action. London: R. Phillips, 1807.
____	____	4. Barry, John Daniel . . . Julia Marlowe. Boston: R. G. Badger & Co., 1899.
____	____	59. King, Robert. North Shields theatres, a history of the theatres at North Shields and the adjoining village of Tynemouth from 1765 . . . Gateshead on Tyne: Northumberland Press, 1948.
____	____	60. Pfeiffer, H. E. Theater in Bonn von seinen Anfängen bis zum Ende der franz. Zeit (1600–1814). Inaug.-diss. Köln, 1933.

Do not store this title	Am doubtful about this title	
_____	_____	5. Heine, Carl. Johannes Velten. Ein Beitrag zur Geschichte des deutschen Theaters im XVII Jahrhundert. Inaug.-diss. Halle: 1887.
_____	_____	61. Henley, John. The Art of speaking in public. London: Printed for N. Cox, 1727.
_____	_____	6. Baden. Laws, Statutes, etc. Das Pressgesetz vom 28. dezember 1831 zusammengestellt von J. Betz. Karlsruhe: G. T. Groos, 1940.
_____	_____	7. Ginisty, Paul. . . . Souvenirs de journalisme et de théâtre. Paris: Les Éditions de France, 1930.
_____	_____	8. Brunöhler, Kurt. Die Redakteure der mittleren und grösseren Zeitungen im heutigen Reichsgebiet von 1800 bis 1848. Inaug.-diss. Leipzig: 1933.
_____	_____	62. Pinto, Vivian de Sola. The Tree of life; an anthology made by V. de Sola Pinto and George Neill Wright. New York: Oxford University Press, 1929.
_____	_____	63. Delepierre, Joseph Octave. La Parodi chez les Grecs, chez les Romains, et chez les modernes. Londres: N. Trübner et cie., 1870.
_____	_____	64. Grasset, Bernard. . . . Remarques sur l'action; suivies de quelques réflexions sur le besoin de créer et les diverses créations de l'esprit. Paris: Gallimard, 1928.
_____	_____	9. Pistorius, G. T. Thesavrvs Paroemiarvm germanoivridicarvm, Teutsch-juristischer sprichwörter-schatz. 5 v. Lipsiae: typ. J. O. Mvlleri, 1716.
_____	_____	65. Brooks, V. W. Emerson and others. New York: E. P. Dutton & Company, 1927.
_____	_____	66. Contemporary American Writers, 1937–1938; A Collection of poetry, short stories and essays. . . . New York: Renaissance Book Company, 1938.
_____	_____	67. Brackenridge, H. H. Adventures of Captain Farrago. 4 v. Philadelphia: T. B. Peterson & Brothers, 1856.
_____	_____	10. Anderson, Florence. Zenaida. Philadelphia: J. B. Lippincott & Co., 1858.
_____	_____	68. Deland, Mrs. Margarent Wade (Campbell). The Iron Woman. New York: Harper & Brothers, 1911.
_____	_____	11. Dole, Nathan Haskell. On the Point; a summer idyl. Boston: J. Knight Company, 1895.
_____	_____	12. Earle, Mary Tracy. The Wonderful Wheel, a novel. New York: The Century Co., 1896.
_____	_____	69. Grant, Robert. The Confessions of a frivolous girl. Boston: A. Williams & Co., 1880.
_____	_____	13. Hornblower, Mrs. Nellie of Trurd. New York: R. Carter & Brothers, 1856.
_____	_____	70. Howells, William Dean. April Hopes. New York: Harper & Brothers, 1888.

Do not store this title	Am doubtful about this title	
___	___	14. Iron, Mrs. N. C. Minna Monté. By "Stella." Philadephia: J. B. Lippincott & Co., 1872.
___	___	15. Kouns, Nathan Chapman. Arius the Libyan. An idyl of the primitive church. New York: D. Appleton and Company, 1884.
___	___	16. Le Gallienne, Richard. The Book-bills of Narcissus. New York: G. P. Putnam's Sons, 1895.
___	___	17. Marsh, Richard. Ada Vernham, Actress. Boston: L. C. Page & Co., 1900.
___	___	18. Nowell, S. A. The Shadow on the pillow. Boston: Tompkins, 1860.
___	___	19. Peterson, Belle. One Word and a tear; or The wounded dove. St. Louis, Mo.: Pub. for the Authoress, 1875.
___	___	71. Bondurant, Agnes Meredith. Poe's Richmond. Richmond: Garrett & Massie, 1942.
___	___	20. Stetson, Mrs. Grace Ellery (Channing). Sea drift, poems. Boston: Small, Maynard & Co., 1899.
___	___	72. Ward, Elizabeth Stuart (Phelps). Old maids, and burglars in paradise. Boston: Houghton, Mifflin and Company, 1885.
___	___	21. Wilder, Marshall. Pinckney. The Sunny Side of the Street. New York: Funk & Wagnalls Company, 1905.
___	___	22. Green, Paul. The Man who died at twelve o'clock, a negro comedy in one act. New York: S. French, 1927.
___	___	23. Kester, Paul and Lewers, William. The Course of true love, a comedy in four acts. New York: S. French, 1930.
___	___	73. Rice, E. L. The Subway; a play . . . New York: S. French, 1929.
___	___	24. Seavey, M. M. Miss Tabitha's garden; a comedy in one act. New York: S. French, 1928.
___	___	25. Stephens, Kate. Workfellows in social progression. New York: Sturgis & Walton Company, 1916.
___	___	26. Truesdell, Amelia Woodward. A California Pilgrimage. San Francisco: S. Carson & Co., 1884.
___	___	74. Phelan, John Joseph. Motion pictures as a phase of commercialized amusement in Toledo, Ohio, by Rev. J. J. Phelan. Toledo, O.: Little Book Press, 1919.
___	___	75. Frederick James Furnivall; a volume of personal record. London: H. Frowde, 1911.
___	___	27. Potter, M. C. Oral and written English. 2 v. Boston: Ginn & Company, 1917.
___	___	76. Hartog, Sir Philip Joseph. The Writing of English. Oxford: Clarendon Press, 1907.
___	___	28. Andrews, Arthur Lynn, ed. Specimens of Discourse. New York: H. Holt and Company, 1905.
___	___	77. Cooley, A. J. A Dictionary of the English language exhibiting the orthography . . . London: W. and R. Chambers, 1861.
___	___	29. Moore, A. W. A Vocabulary of the Anglomanx dialect . . . London: H. Milford, Oxford University Press, 1924.

Do not store this title	Am doubtful about this title	
_____	_____	30. Lenz, K. ie. J. K. Zur Lautlehre der französischen elemente in den schottischen dichtungen von 1500–1550. Inaug.-diss. Marburg: 1913.
_____	_____	31. Peebles, R. J. The Legend of Longinus in ecclesiastical tradition. Bryn Mawr thesis. Baltimore: J. H. Furst Company, 1911.
_____	_____	78. Robinson, Gertrude. In a Medieval Library; a study in pre-reformation religious literature. London: Sands & Co., 1918.
_____	_____	79. Vriend, Joannes. The Blessed Virgin Mary in the medieval drama of England. Purmerend, Holland: Muusses, 1928.
_____	_____	32. Ellis, George, ed. Specimens of the early English poets. 3 v. London: W. Bulmer & Co., for G. and W. Nicol, 1801.
_____	_____	33. Coppée, Henry. A Gallery of famous English and American poets. Philadelphia: J. M. Stoddart & Co., 1874.
_____	_____	80. Oliphant, Thomas. La Musa madrigalesca; or a collection of madrigals, ballets, roundelays . . . London: Calkin & Budd, 1837.
_____	_____	81. Piercy, Josephine Ketcham, ed. Modern Writers at Work. New York: The Macmillan Company, 1930.
_____	_____	34. Zickner, Bruno. Syntax und stil in Reginald Pecock's "Repressor" . . . Berlin: Mayer & Müller, 1900.
_____	_____	82. Bartholomaeus Anglicus, 13th cent. Medieval Lore: an epitome of the science, geography, animal and plant folk-lore and myth of the middle ages . . . London: E. Stock, 1893.
_____	_____	83. Montrose, James Graham, 1st Marquis of. Poems , . . . London: J. Murray, 1938.
_____	_____	84. Taylor, John. A Kicksey Winsey; or a lerry cometwang. London: N. Okes, 1619.
_____	_____	85. Greene, Robert. The History of Orlando Furioso. London: H. Hart, Oxford University Press, 1907.
_____	_____	86. *Marlowe, Christopher. Eduard II. Tragödie von C. Marlowe. Tr. Alfred Walter Heymel. Leipzig: Insel-Verlag, 1914.
_____	_____	87. New Shakspere Society, London. . . . Critical and historical program of the . . . second annual musical entertainment at Union College. London: Pub. for the Society by Clay and Taylor, 1884.
_____	_____	88. Theobald, Bertram Gordon. Exit Shakspere. London: C. Palmer, 1931.
_____	_____	35. Four Hudibrastick Canto's, being poems on four of the greatest heroes that liv'd in any age since Nero's Don Juan Howlet, Hudibras, Dicko-ba-nes and Bonniface. London: J. Roberts, 1715.
_____	_____	36. The Generous Briton, or the authentic memoirs of William Goldsmith esq. . . . 2v. London: printed for C. Henderson, 1765.
_____	_____	37. Cowley, Mrs. H. (p.) The Fate of Sparta; or the rival kings. London: G. G. J. and J. Robinson, 1788.
_____	_____	89. Delacour, James, supposed author. Abelard to Eloisa. London: J. Bettenham, 1725.

*Indicates an English edition of this title is held by the Library.

Do not store this title	Am doubtful about this title	
_____	_____	90. Goldsmith, Oliver. Select Works. Berlin: Printed for G. C. Nauck, 1803.
_____	_____	38. Hawthorn, John. Poems. Salisbury: Printed for the author, 1779.
_____	_____	39. The Story of the tragedy of Agis. London: M. Cooper, 1758.
_____	_____	91. Jerningham, Edward. Enthusiasm: a Poem. London: J. Robson and W. Clarke, 1789.
_____	_____	40. Miller, James. Seasonable Reproof, a satire, in the manner of Horace. London: Printed for L. Gulliver, 1735.
_____	_____	41. Sheridan, Mrs. F. C. The history of Nourjahad. London: Printed for J. Dodsley, 1792.
_____	_____	92. Baillie, Joanna. The Separation. A Tragedy. 1850.
_____	_____	93. Ross, John Sawson. Robert Burns and his rhyming friends. Stirling, Scotland: E. Mackay, 1928.
_____	_____	42. Holloway, William. Scenes of Youth. London: Vernor and Hood, 1803.
_____	_____	43. James, George Payne Rainsford. The Gipsy; a tale. London: Longman, Rees, Orme, Brown, Green & Longman, 1835.
_____	_____	44. Reade, J. E. Cain the Wanderer: A Vision of heaven; Darkness and other poems . . . London: Whittaker, Treacher & Co., 1829.
_____	_____	94. Ingpen, Roger. Shelley in England; New facts and letters from the Shelley-Whitton Papers. London: Kegan, Paul, Trench, Trubner & Co., Ltd., 1917.
_____	_____	45. Smibert, Thomas. The Conde's Wife. London: W. D. Orr & Co., 1843.
_____	_____	95. Stevenson, R. L. The Works of. 4v. New York: P. F. Collier & Son Company, 1912.
_____	_____	46. Young, Sir C. L. bart. Yellow Roses; a dramatic sketch in one act. New York: S. French, 19——.
_____	_____	96. Collis, Robert. The Silver Fleece, an autobiography. Garden City, New York: Doubleday, Doran & Company, Inc., 1937.
_____	_____	47. Hamilton, John. In a Bengal Backwater. Calcutta & Simla: Thacker, Spink & Co., 1920.
_____	_____	97. Hamilton, Robert. W. H. Hudson; the Vision of earth. London: J. M. Dent and Sons Ltd., 1936.
_____	_____	48. Jacob, Violet. Songs of Angus . . . London: J. Murray, 1916.
_____	_____	98. Babb, James Tinkham. A bibliography of the writings of William McFee. Garden City, N.Y.: Doubleday, Doran & Company, Inc., 1931.
_____	_____	99. Palmer, Nettie. . . . Modern Australian Literature (1900–23). Melbourne and Sydney: Lothian Book Publishing Company pty., Ltd., 1924.
_____	_____	100. Lucas, Edward Verrall. The Colvins and their friends. London: Methuen & Co., Ltd., 1928.

G. Procedures and supplementary data for the samples taken at Yale, Northwestern, and the University of California at Berkeley

I. Difference in classification groups in comparative samples at paired institutions

II. Overlap in holdings between institutions

III. Bias in comparative samples

IV. Summary of the use records and classification systems used in a number of major research libraries

I. Difference in classification groups in comparative samples at paired institutions

Table G-1 shows the number of titles in each joint-holdings sample that were *not* classified in comparable subject areas at the University of Chicago and the paired institution. For example, of the group of 209 titles in the biology random systematic sample taken at the University of Chicago that were *also* held at the University of California, 12 were not classified under "biology" in the California shelf list.

II. Overlap in holdings between institutions

The extent to which the Chicago samples could be matched at the other libraries is given in table G-2. An example of the way in which this table may be read is as follows: Of the 392 titles in the original sample in biology taken at the University of Chicago, Yale held some edition of 205 of the titles, and California of 209.

III. Bias in comparative samples

The *average* use shown by titles in these joint-holdings samples is considerably higher than the average use shown by all titles in these subject areas in any *one* of the libraries. We would certainly expect this effect to occur since titles that are held in common are almost certainly more popular than titles not held commonly.

To determine the nature of these joint-holdings samples and their biases, we may compare their mean use with the mean use of inclusive random systematic samples.

The statistics for the joint-holdings samples (tables 18–20) differ from the statistics shown in table G-3 because the latter includes titles for which the use had been estimated in the sample.

TABLE G-1

Differences in classification of groups of titles in joint-holdings samples at pairs of institutions

Libraries	Subject	No. of titles in joint-holdings sample	No. of titles classified differently
Yale and Chicago	Philosophy	253	55
	Teutonic lang. and lit.	215	43
	Biology	205	15
Northwestern and Chicago	Economics	117	12
	Teutonic lang. and lit.	109	3
	Physics	98	15
California and Chicago	Economics	197	25
	Teutonic lang. and lit.	245	15
	Biology	209	12

TABLE G-2

Number of titles in each list held jointly by Chicago and comparison libraries
(These include joint holdings for which the use data were missing)

	Teutonic lang. & lit.	Economics	Biology	Philosophy	Physics
Number of titles on original list of random systematic samples taken at Chicago......	436	353	392	424	360
Number of titles held jointly by Chicago and Yale............................	215		205	253	
Number of titles held jointly by Chicago and Northwestern.....................	109	117			98
Number of titles held jointly by Chicago and California.......................	245	197	209		

TABLE G-3

A comparison of the mean use in 1954–58 for the random systematic and joint-holdings
samples at Northwestern University and the University of California at Berkeley

Subject	Northwestern random	Northwestern joint holdings	Calif. random	Calif. joint holdings
Teutonic languages and literatures ..	.57	1.03	1.03	1.91
Economics......................	1.15	1.32	2.35	5.18
Biology........................			2.19	5.01
Physics........................	1.80	3.34		

The titles in this sample *include* estimated-use titles.

IV. Summary of the use records and classification systems used by a number of major research libraries

CHARGING SYSTEM

	Book cards	Date due slips	Key-sort	Time period covered	Notes

A. Libraries using the Libraries of Congress classification system

Cornell University   ×   (1)*   Still a large number of books in local Harris system.

Indiana University   Has been keeping all call slips for some time.

* (1) No time period is mentioned specifically, but the system has been used for at least ten years and information is available on those books which are not heavily used. Heavier-use books probably have had book cards and/or date due slips removed.

CHARGING SYSTEM

	Book cards	Date due slips	Key-sort	Time period covered	Notes
Johns Hopkins University	×	×		(1)	Library of Congress system used with modifications.
Ohio State University	Until 1951		Since 1951		Book cards removed as books are charged out.
State University of Iowa		×		(1)	
University of California	Until 1943	Since 1943		Since accession	Some literature in Rowell system.
University of Colorado	Until 1959	×	Since 1959 fall	(1)	Accessions before 1958 in Dewey.
University of Michigan	No information available.				
University of North Carolina		×	Changing to Key-sort	(1)	Accessions before Sept. 1958 in Dewey.
University of Virginia		×		(1)	Can produce information.

B. Libraries using the Dewey system of classification

	Book cards	Date due slips	Key-sort	Time period covered	Notes
Brown University			×	If circulated in last 10 years	150,000 volumes still Cutter.
Duke University	Uses transaction numbered method.				
Massachusetts Inst. of Technology	×	×		(1)	
Pennsylvania State University		×		(1)	
University of Illinois		×		(1)	
University of Kansas	×	×		(1)	
University of Minnesota	×			(1)	Dewey system used with exceptions.
University of Nebraska	System will provide information wanted.				
University of Oregon	×	×		(1)	

CHARGING SYSTEM

	Book cards	Date due slips	Key-sort	Time period covered	Notes
University of Pennsylvania	×	×		(1)	
University of Texas		×		May go back 25 yrs. in little-used books.	Dewey system used with some exceptions.

C. Libraries using other classification systems

Harvard University	Widener has information and departmental libraries may have.		(1)	No single classification system.
Princeton University	×		(1)	Local classification system: Richardson.

D. Libraries for which no information about classification system was received

Boston Public Library	Record of books circulated kept on film for 2 years.
Columbia University	× But not used in the last 10 years.
University of Missouri	No information available.

H. Distribution of books by the frequency of their use

The assumption of a stochastic model does not suggest that the Poisson distribution will approximate the distribution of books within a library (or within a given subject area) by the frequency of their use during some period of time. If a library contained 10 books, each with an expectation of 1,000 uses per year, and 100 books with an expectation of .01 uses per year, the expected distribution of a sample drawn from such a library, instead of being Poisson will show a scatter of books around 1,000 uses, and a scatter of books at zero use and slightly above, with practically nothing between the scatters. We make this point because the fast-falling, convex-to-the-origin curve stemming from a binomial process may immediately suggest the Poisson to many readers.

In fact, the observed distributions do not resemble the Poisson closely but have a much higher variance. There are too many observations at zero and at multiple use points. Figures H-1 and H-2 show distribution of numbers of uses for monographs in economics and Teutonic languages and literatures samples, with the points of a Poisson distribution of the same mean superimposed on the actual distributions.

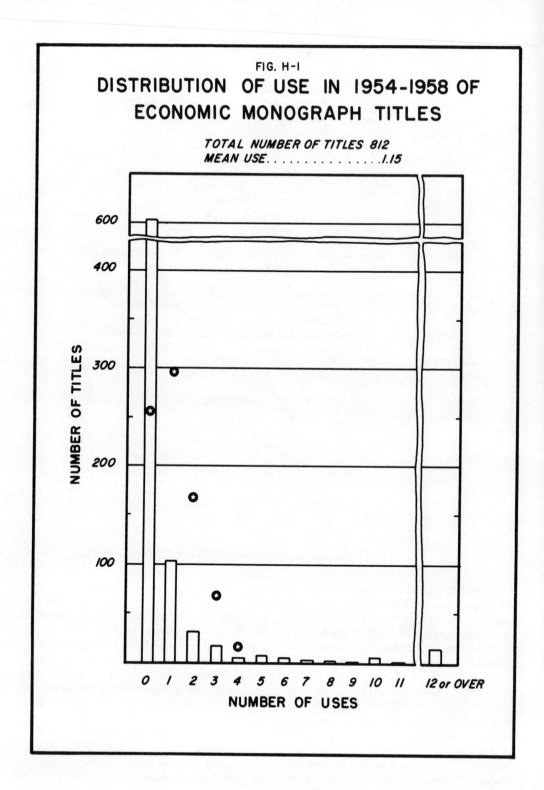

FIG. H-I

DISTRIBUTION OF USE IN 1954-1958 OF ECONOMIC MONOGRAPH TITLES

TOTAL NUMBER OF TITLES 812
MEAN USE.................1.15

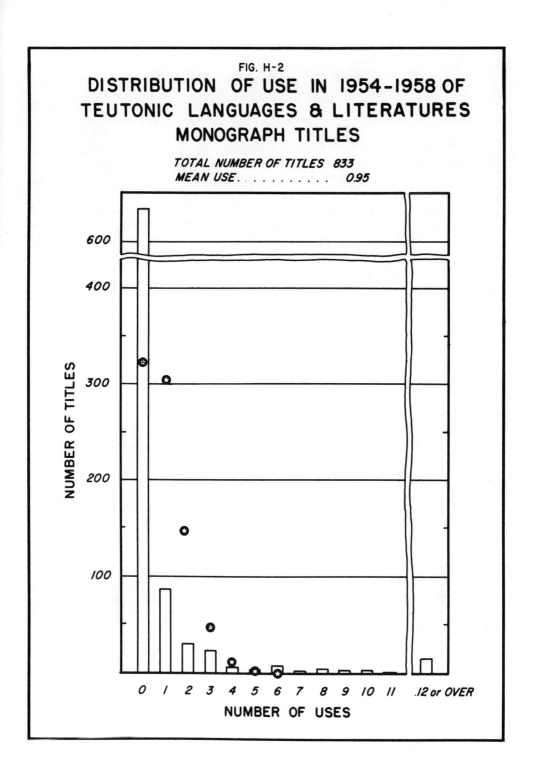

FIG. H-2

DISTRIBUTION OF USE IN 1954-1958 OF TEUTONIC LANGUAGES & LITERATURES MONOGRAPH TITLES

TOTAL NUMBER OF TITLES 833
MEAN USE. 0.95

I. Rejected investigative techniques

The two methods of investigation that were rejected are as follows:

1. Analysis of the books charged out at a single point in time, or during a short period of time

The apparent advantage of this approach is a practical one: For a relatively slight expenditure of time and money it is possible to identify immediately those classes of books that are used most. But the fallacy in this method can be illustrated by applying it to an attempt to estimate how good an outfielder is by examining the number of fly balls he caught in a season. We would have to know how many fly balls were hit in his direction, as well as the numbers hit toward other outfielders, before we could determine whether he was a good outfielder or just happened to have many opportunities to make catches.

Similarly, such an approach offers no way of determining whether the appearance (in the collection of books that were charged out in the sampling period) of many members of one group of books (for example "Published in English between 1910 and 1920") indicates a high average use for that group, or whether it indicates simply that there are many of that group of books in a library's collection. Therefore this kind of data must be supplemented with data from other sources if the analysis is to be interpreted sensibly.[1]

Such analysis of current circulation also has the defect that whatever period is chosen for data collection would be subject to some kind of seasonal variation. It is possible that different kinds of library patrons withdraw different kinds of books in the spring than in the fall. During school vacations, faculty

[1] Since our samples did provide such supplementary data, we were able to use this kind of analysis as a check on the results obtained.

use is probably a higher proportion of the total use than it is during the terms, and faculty use patterns are probably quite different from those of the student body. An accurate and unambiguous picture would require that we collect this kind of data throughout the year.

Current circulation records can also be biased in terms of the velocity of circulation of different types of material, and different circulation rules apply in different situations.

2. Limitation of sampling frame to infrequently used books

It has been argued that if the purpose is to select for storage those books that are used least, it is merely necessary to proceed through the book stacks and store those volumes that show no use since some arbitrarily chosen date. This suggestion is complicated by the fact that many libraries have no records of past book use. The solution suggested here would be to stamp every book that goes out during an arbitrary period of time, of perhaps three years, and at the end of that time to remove all those that have not been stamped. Proponents of this view argue that the plan eliminates the need for a study of the present type.

There are several working objections to this alternative. First, it may result in storing new books that have not been in the library long enough to have had a great deal of use, although this disadvantage could be overcome relatively easily by examining the acquisition dates of books.

Another difficulty is that such a program would offer no advance estimate of the proportion of a library that would be removed by storing all the books that showed no use since any single arbitrary date. This program would therefore be unable to accommodate itself to some planned size of conventional stack library without successive stages of examination. Several examinations would increase the cost so greatly that some or all of the value of the simple examination procedure would be lost.

The strongest objection to this scheme is that the past use of a single book is but one estimate of its future use. The characteristics of the group to which it belongs may—and do, as we shall show—also predict the use of its members. With these two pieces of information we may well be in a better position to predict the future use of a single book than with either piece of information alone.

J. Advantages, disadvantages, and bias in measured systematic sampling and random sampling plans

1. Description of the "random" sample[1]

This procedure was employed only for the second sample in Teutonic languages and literatures, taken in this manner for comparison purposes. A series of 600 approximately equal intervals were measured systematically through the shelf list cards for the area being sampled. A flag was placed on the boundary card at each interval. A number was chosen which was believed to be just larger than the greatest number of cards in any of the 600 intervals. A random number was chosen, of which the first three digits referred to the flag number and the second two (or three) digits to the card within the chosen interval. If the first three digits were less than 601, and the next two (or three) digits were less than the arbitrarily chosen large number, the correct flag was found by number. The cards in the interval were counted until the number of the digits was reached, and the card that corresponds to the digit was the choice card. If the number of cards in the interval was less than the number of the digits, the interval was skipped.

2. Advantages and disadvantages of the random and systematic methods

a. With respect to the variance, the random method has the advantage that the

1 This method was suggested by Professor Lawrence Fisher. If a mechanical counter were available it would certainly be the most desirable method.

sampling variability is completely knowable, whereas there is no way of establishing the variability of a systematic sample. However, if we assume that there are no regular periodic variations in the shelf list (i.e., that every tenth card or titles are not more like each other than they are like the fifth cards or titles), then the variability of the systematic sample should be less than that of the random sample. We tested a subject area for cyclical effects and found none.

b. With respect to bias, the measured systematic sample had the danger that variations in the numbers of cards per interval might cause variations in the probability of selection of individual items in the universe. If the variation in number of cards to the interval is related to some variable that enters into the analysis, the variation may cause a bias. The most obvious cause of such variation is the thickness of cards. Old shelf list cards tend to be thicker than new ones, and if old and new cards are not distributed randomly throughout the shelf list, more than a fair proportion of old cards will enter into the analysis.

We tested for this effect by comparing the results obtained with our systematic measured sample against the results obtained if we weighted our observations by their true probability of entering the sample. (We established this true probability by counting cards in the sample intervals.) The results were that the age of cards was biased in the direction of being 0.5 years too old, but the

TABLE J-1

Distribution of titles by use and publication date as shown by two methods of
sampling Teutonic languages and literatures monograph titles

Measured Systematic Sample									"Random" Sample								
Publication date	No. of cases having these numbers of uses 1954–58						Total uses in 1954–58	Total restricted use 1954–58*	Publication date	No. of cases having these numbers of uses 1954–58						Total uses in 1954–58	Total restricted use 1954–58*
	0	1	2	3	4	5+				0	1	2	3	4	5+		
1689–1823	24	0	0	0	0	0	0	0	1634–1823	29	1	1	0	0	1	57	8
1824–63	42	0	1	1	0	2	22	15	1824–63	31	0	0	0	0	0	0	0
1864–78	28	2	1	0	0	1	27	9	1864–78	21	3	1	0	0	2	79	15
1879–93	37	3	2	3	1	2	47	30	1879–93	37	4	1	2	1	1	22	21
1894–1903	28	2	1	0	0	1	20	9	1894–1903	19	3	1	2	0	1	27	16
1904–13	38	5	1	1	0	2	46	20	1904–13	33	3	3	0	0	1	15	14
1914–23	44	11	1	1	1	5	50	45	1914–23	38	5	4	1	0	3	48	31
1924–33	42	9	2	2	0	5	100	44	1924–33	43	10	6	2	0	3	56	43
1934–43	38	5	2	0	1	1	18	18	1934–43	35	6	0	0	0	2	21	16
1944–53	18	7	1	5	1	4	66	48	1944–53	19	6	2	1	2	5	68	46
	339						396	238		305						393	210
									Adjusted for sample size	336						432	231

* Restricted use has a range of 0–5; all uses of more than 5 are counted simply as 5.

bias for age of titles—the relevant figure—was only 0.3 years too old, even though the variance for age of titles is greater than the variance for age of cards. We considered that that amount of bias was not very important.

The random sampling method is subject to unknown biases because the data collectors, in a hand-counted sample, may err in systematic fashions. This could raise the probability of observations coming from some portions of the universe, and lower it for others.

Perhaps the most satisfactory method of considering the effects of possible biases is to compare the measured systematic sample against a random sample.

Figure J-1 shows the distribution of books by various publication dates that fall into a counted random sample in Teutonic languages and literatures, and into a measured systematic sample in the same subject. The counted sample contained 395 titles and the systematic sample 435 titles, but the two samples were adjusted for the difference in sample size for the purpose of comparison.

Figure J-2 shows a similar distribution by accession dates.

The distributions within each pair seem to be sufficiently similar, with no trend apparent, that it is unnecessary to test whether the differences could be due to chance.

In general, there do not seem to be any salient differences between the two samples, especially in the important dimension of total use. Table J-1 gives the basic information about the use of the two samples.

If there were bias in the measured systematic sampling method, it would necessarily be in the direction of producing lower use for the sample as a whole, because of the too-large probability of old books entering the sample. In the 1954–58 period, the systematic sample showed slightly lower use than the random sample by one measure and slightly higher use by another measure (after adjusting the samples for number of observations).

As to the effect of bias upon the conclusions, we may note first that there will be

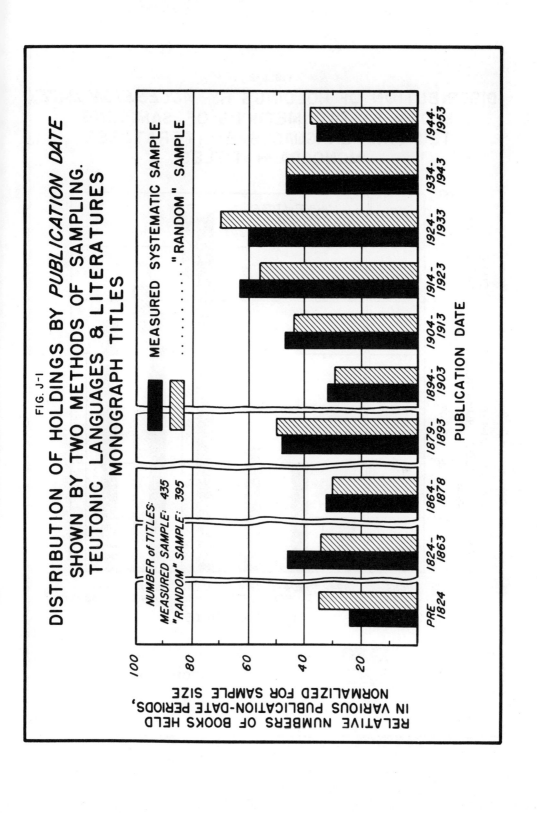

FIG. J-I

DISTRIBUTION OF HOLDINGS BY *PUBLICATION DATE* SHOWN BY TWO METHODS OF SAMPLING. TEUTONIC LANGUAGES & LITERATURES MONOGRAPH TITLES

MEASURED SYSTEMATIC SAMPLE

"RANDOM" SAMPLE

NUMBER of TITLES:
MEASURED SAMPLE: 435
"RANDOM" SAMPLE: 395

PUBLICATION DATE

PRE 1824   1824– 1863   1864– 1878   1879– 1893   1894– 1903   1904– 1913   1914– 1923   1924– 1933   1934– 1943   1944– 1953

RELATIVE NUMBERS OF BOOKS HELD IN VARIOUS PUBLICATION-DATE PERIODS, NORMALIZED FOR SAMPLE SIZE

100   80   60   40   20

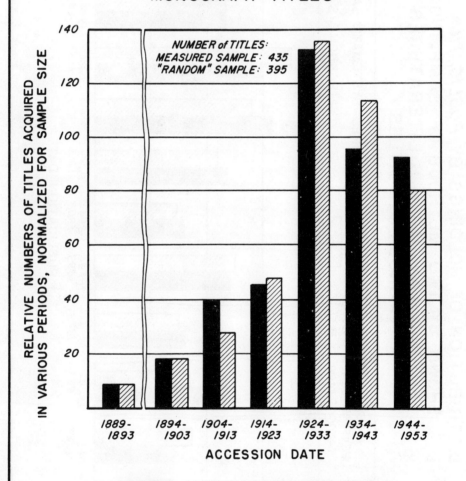

FIG. J-2

DISTRIBUTION OF HOLDINGS BY *ACCESSION DATE* SHOWN BY TWO METHODS OF SAMPLING. TEUTONIC LANGUAGES & LITERATURES MONOGRAPH TITLES

NUMBER of TITLES:
MEASURED SAMPLE: 435
"RANDOM" SAMPLE: 395

RELATIVE NUMBERS OF TITLES ACQUIRED IN VARIOUS PERIODS, NORMALIZED FOR SAMPLE SIZE

ACCESSION DATE

 MEASURED SYSTEMATIC SAMPLE

..........."RANDOM" SAMPLE

no effect upon any regression functions developed to predict use. In fact, the bias should help the regression estimate slightly by placing more cases at the older end of the scale where there are relatively few cases. It might lead to a slight underestimation of total use. Concerning the estimates of numbers of titles in the various age categories in the population, our measurement of the bias should allow us to make accurate corrections.

Perhaps the final test for bias within the sampling process would be a test for differences in coefficients of linear discriminant functions derived from a sample taken with our standard technique and a sample taken in random fashion. If there is no difference between the discriminant functions, then no matter what biases may enter the sampling we can assert that they do not materially

affect our prediction of book use. A technique suggested by Rao[2] would be appropriate, but we do not believe that the evidence as to bias is sufficient to warrant a further test.

c. There were more important administrative differences between the two sampling methods. The extra cost of counting several hundreds of thousands of shelf list cards by hand would have been very great. Furthermore, data collectors showed extreme resistance to performing this dreary task when we experimented with the technique. And much extra and difficult supervision would have been required for the random method. Taking into account the costs, the psychological resistance of employees, and the lack of strong evidence concerning bias, the decision to use a measured systematic sample seems well advised.

K. Monotonicity in use as a function of age (Supplement to chapter 2)

We may inquire into the question of monotonicity in several ways. Perhaps the most conclusive demonstration is to look at several samples from the same population to determine whether they show the same disturbances. If there are true departures from monotonicity, we would expect that several samples would depart from monotonicity in the same publication date periods. On the other hand, if the apparent departures are the result of sampling variability, we would not expect the departures to occur in the same periods in the various samples.

We have three separate samples in economics and three in Teutonic languages and literatures. In each area one of the samples is stratified, and two are not (see discussion of stratification, and stratification plan, in chapter 1). The best practice would be to lump the samples in each area and draw groups randomly from the lumped data, but it does not seem necessary to do so in this case.

Let us first look at economics. In figure 2 (chapter 2) we see that for the three functions involving the three dependent variables there is a minor departure from monotonicity in the period 1864–78 and a major departure in 1904–13. In table K-2 we read that only one sample (the first random sample) on one measure of the dependent variable (Proportion) contradicts the departure in 1864–78.

Another way to test the monotonicity assumption is to compare the behavior in successive five-year periods of titles whose use records were complete and require no estimation. We consider only the nonestimated use titles to avoid the dependence between time periods introduced by the estimation process. But given our basic assumption of stable underlying parameters of probability of use for each title, we expect correlation from time period to time period for the same

[2] C. Radhakrishna Rao, *Advanced Statistical Methods in Biometric Research* (New York: John Wiley, 1952), p. 250.

TABLE K-1

Use in 1954–58 as a function of age in various subsamples. A test for monotonicity.
Teutonic languages and literatures monograph titles

	Publication Dates									
	Pre-1824	1824–63	1864–78	1879–93	1894–1903	1904–13	1914–23	1924–33	1934–43	1944–53
Number of titles										
First unstratified measured sample	24	46	32	48	32	47	63	60	47	36
Second unstratified measured sample	32	31	27	46	26	40	51	64	43	35
Stratified sample	1	0	27	68	31	15	0	0	20	10
Average use										
First unstratified measured sample	0	.48+	.34+	.98+	.63−	.98+	.79−	1.67+	.38−	1.83+
Second unstratified measured sample	1.78	0−	2.93+	.48−	1.04+	.38−	.94+	.88−	.49−	1.94+
Stratified sample	0		.48+	1.60+	.52−	.67+			.52−	1.18+
0–5+ uses										
First unstratified measured sample	0	.33+	.28−	.63+	.33−	.43+	.71+	.73+	.38−	1.33+
Second unstratified measured sample	.25	0−	.56+	.46−	.62+	.35−	.61+	.67+	.37−	1.31+
Stratified sample	0		.48+	.44−	.52+	.60+			.52−	1.18+
Proportion used										
First unstratified measured sample	0	.09+	.13+	.23+	.13−	.19+	.30+	.30−	.19−	.50+
Second unstratified measured sample	.09	0−	.22+	.20−	.27+	.18−	.25+	.33+	.19−	.46+
Stratified sample	0		.22+	.21−	.19−	.27+			.19−	.36+

+ and − indicate whether the trend is up or down.

titles. For that reason, this test would only be of interest if it contradicted our initial impressions of departures from monotonicity.

Tables K-3 and K-4 show the values of the three dependent variables for the non-estimated use titles in the overall economics and Teutonic samples by the period in which the titles were published. The values are shown for the two observation periods, 1949–53 and 1954–58. We find (table K-4) that the departure from monotonicity in economics in 1864–78 is contradicted on two of the three dependent variables in the period 1949–53. This finding is sufficient to support our assumption that monotonicity is not disproved for this period.

On the other hand, all three economics samples (table K-2) agree in the departure from monotonicity in 1904–13 on all three dependent variables, and the overall samples

TABLE K-2

Use in 1954–58 as a function of age in various subsamples.
A test for monotonicity. Economics monograph titles

	Publication Dates									
	Pre-1824	1824–63	1864–78	1879–93	1894–1903	1904–13	1914–23	1924–33	1934–43	1944–54
Number of titles										
Unstratified measured systematic sample	16	18	15	21	22	34	49	67	72	39
Random sample	10	22	20	25	32	56	59	78	90	67
Stratified sample	0	0	43	93	49	41	24	1	0	0
Average use										
Unstratified measured systematic sample	.13	.22+	.20−	.24+	.18−	.18−	1.10+	.33−	2.39+	2.87+
Random sample	.30	.23−	.20−	.24+	.16−	.11−	.58+	1.45+	1.22−	3.96
Stratified sample			.16	.45+	.55+	.32−	.08−	0−		
0–5+ use										
Unstratified measured systematic sample	.13	.22+	.20−	.24+	.18−	.18−	.35+	.33−	.99+	1.59+
Random sample	.30	.23−	.20−	.24+	.16−	.11−	.41+	.53+	.80+	1.63+
Stratified sample			.16	.19+	.45+	.27−	.08−	0−		
Proportion used										
Unstratified measured systematic sample	.06	.11+	.13+	.19+	.14−	.12−	.18+	.19+	.38+	.56+
Random sample	.30	.23−	.15−	.24+	.13−	.11−	.20+	.27+	.32+	.51+
Stratified sample			.09	.12+	.34+	.17−	.08−	0−		

+ and − indicate whether the trend is up or down.

agree in both periods (table K-4). This pattern should be sufficient evidence to conclude that the function is not monotonic for this period.

No probability statements have been made to support our assertions about departures from monotonicity. We might make such statements if we confined our examination to tables K-2 and K-4 and let

$$\frac{\text{total number of departures}}{\text{total number of period intervals examined for departures}}$$

stand for the probability of departure in any period. We might then test the hypothesis that the number of coinciding departures occurring in the several samples is to be expected by chance, against the hypothesis that they coincide in numbers greater than chance.

This would be a very different problem from merely setting out the probability of five of six cells being negative for 1864–78 (economics) and nine of nine being negative for 1904–13 (also economics) and then testing against a hypothesis of chance. The

TABLE K-3

Use in 1949–53 versus 1954–58 as a function of publication date.
Teutonic languages and literatures monograph titles

				Publication Dates						
	Pre-1824	1824–63	1864–78	1879–93	1894–1903	1904–13	1914–23	1924–33	1934–43	1944–53
Number of titles										
1949–53	53	69	79	148	80	95	107	113	96	22
1954–58	54	71	79	148	80	97	108	115	104	73
Average use										
1949–53	.06	.35+	.18−	.26+	.40+	.38−	.51+	.90+	.26−	.60+
1954–58	.06	.31+	.20−	.36+	.30−	.31+	.59+	.60+	.28−	1.29+
0–5 Use										
1949–53	.06	.23+	.18−	.25+	.40+	.32−	.50+	.79+	.25−	.55+
1954–58	.06	.21+	.20−	.34+	.30−	.29−	.55+	.51−	.28−	1.08+
Proportion used										
1949–53	.06	.10+	.11+	.16+	.25+	.15−	.25+	.30+	.15−	.32+
1954–58	.04	.06+	.14+	.17+	.16−	.16+	.26+	.28+	.16−	.42+

+ and − indicate whether the trend is up or down.

TABLE K-4

Use in 1949–53 versus 1954–58 as a function of publication date.
Economics monograph titles

				Publication Dates						
	Pre-1824	1824–63	1864–78	1879–93	1894–1903	1904–13	1914–23	1924–33	1934–43	1944–53
Number of titles										
1949–53	24	36	73	129	96	117	126	133	146	36
1954–58	25	40	76	138	100	125	129	134	150	88
Average use										
1949–53	.13	.28+	.26−	.26+	.47+	.25−	.50+	.87+	1.62+	3.33+
1954–58	.16	.23+	.14−	.15+	.30+	.10−	.26+	.32+	.85+	1.49+
0–5 use										
1949–53	.13	.28+	.26−	.22−	.38+	.25−	.46+	.77+	1.17+	1.75+
1954–58	.16	.23+	.14−	.15+	.25+	.10−	.26+	.32+	.65+	1.17+
Proportion used										
1949–53	.04	.17+	.14−	.15+	.24+	.15−	.26+	.34+	.45+	.58+
1954–58	.12	.18+	.09−	.12+	.17+	.10−	.16+	.20+	.31+	.47+

+ and − indicate whether the trend is up or down.

fact that we are examining all the periods for departures from monotonicity greatly raises the chances of an unlikely event.

Furthermore, the use of the same titles in periods 1949–53 and 1954–58 is certainly not independent, and we should be hard put to develop a satisfactory test that would properly weight that interdependence as well as take into account the two types of evidence (the comparison of two time periods for the same group and the comparison of several groups in the same time period).

Nor would any test of binomial proportions for the combined samples be conclusive, since titles within the same time period are not independent but may be complementary. A single scholar interested in the literature of a single short period could easily withdraw enough titles to affect the use values for that period. Such a test also faces

the difficulty outlined above, that of testing the most negative cell or relation within a group of cells or relations.

The implications of departures from monotonicity depend upon the particular library situation. At the University of Chicago, for example, if storage were indicated for the books published in 1894–1903, there would be no problem. But if the cutting point (in terms of the assessment of utility, employing use as an indicator of utility) fell between the values for 1904–13 and 1894–1903, then a decision would have to be made whether or not to store the 1904–13 books instead of the 1894–1903 books. The decision would be made on the basis of operational conditions and attitudes toward age integrity and age consistency of the collection as a whole.

L. Multiple regression techniques (Supplement to chapter 2)

There are two properties of the regressions we have discussed: (a) They are linear models, and (b) "language" is not a quantified, scaled variable (at least in its raw form).

For explicit, formal regressions, we have limited ourselves to linear models, and, for the most part, to linear functions of the variables. The former limitation was imposed because of the linear regression program available on the UNIVAC. The latter limitation stemmed from the limited amount of time available to experiment with functions of other forms.

We treated nonscaled variables as "dummy" (i.e., binary) variables, a technique that boils down to adding a constant for each observation where the variable is present. For example, if we wished to use the variables "English," "French," "German," and "other," each French book would have added

to its other values some value "a," German books "b," and English books "c." The constants were developed by setting up three separate variables "French versus not-French" (French books received a value "1," not-French received "0"), "German versus not-German," and "English versus not-English."

For some regressions we used a dummy variable coding technique to handle publication date and other quantitative variables. This was done because of the apparent nonlinearity of the variable over the revealed ranges. In those cases we set up several variables. One would be "Published before 1824 ("1")," or "Published after 1824 ("0")," another would be "Published between 1825 and 1879," or "Not published between 1825 and 1879," and so on.

The problem that arises with this kind of

a procedure is that because of the large number of independent variables (UNIVAC's capacity is 18, though we never used that many) relative to the number of observations, it is possible to get a speciously good fit of the regression surface when we do not restrict the function to monotonicity. This may be analogous to fitting polynomials to

scale by plotting the values of the proportions of books used by time periods for a great many titles in many subject areas, then choosing intervals along the publication date axis in such a way that the means of the arbitrary time periods created were linear when plotted against the order of the time periods.

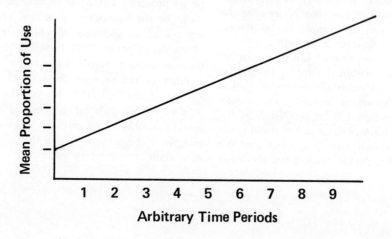

observations: If there are "n" observations, a polynomial of degree n–1 will pass through every point.

We may also construct regression functions using various measures of use as the dependent variable. The measures which we employed in our investigation were: "average use"; "average use with the restriction to 5 uses"; "proportion used (average use with the restriction to 1 use)." The regression functions that we computed were "least-squares" fits, and a single, very highly used title observation could have a major effect upon an average use function. It is for this reason that we decided to employ the restrictions on use.

Functions 8a, 8b, and 8c employed a scaled variable for publication date. We created the

The important point is that this linear scale was created arbitrarily by making the time periods of different and arbitrary lengths. We then applied this scale, generated on a large and heterogeneous sample, to our samples of economics, and Teutonic languages and literatures.

Note that this technique is the most general technique possible. No matter what the underlying distribution of the population, as long as it is monotonic, whether it be linear, quadratic, exponential, or anything else, this technique should develop the correct function within the limits of sampling errors (considering only the simple independent variables of publication date).

This function also included language as a variable.

M. Data on the cost of book space

I. Skidmore, Owings, and Merrill memorandum on construction costs
II. University of Michigan storage building costs for 1959–60
III. Midwest Inter-Library Center space costs 1955–56 through 1959–60

SKIDMORE, OWINGS & MERRILL

Architects / Engineers   30 West Monroe Street, Chicago 3, Illinois

August 23, 1960

Mr. Herman H. Fussler
Director of University Library
University of Chicago
Chicago 37, Illinois

Re: The University of Chicago Book Storage Study

Dear Herman:

Attached to this letter is a compilation of estimated costs and areas for a Working Library Stack and a Warehouse Stack. The costs for a Working Library Stack have been developed, based upon library work presently in process by this office. We have attempted to assign costs to this work so that everything necessary for the stack is included with the exception of vertical transportation. The reason this was omitted was the difficulty in comparing on an area basis as well as on a cost basis with no layout in hand. It was also assumed in Working Library Stack that this particular area would bear the cost of some outside walls, because it does not seem probable that the stack would be buried as an interior space. The stack is figured as an air conditioned space.

The estimated costs for a Warehouse Stack are based upon an extremely simple structure which is intended for the storage of books with very little access required. The structure is considered as air conditioned but is certainly not finished in the same manner as a Working Library Stack. We have used two different types of shelving in the Warehouse compilations; one the standard library shelving and the other a standard warehouse type of fixed steel shelving. We explored the possibilities of multi-tiered warehouse type steel shelving with The Art Metal Company and were informed because of the special nature of fabrication that multi-tiered warehouse type shelving would run more than multi-tiered library shelving. This direction of research was abandoned.

The structures which we assumed for the warehouse (subject to review by the City of Chicago) would be satisfactory under the Chicago Building Code and accounts for the fact that the four tier self-supporting stack is enclosed in a warehouse shell with a separate structural system. All our costs are based upon the Chicago area and of course are limited to the year 1960. No architectural fees are included in the various cost figures.

Area studies are attached indicating the areas which would be required for the various single faced 7'–6" high section of stack. In the Warehouse Stack we have carried this one step farther in spacing the sections closer together as well as adding one additional shelf to determine the effect this has upon the area required. These two variations appear justifiable, based upon the lack of need for frequent access to the warehouse collection and the considerable reduction in area experienced.

It has been a pleasure to discuss these matters with you and it is hoped this information will be of help in compiling your report. Do not hesitate to call if the data transmitted needs additional explanation and we hope we can be of service to you at some future date.

Very truly yours,

SKIDMORE, OWINGS & MERRILL

WVP/g   Wesley V. Pipher (signed)

Chicago 1960

I *COST*

  A. Working Library Stack

    1. Free-standing Shelving
      Stack using free-standing steel library shelving on concrete structure four stories high (shelving $3.50 per sq. ft. included)
        $19.00 to $21.00 per sq. ft.

    2. Self-supporting Shelving
      Stack using four-tier self-supporting library shelving enclosed by the building structure (shelving & slabs $6.00 per sq. ft. included)
        $18.00 to $20.00 per sq. ft.

  B. Warehouse Stack

    1. Free-standing Shelving
      a) One-story warehouse building using free-standing steel library shelving (shelving $3.50 per sq. ft. included)
        $13.00 to $15.00 per sq. ft.
      b) One-story warehouse building using free-standing steel warehouse shelving (shelving $1.75 per sq. ft. included)
        $11.35 to $13.25 per sq. ft.

    2. Self-supporting Shelving
      a) One-tier self-supporting steel shelving supporting its own roof (shelving & slabs with roof slab $6.00 per sq. ft. included)
        $14.00 to $16.00 per sq. ft.
      b) Four-tier self-supporting steel shelving in a warehouse shell (shelving & slabs $6.00 per sq. ft. included)
        $15.00 to $17.00 per sq. ft.

II *AREA* (for 500,000 Volumes)

  A. Working Library Stack

    126 vol. per single-faced 7'–6" high section at 4'–6" on center or 15 vol. per sq. ft. therefore ($500,000/15 = 33,000$ sq. ft.) 33,000 sq. ft. will be required.

  B. Warehouse Stack

    1. 250 vol. per single-faced 7'–6" high section at 4'–6" on center or 29.4 vol/ per sq. ft. therefore ($500,000/29.4 = 17,000$ sq. ft.) 17,000 sq. ft. will be required.
    2. Same shelving as 1. at 4'–0" on center will require 15,000 sq. ft.
    3. Same spacing as 2. but one shelf higher will require 13,500 sq. ft.

UNIVERSITY OF MICHIGAN
PLANT DEPARTMENT

Central Service & Stock Building
Costs for 1959–60

Repairs & Maintenance		*Cost per sq. ft.*
Painting	$ 32.33	
Lamp Replacements & Ltg. Repairs	210.12	
Plumbing	25.92	
Heating & Ventilating Repairs	616.45	
Pump Inspection & Repair	73.73	
Interior Bldg. Repairs	70.17	
Air Conditioning	191.93	.00956
Filters	226.97	
Elevator Repairs	67.18	
Window Washing	70.40	
Mech. Equip. for Process Air & Steam	48.60	
Boiler Operation	1,529.51	
Total Repairs & Maintenance	$3,163.31	.15756
(Repairs & Maint. without Air Cond.	2,971.38	.14800)
Fuel cost—18,445 gal. oil	2,515.62	.12530
Custodial Service	3,373.00	.16800
Water & Sewer	477.91	.02380
Electricity		n.a.
		.46966

Midwest Inter-Library Center Space Operating Costs, 1955/56–1959/60
(Excludes Overhead and Insurance)

	1955/56	1956/57	1957/58	1958/59	1959/60
A1 Personnel	$ 4,839.60	$ 5,028.60	$ 5,159.40	$ 5,257.80	$ 5,526.60
A3 Repairs & Equipment	351.35	1,397.32	1,519.15	398.96	94.10
A4 Supplies	*	*	*	*	774.08
A7 Heat, Light, Supplies	9,875.46	10,658.81	7,867.52	9,831.44	9,947.05
* Included in A7					
	$15,066.41	$17,084.73	$14,546.07	$15,488.20	$16,341.83

Square feet in Building:

61,740 stacks
11,100 ground floor, work and office space and basement
 2,100 cubic area (studies)

74,940

$78,527.24 (total expenditures) ÷ 74,940 (sq. ft.) = $1.047 per sq. ft.

Index